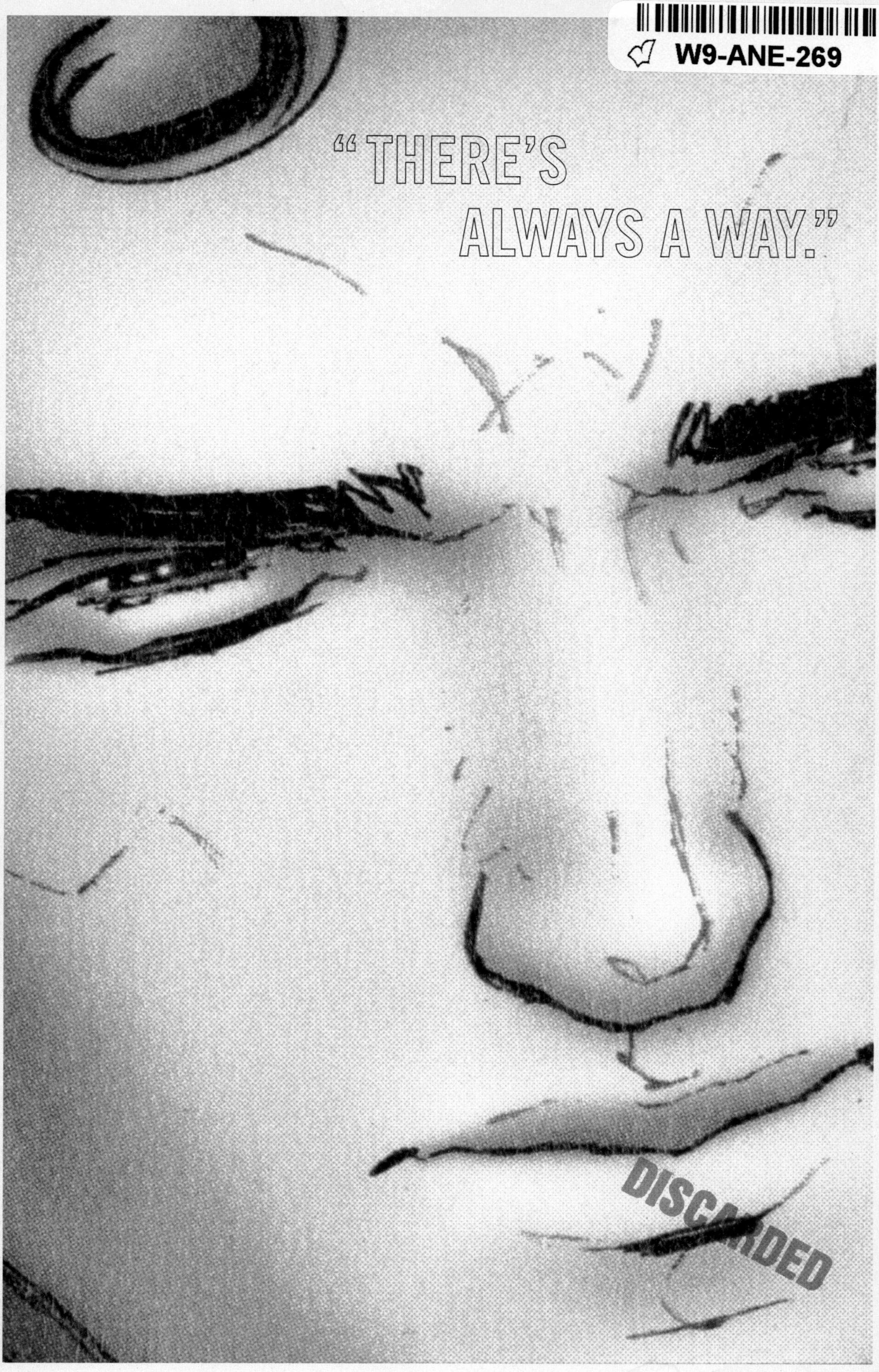
"THERE'S
ALWAYS A WAY."
DISCARDED

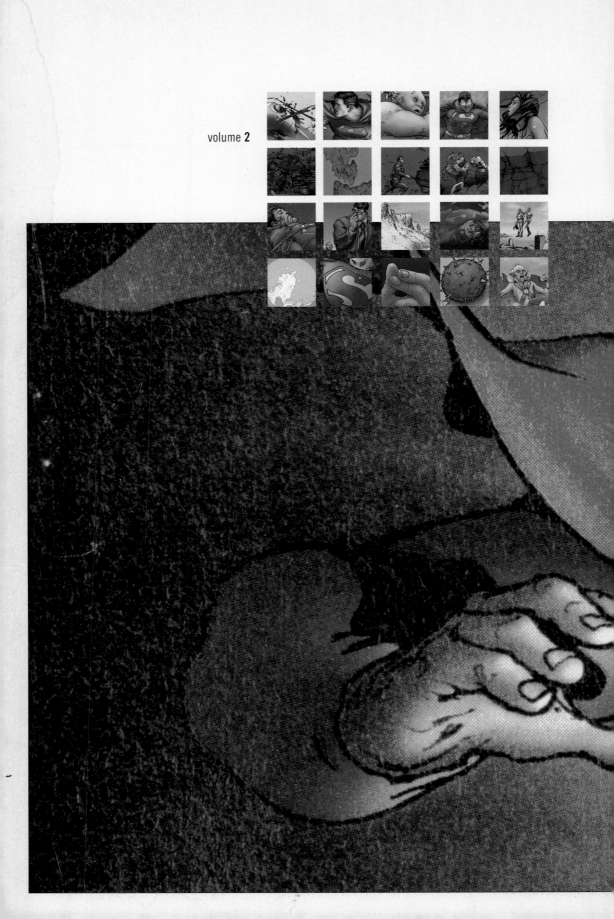

volume **2**

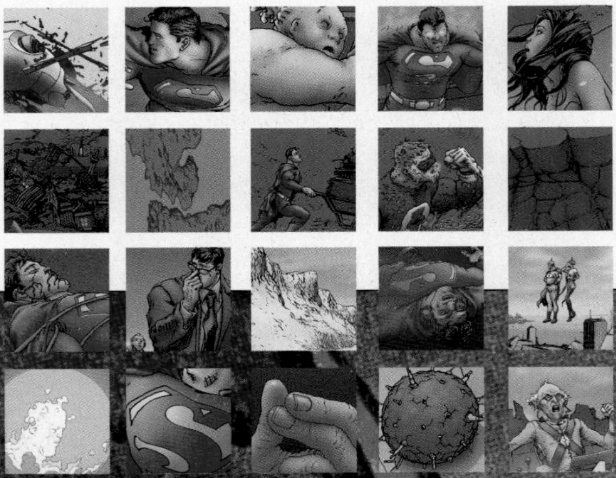

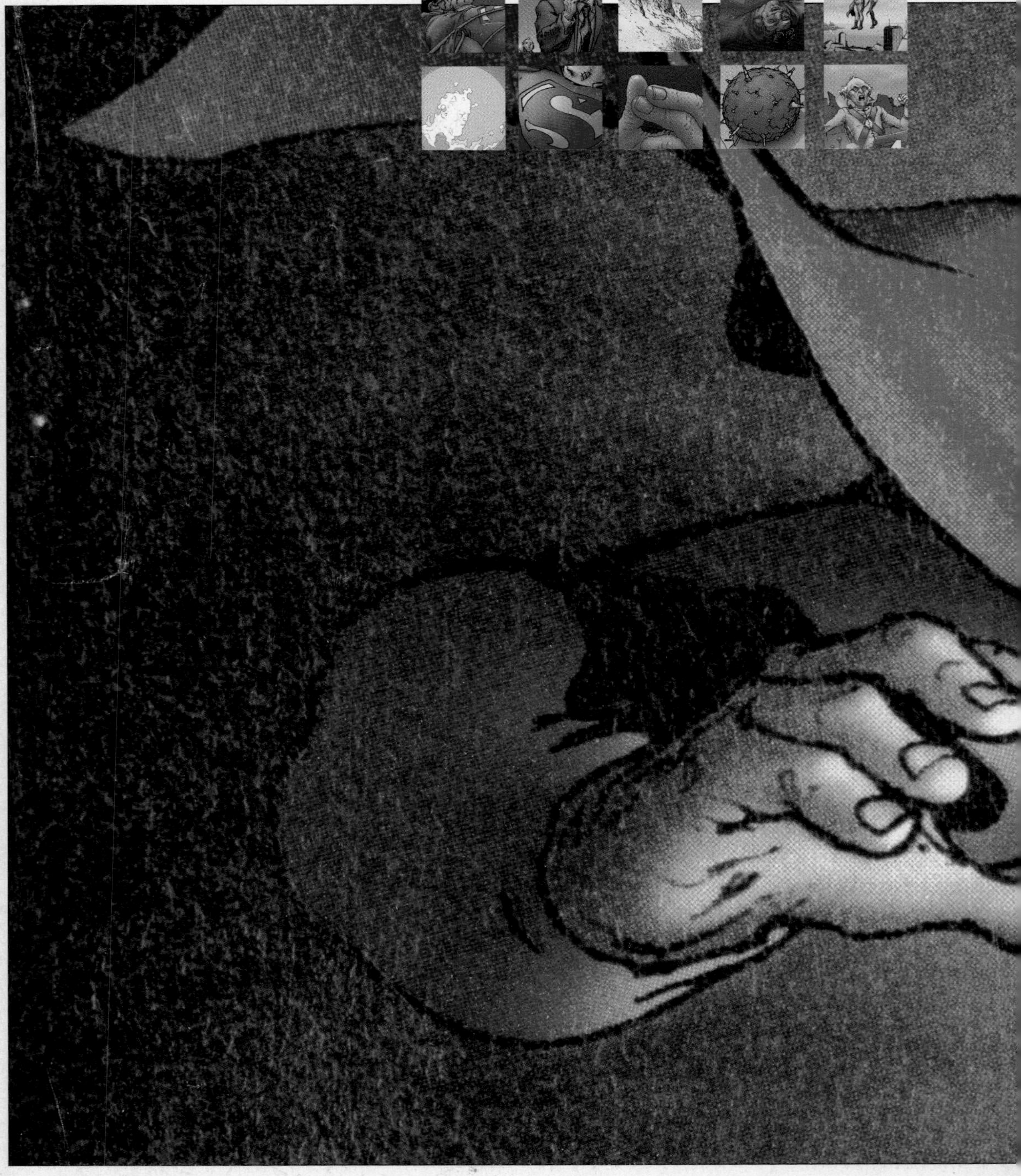

ALL-STAR SUPERMAN

Written by **Grant Morrison** Pencilled by **Frank Quitely** Digitally inked & colored by **Jamie Grant**

Lettered by **Phil Balsman & Travis Lanham** Introduction by **Mark Waid**

Superman created by **Jerry Siegel & Joe Shuster**

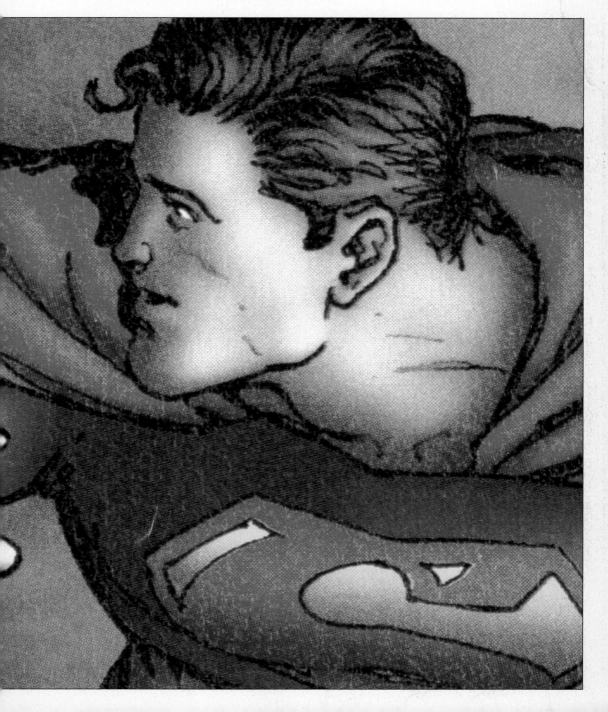

DC Comics

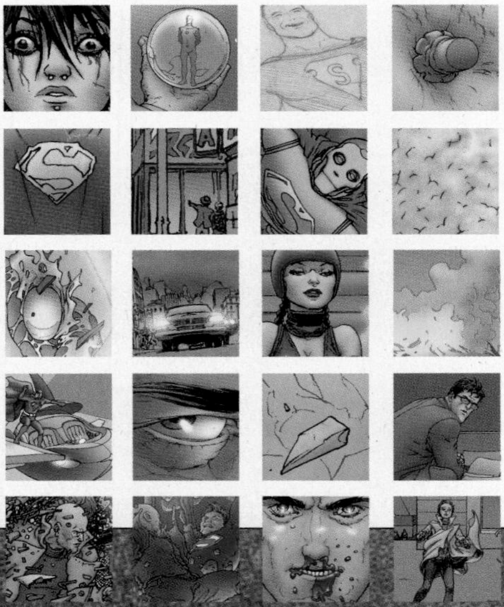

Dan DiDio
Senior VP-Executive Editor

Bob Schreck
Editor-original series

Brandon Montclare
Assistant Editor-original series

Bob Joy
Editor-collected edition

Robbin Brosterman
Senior Art Director

Paul Levitz
President & Publisher

Georg Brewer
VP-Design & DC Direct Creative

Richard Bruning
Senior VP-Creative Director

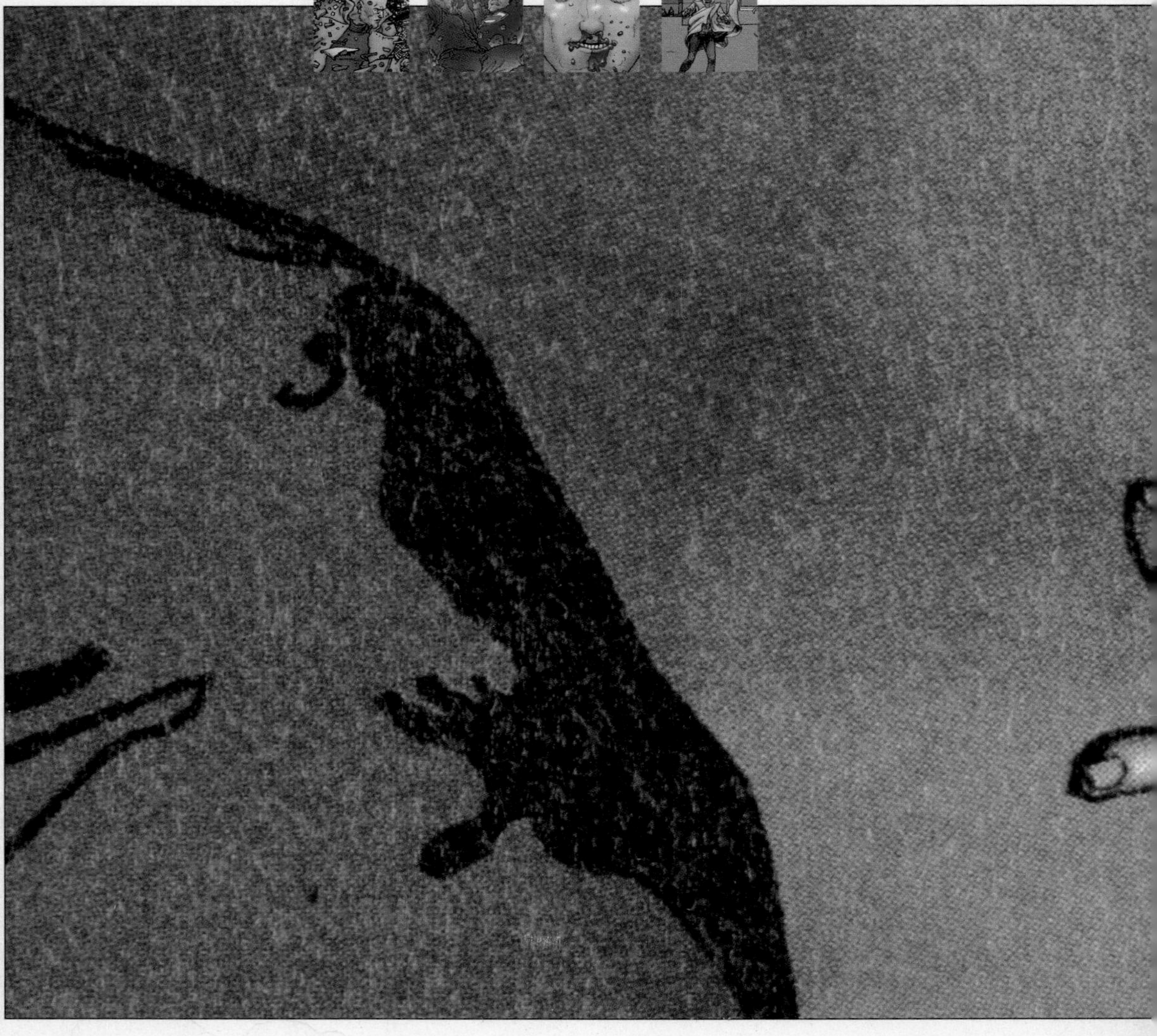

Patrick Caldon
Executive VP-Finance & Operations

Chris Caramalis
VP-Finance

John Cunningham
VP-Marketing

Terri Cunningham
VP-Managing Editor

Amy Genkins
Senior VP-Business & Legal Affairs

Alison Gill
VP-Manufacturing

David Hyde
VP-Publicity

Hank Kanalz
VP-General Manager, WildStorm

Jim Lee
Editorial Director-WildStorm

Gregory Noveck
Senior VP-Creative Affairs

Sue Pohja
VP-Book Trade Sales

Steve Rotterdam
Senior VP-Sales & Marketing

Cheryl Rubin
Senior VP-Brand Management

Alysse Soll
VP-Advertising & Custom Publishing

Jeff Trojan
VP-Business Development, DC Direct

Bob Wayne
VP-Sales

Cover art by **Frank Quitely** and **Jamie Grant**.
Logo design by **Chip Kidd**.

ALL-STAR SUPERMAN Volume Two
Published by DC Comics. Cover, introduction and
compilation Copyright © 2009 DC Comics.
All Rights Reserved. Originally published in single
magazine form in ALL-STAR SUPERMAN 7-12
Copyright © 2007, 2008 DC Comics.
All Rights Reserved. All characters, their
distinctive likenesses and related elements
featured in this publication are trademarks of
DC Comics. The stories, characters and incidents
featured in this publication are entirely fictional.
DC Comics does not read or accept unsolicited
submissions of ideas, stories or artwork.

DC Comics, 1700 Broadway, New York, NY 10019
A Warner Bros. Entertainment Company
Printed in USA. First Printing.

ISBN: 978-1-4012-1837-9
ISBN SC: 978-1-4012-1860-7

INTRODUCTION

"And to Clark Kent...I leave the headline of the century."

That may be the most electrifying line I have ever read in a Superman story, and I have read all of them.

And...and...it comes only ten pages after the most perfect line. I can't decide which one I like more. Let's discuss.

ALL-STAR SUPERMAN Volume Two completes Grant Morrison and Frank Quitely's celebration of the world's best-loved fictional hero, and — as you are about to see — it ends as skillfully and as lyrically as it began. Within these pages is the conclusion to Superman's greatest adventure, his greatest challenge and his greatest triumph.

Superman is dying. Poisoned with solar radiation by his nemesis, Lex Luthor, the Man of Tomorrow must finally face his own mortality and races the clock to compress a lifetime's worth of super-achievements into what little time he has left — the Twelve Labors of Superman, as augured by the time-traveler Samson back in Chapter Three. Some of these labors — answering the unanswerable question, chaining the Chronovore, alchemizing the Super-Elixir — he has already accomplished in previous chapters. The remaining feats of legend he faces here with no less courage and fortitude than one would hope for

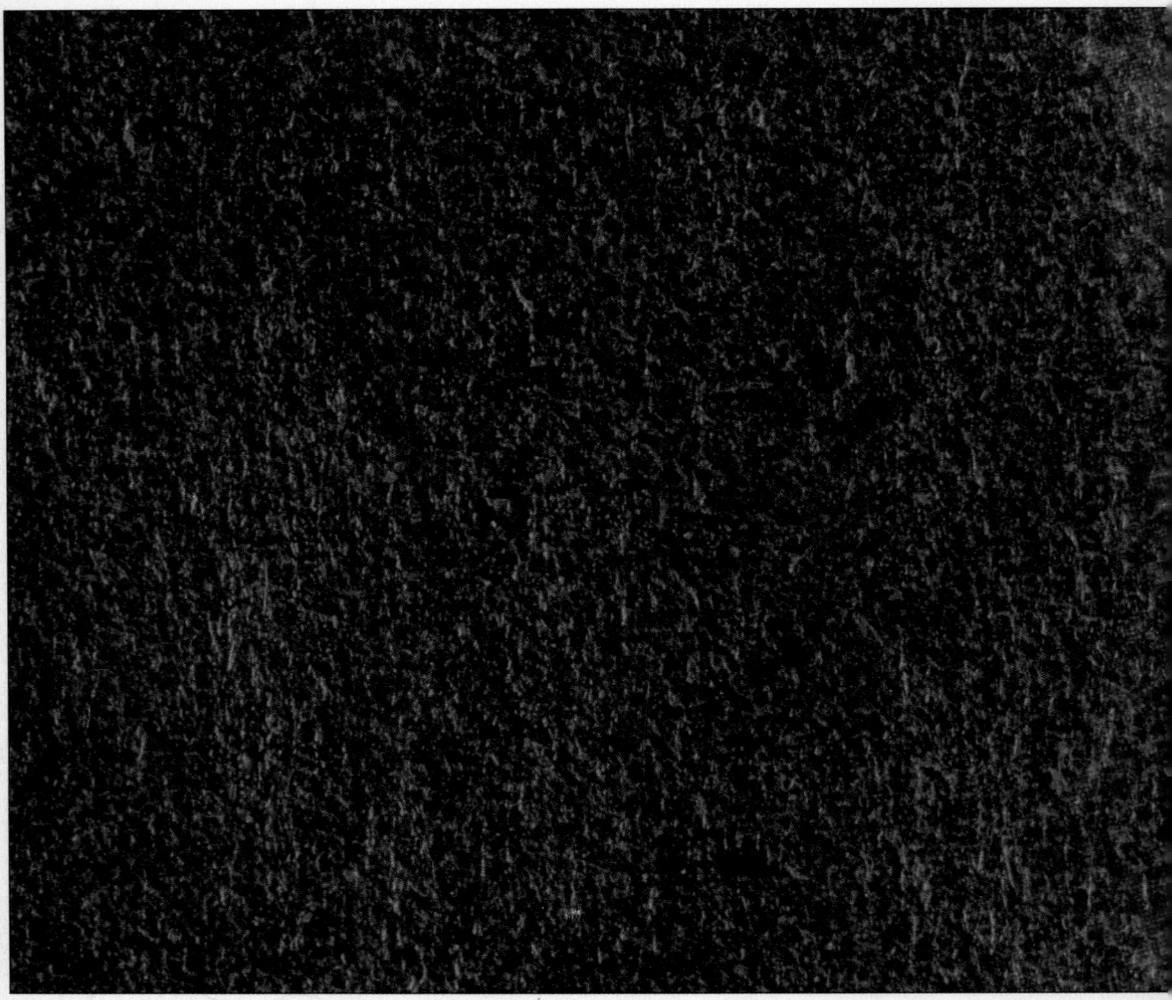

from Kal-El of Krypton. But along the way, as all men must, he takes the time to craft a Last Will and Testament. The fact that, as he writes it, he bequeaths something remarkable and prescient to Lois is touching but expected; that he concludes by leaving his own secret identity, as a gift, a final chance to keep the space-time continuum aright (as the future newspaper displayed in Chapter Three dictates someone must) is an idea that crackles off the page. It's a great turn, and as I mentioned before, it comes ten short pages after the perfect line — Superman's great secret.

There is a never-ending debate among Superman aficionados as to the value of the character's uniqueness. There are some who contend, stridently, that super-dogs and super-girlfriends and miniature super-survivors from a bottled city diminish Superman's purity as the Last Son of Krypton. Morrison and Quitely tackle that argument head on by making the superdoppelgänger such a recurring motif in ALL-STAR SUPERMAN that it masterfully underscores through contrast exactly what does make Superman unique. It's not his powers, it's not his costume, it's not his heritage. It's that, unlike his myriad counterparts, he has more faith in us than we have in ourselves, and ALL-STAR SUPERMAN is the story of how transcendently that faith elevates and redeems the human race. Everyone Superman encounters, from Zibarro to Bar-El and Lilo to Leo Quintum, inherits some of Superman's values just by being in contact with him. Read Chapter Twelve closely. Notice how the men and women of Superman's world, from Perry White to Jimmy Olsen to even the loutish Steve Lombard, have so clearly been fortified with

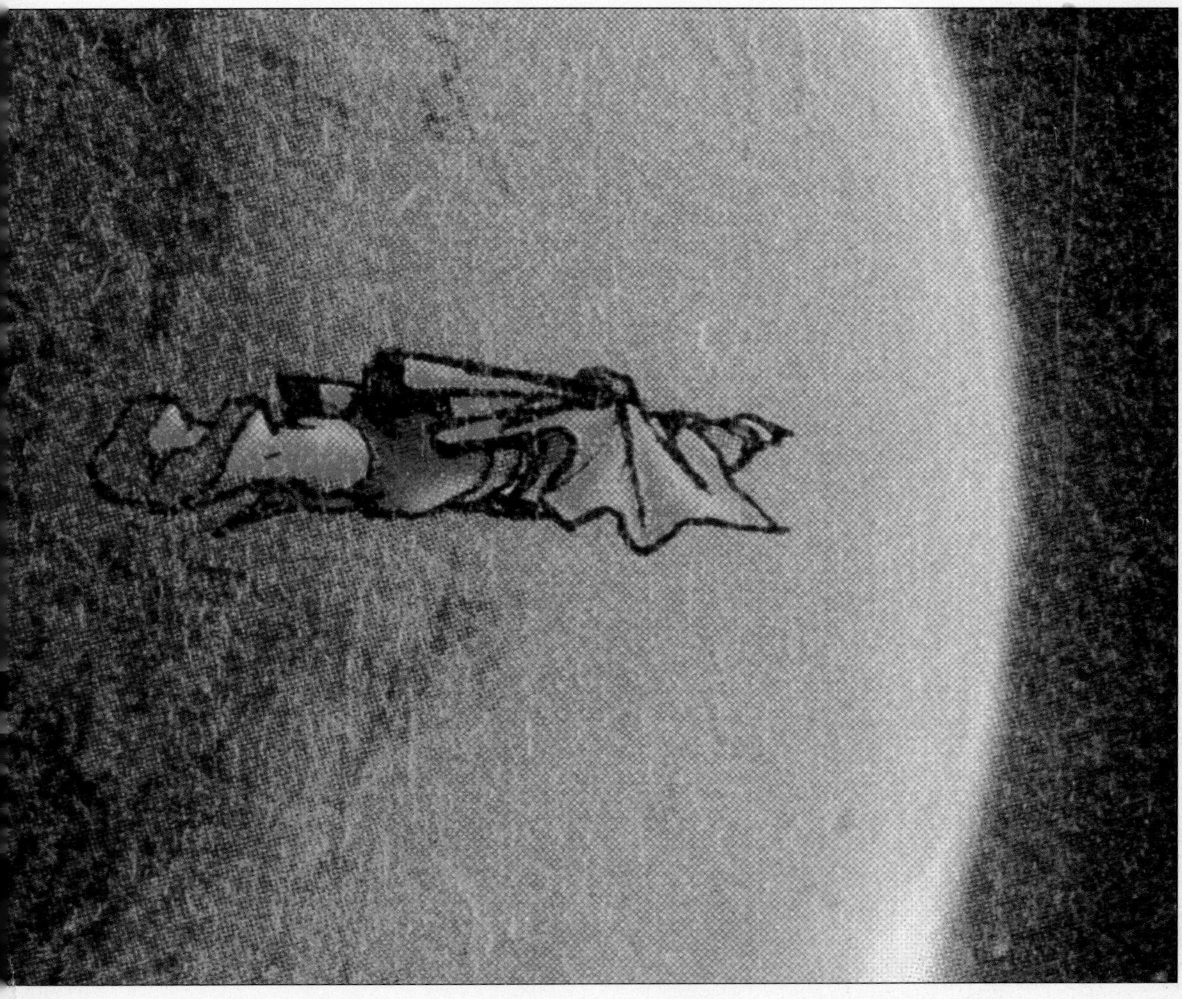

Superman's courage and reverence for truth and life. And, most important, watch how Superman achieves his ultimate victory — not with a swing of his invulnerable fist but with a gift of understanding. In every fight, Superman punches when he must and grapples when he has to, but at the end of every battle, he wins his best and most decisive victories when he allows his foes to see their world — our world — through his eyes.

ALL-STAR SUPERMAN is filled to the brim with wonderful tiny details. The way Quintum's Kandorian chair is malformed by his weight in Chapter Ten. The way Zibarro's costume in Chapter Seven looks for all the world like a modified Clark Kent suit. Bar-El glimpsed as the warden of the Phantom Zone in Chapter Eleven. The way the very last page illuminates a garbled comment from the Unknown Superman back in Chapter Two. But the big moment is the perfect line of dialogue. It comes in Chapter Ten, when Superman, without a second's hesitation, takes time from his world-building feats to embrace and comfort a suicidal young girl. When he tells her, "You're much stronger than you think you are," they become the most moving words we have ever read in a Superman story. And they are perfect because they reveal, in one sentence, the fundamental secret of Superman and why we love him so:

Gods achieve their power by encouraging us to believe in them.

Superman achieves his power by believing in us.

Mark Waid
Who Really Has Read Every Superman Story And Never One Better
2008

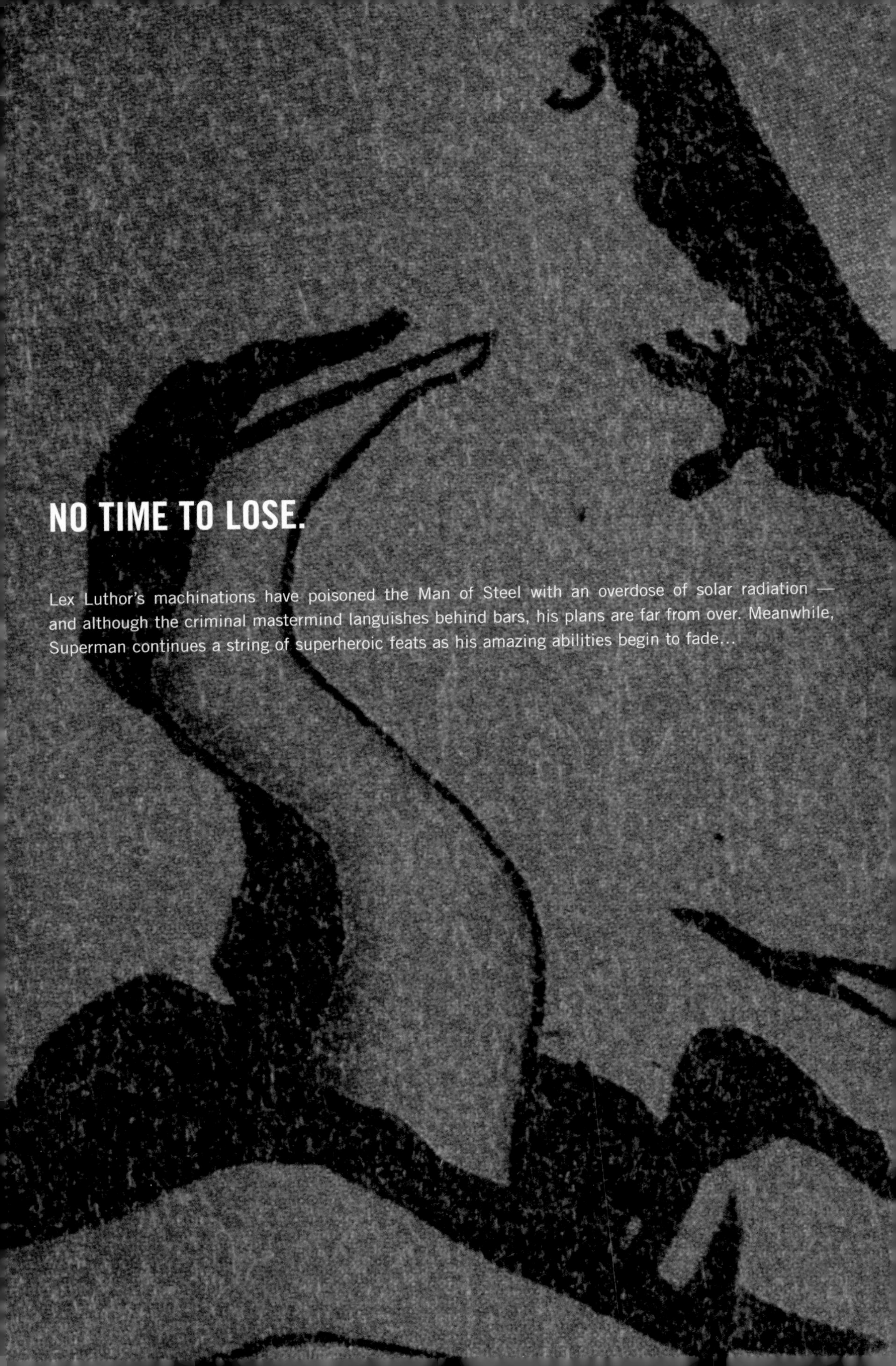

NO TIME TO LOSE.

Lex Luthor's machinations have poisoned the Man of Steel with an overdose of solar radiation — and although the criminal mastermind languishes behind bars, his plans are far from over. Meanwhile, Superman continues a string of superheroic feats as his amazing abilities begin to fade...

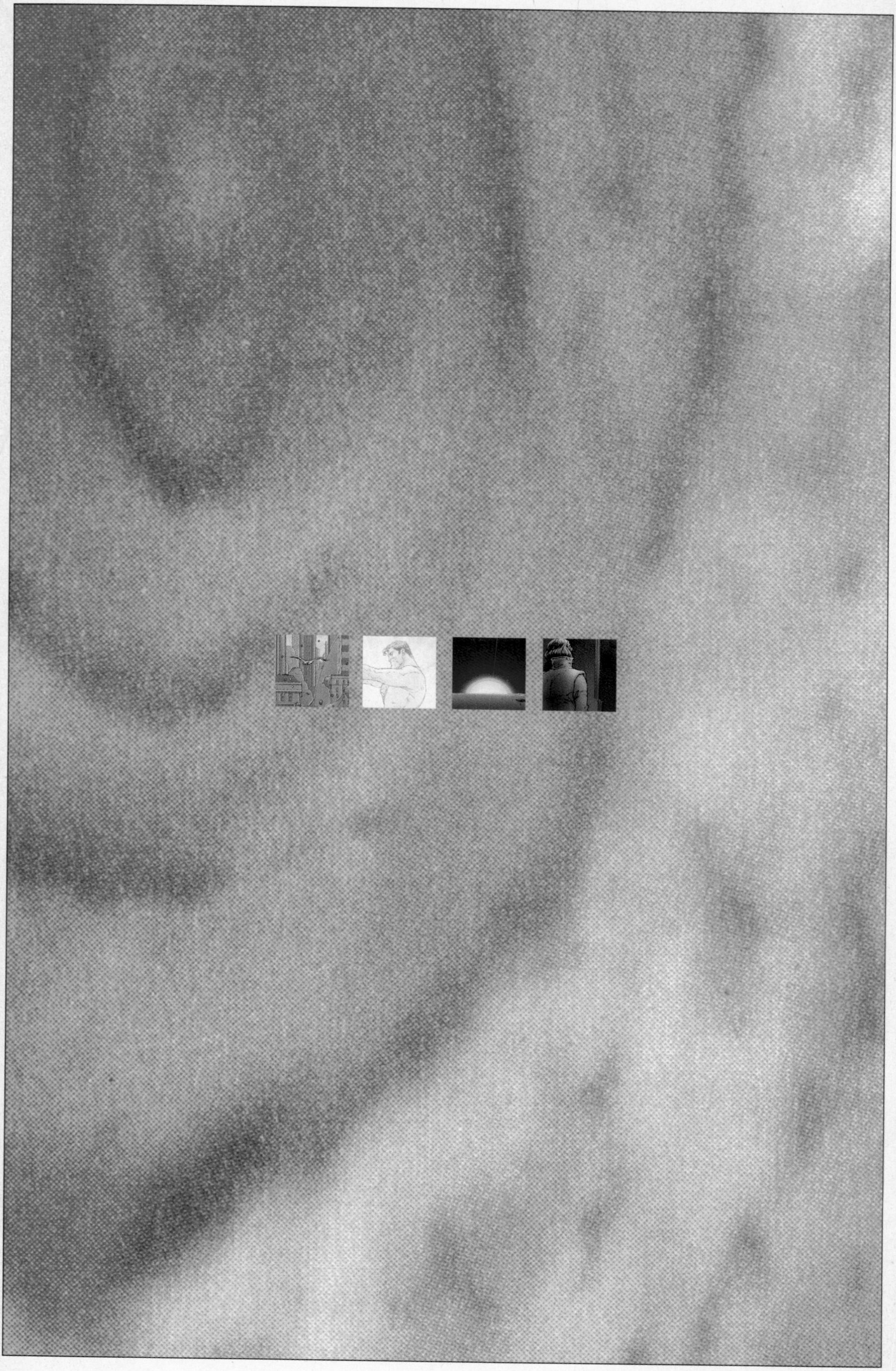

Episode 7

BEING BIZARRO

Cover FRANK QUITELY

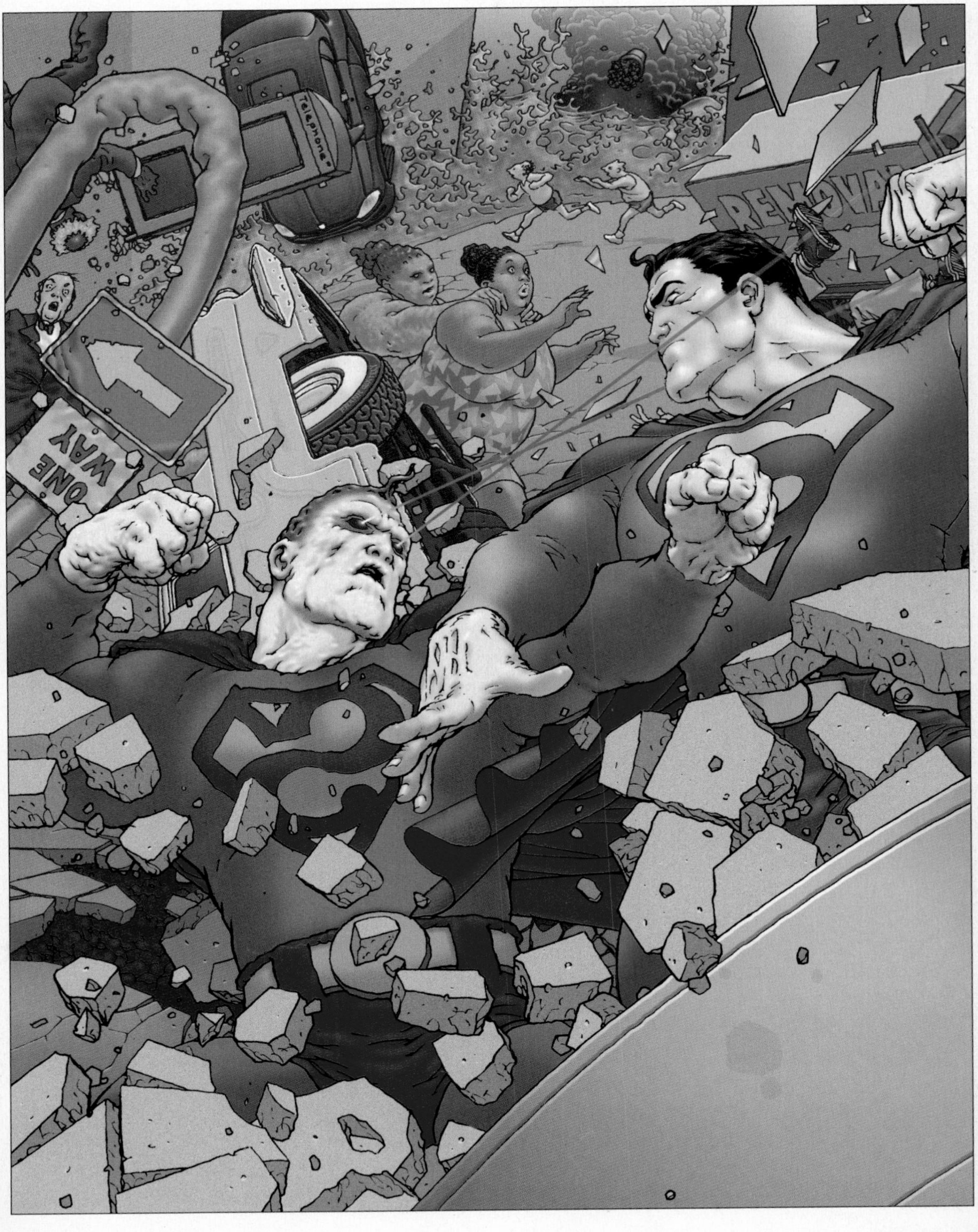
Telephone
ONE WAY

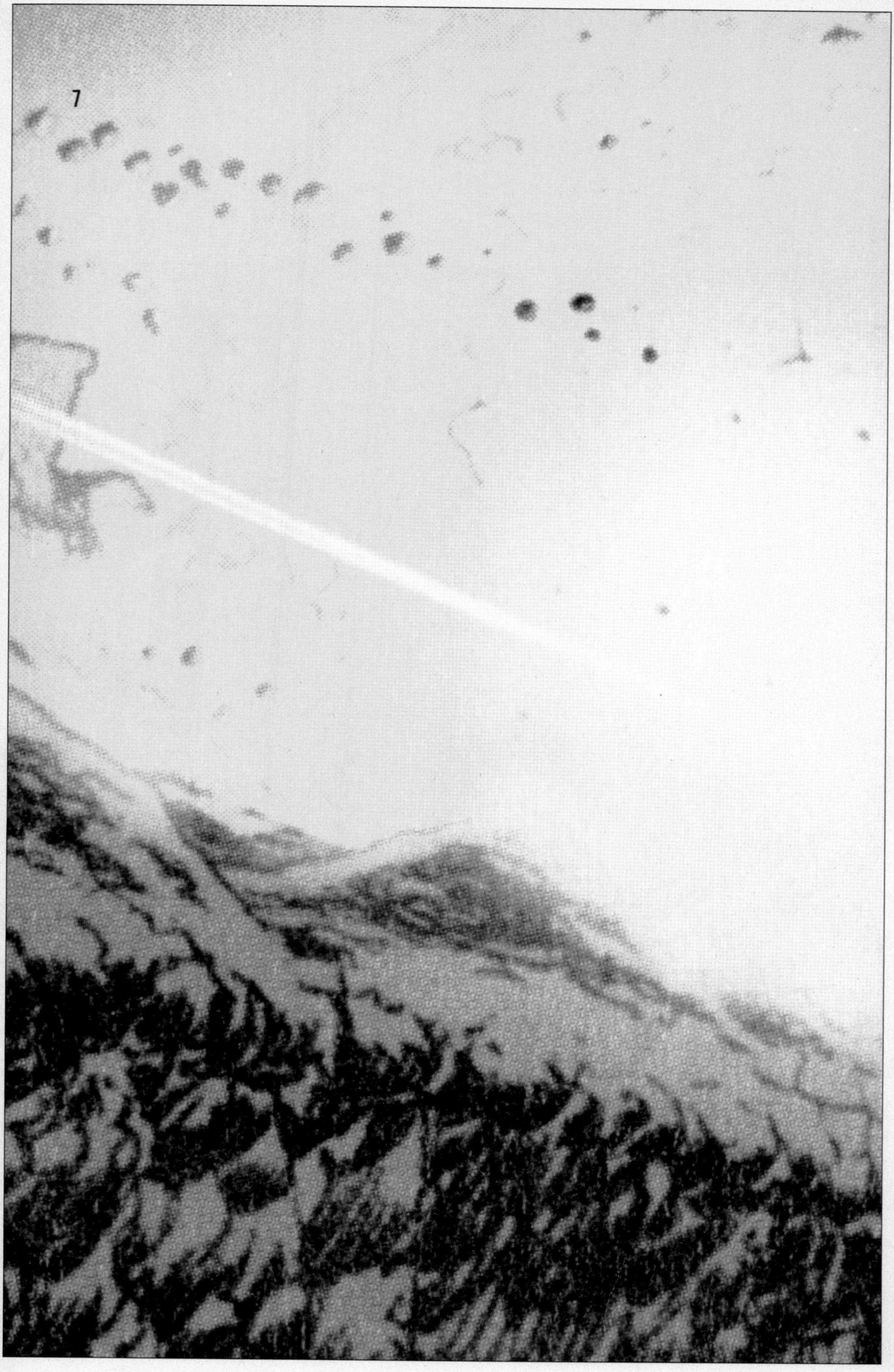

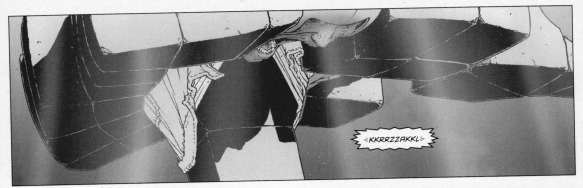

-KKRRZZAKKL-

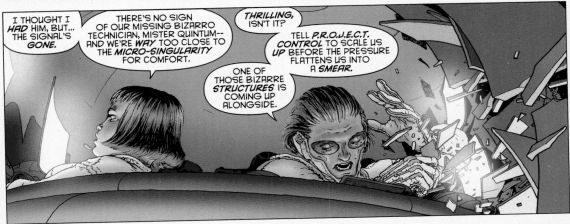

I THOUGHT I *HAD* HIM, BUT... THE SIGNAL'S *GONE.*

THERE'S NO SIGN OF OUR MISSING BIZARRO TECHNICIAN, MISTER QUINTUM-- AND WE'RE *WAY* TOO CLOSE TO THE *MICRO-SINGULARITY* FOR COMFORT.

THRILLING, ISN'T IT?

TELL *P.R.O.J.E.C.T. CONTROL* TO SCALE US *UP* BEFORE THE PRESSURE FLATTENS US INTO A *SMEAR.*

ONE OF THOSE BIZARRE *STRUCTURES* IS COMING UP ALONGSIDE.

...KZZZKTT CONDITIONS HERE IN THE *UNDERVERSE* MAKE FURTHER EXPLORATION *UNTENABLE* KZZZ...

...AND TELL THEM... ZZAKKTTLLL...

TELL THEM I THINK THERE MAY BE A *LIFEFORM* DOWN HERE.

SOMETHING BIG.

COMING CLOSER.

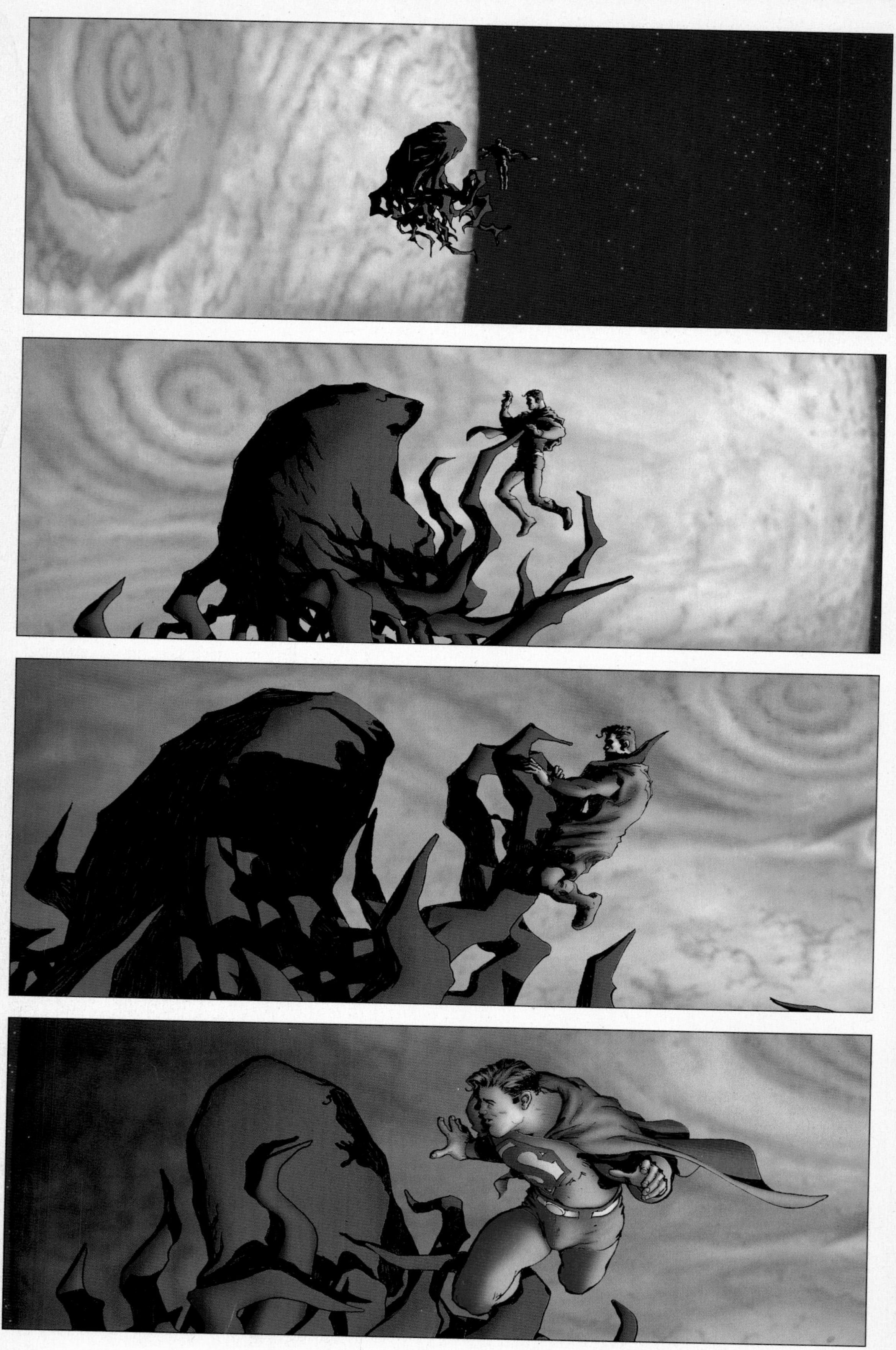

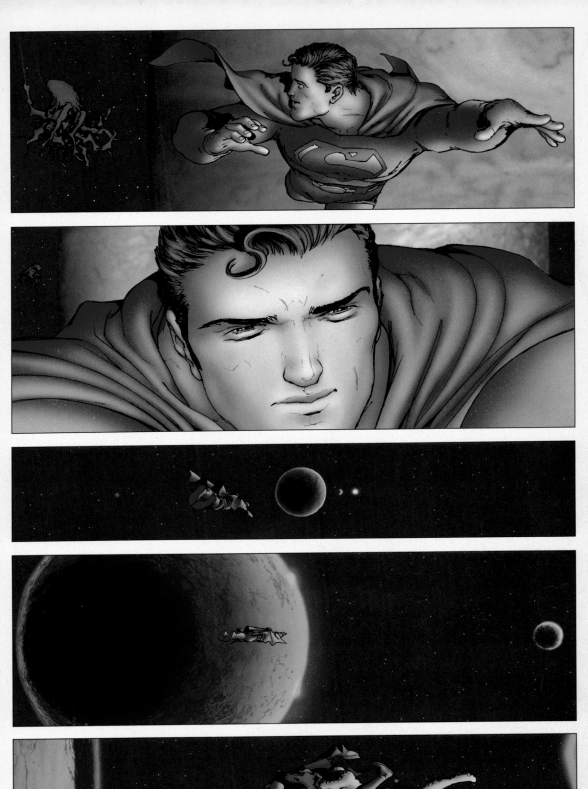

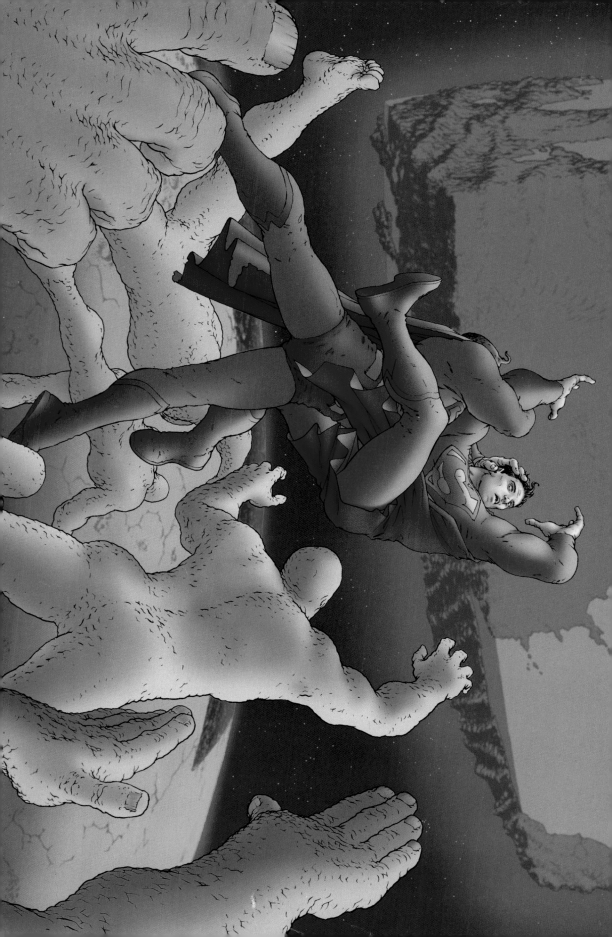

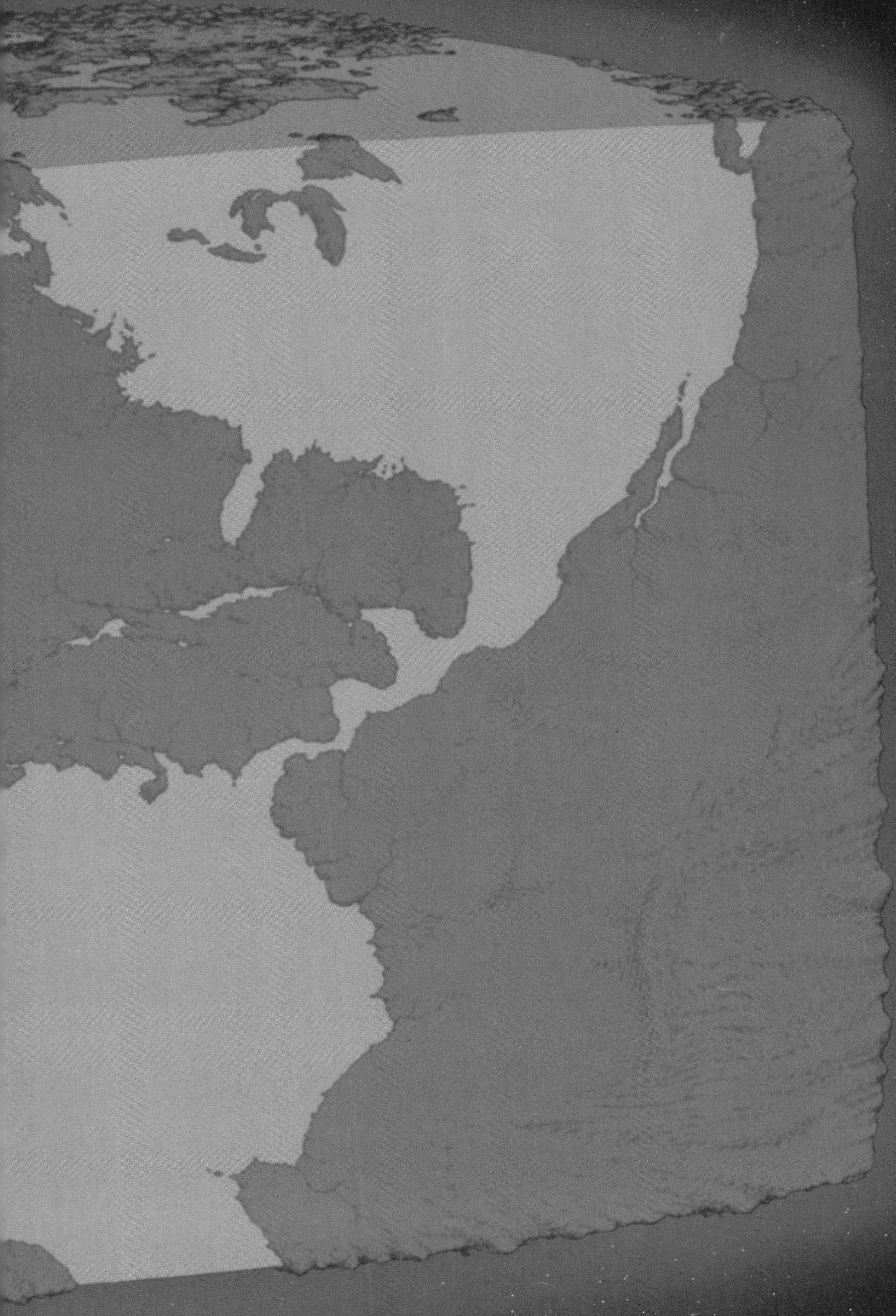

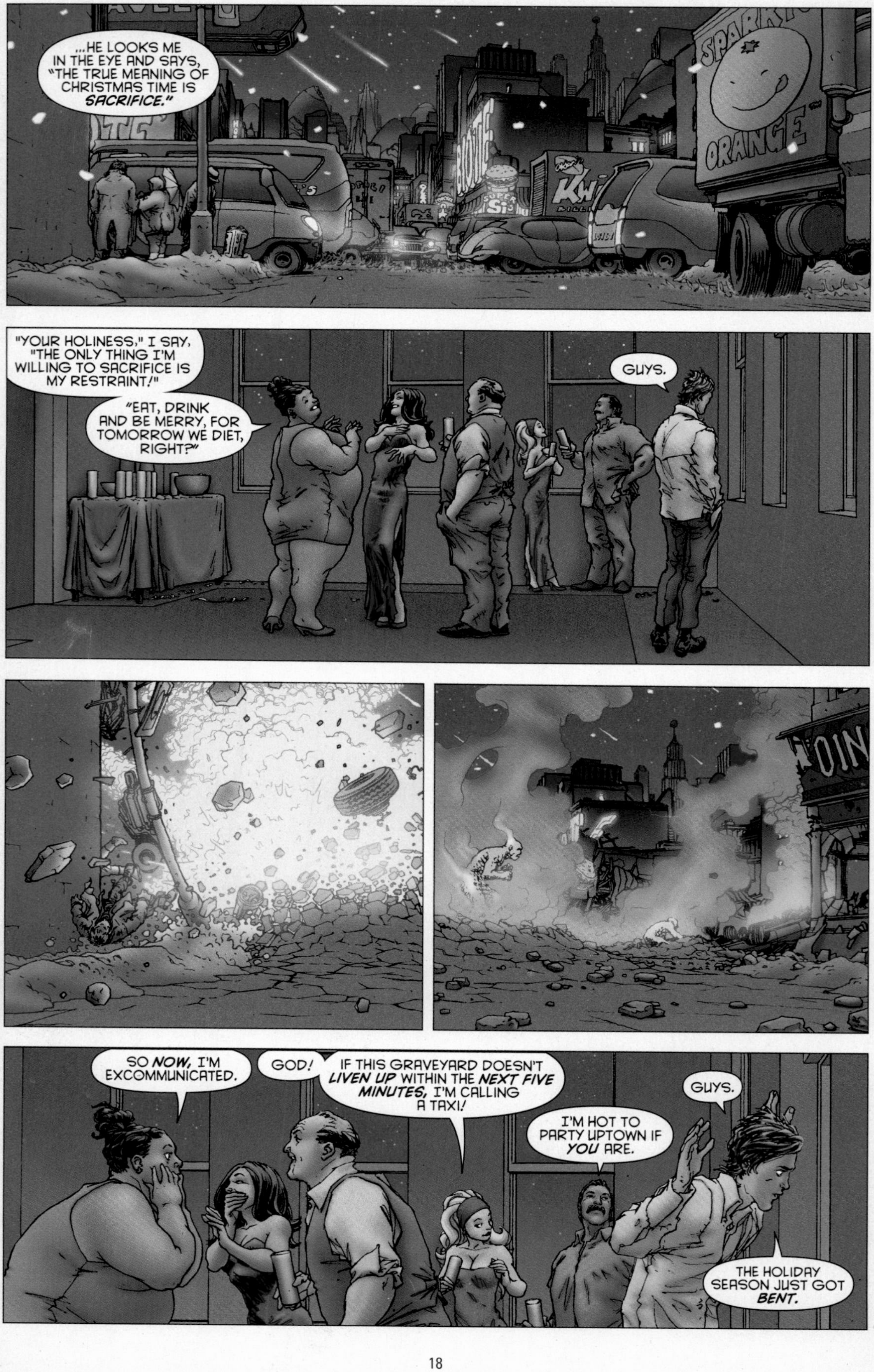
...HE LOOKS ME IN THE EYE AND SAYS, "THE TRUE MEANING OF CHRISTMAS TIME IS *SACRIFICE.*"
ORANGE
"YOUR HOLINESS," I SAY, "THE ONLY THING I'M WILLING TO SACRIFICE IS MY RESTRAINT!"
"EAT, DRINK AND BE MERRY, FOR TOMORROW WE DIET, RIGHT?"
GUYS.
SO *NOW,* I'M EXCOMMUNICATED.
GOD!
IF THIS GRAVEYARD DOESN'T *LIVEN UP* WITHIN THE *NEXT FIVE MINUTES,* I'M CALLING A TAXI!
I'M HOT TO PARTY UPTOWN IF *YOU* ARE.
GUYS.
THE HOLIDAY SEASON JUST GOT *BENT.*

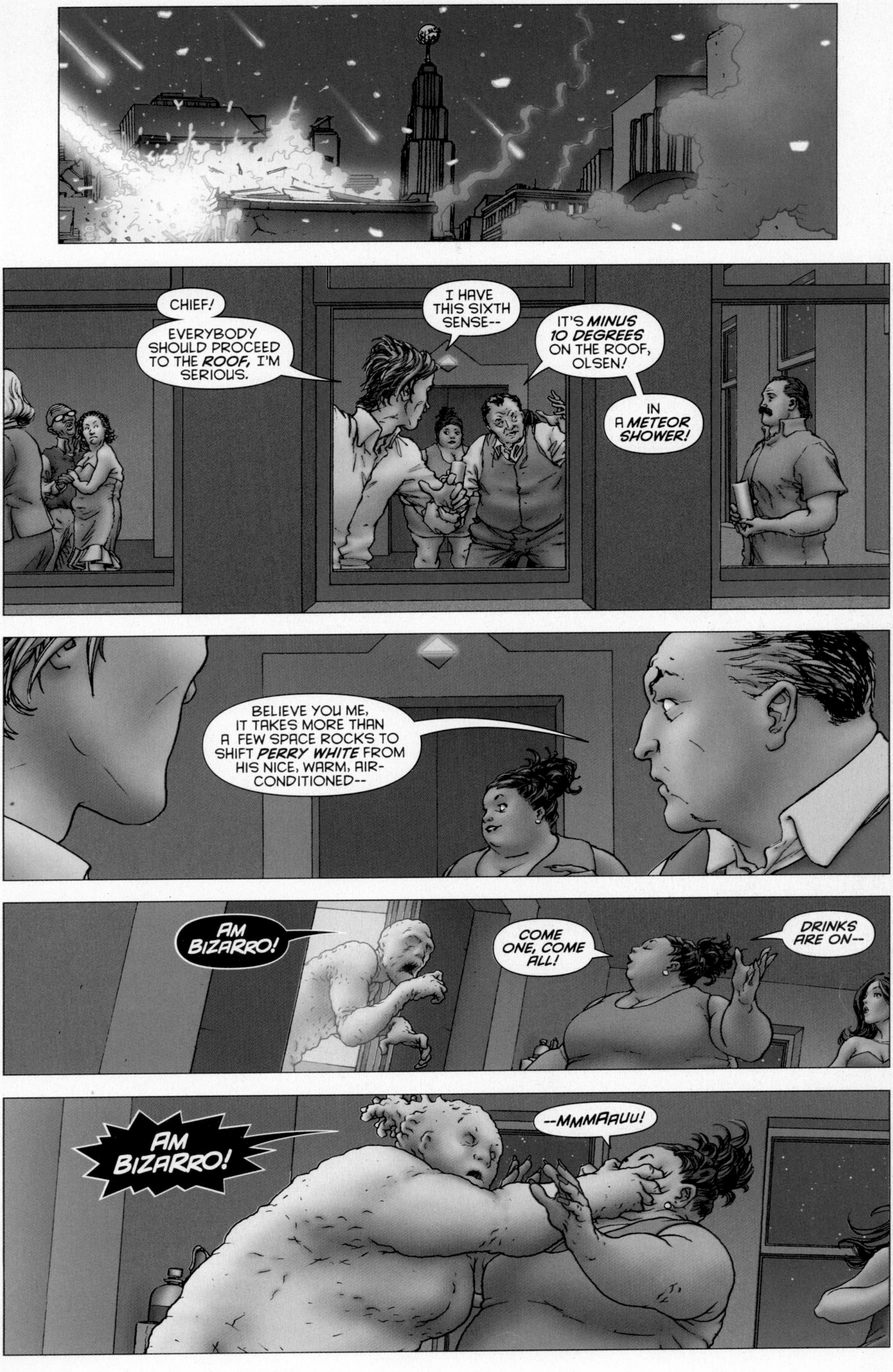
CHIEF!
EVERYBODY SHOULD PROCEED TO THE ROOF, I'M SERIOUS.
I HAVE THIS SIXTH SENSE--
IT'S MINUS 10 DEGREES ON THE ROOF, OLSEN!
IN A METEOR SHOWER!
BELIEVE YOU ME, IT TAKES MORE THAN A FEW SPACE ROCKS TO SHIFT PERRY WHITE FROM HIS NICE, WARM, AIR-CONDITIONED--
AM BIZARRO!
COME ONE, COME ALL!
DRINKS ARE ON--
AM BIZARRO!
--MMMAAUU!

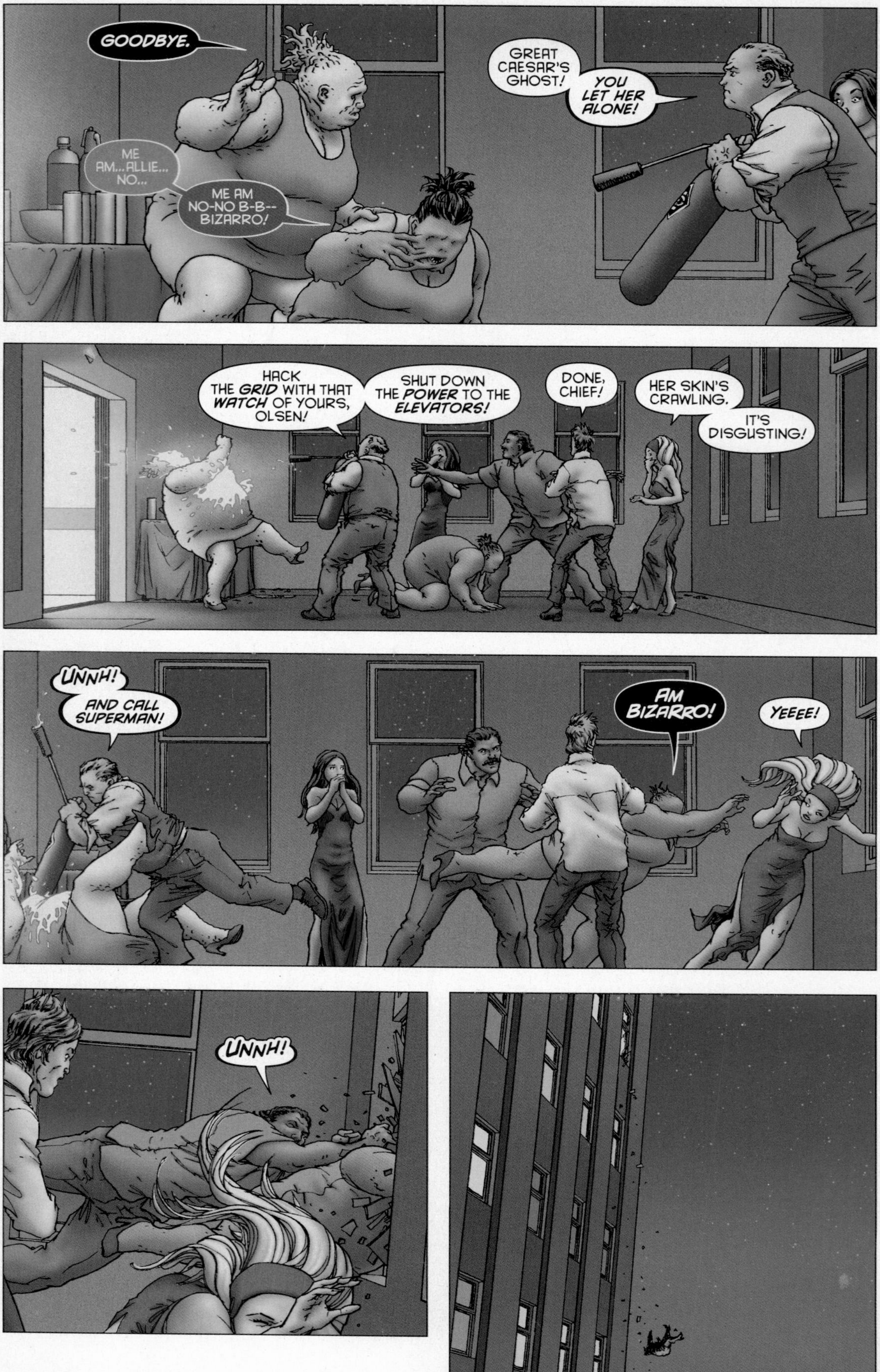
GOODBYE.
ME AM...ALLIE... NO...
ME AM NO-NO B-B-- BIZARRO!
GREAT CAESAR'S GHOST!
YOU LET HER ALONE!
HACK THE GRID WITH THAT WATCH OF YOURS, OLSEN!
SHUT DOWN THE POWER TO THE ELEVATORS!
DONE, CHIEF!
HER SKIN'S CRAWLING.
IT'S DISGUSTING!
UNNH!
AND CALL SUPERMAN!
AM BIZARRO!
YEEEE!
UNNH!

ALL RIGHT! SHE *TOUCHED* ME, WHAT CAN I SAY?

BUT I HAVEN'T *CHANGED,* LIKE ALLIE DID...

...I'M *IMMUNE* TO IT!

OH LORD, POOR *ALLIE!*

I JUST THREW HER OUT THE WINDOW LIKE A *FOOTBALL.*

STILL NO RESPONSE FROM *SUPERMAN.*

ZEEE ZEEEE

SUPERMAN?

DON'T FORGET WHO JUST SAVED *ALL* OUR LIVES.

FIRE EXIT

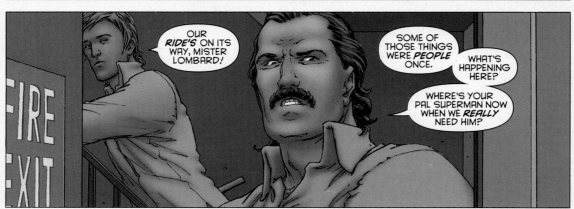

OUR *RIDE'S* ON ITS WAY, MISTER LOMBARD!

SOME OF THOSE THINGS WERE *PEOPLE* ONCE.

WHAT'S HAPPENING HERE?

WHERE'S YOUR PAL SUPERMAN NOW WHEN WE *REALLY* NEED HIM?

FIRE EXIT

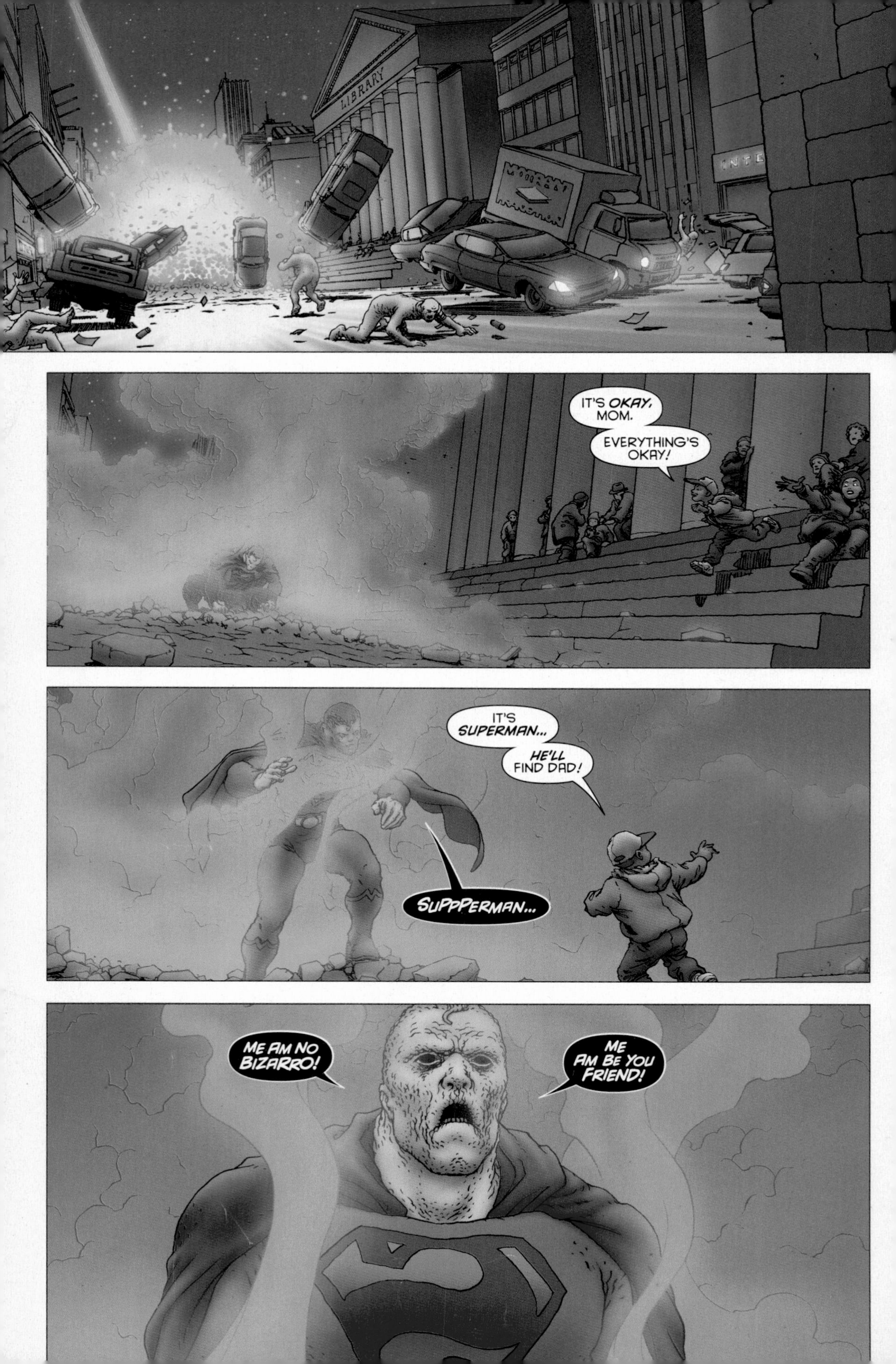
LIBRARY
IT'S *OKAY*, MOM.
EVERYTHING'S OKAY!
IT'S *SUPERMAN*...
HE'LL FIND DAD!
SUPPPERMAN...
ME AM NO BIZARRO!
ME AM BE YOU FRIEND!

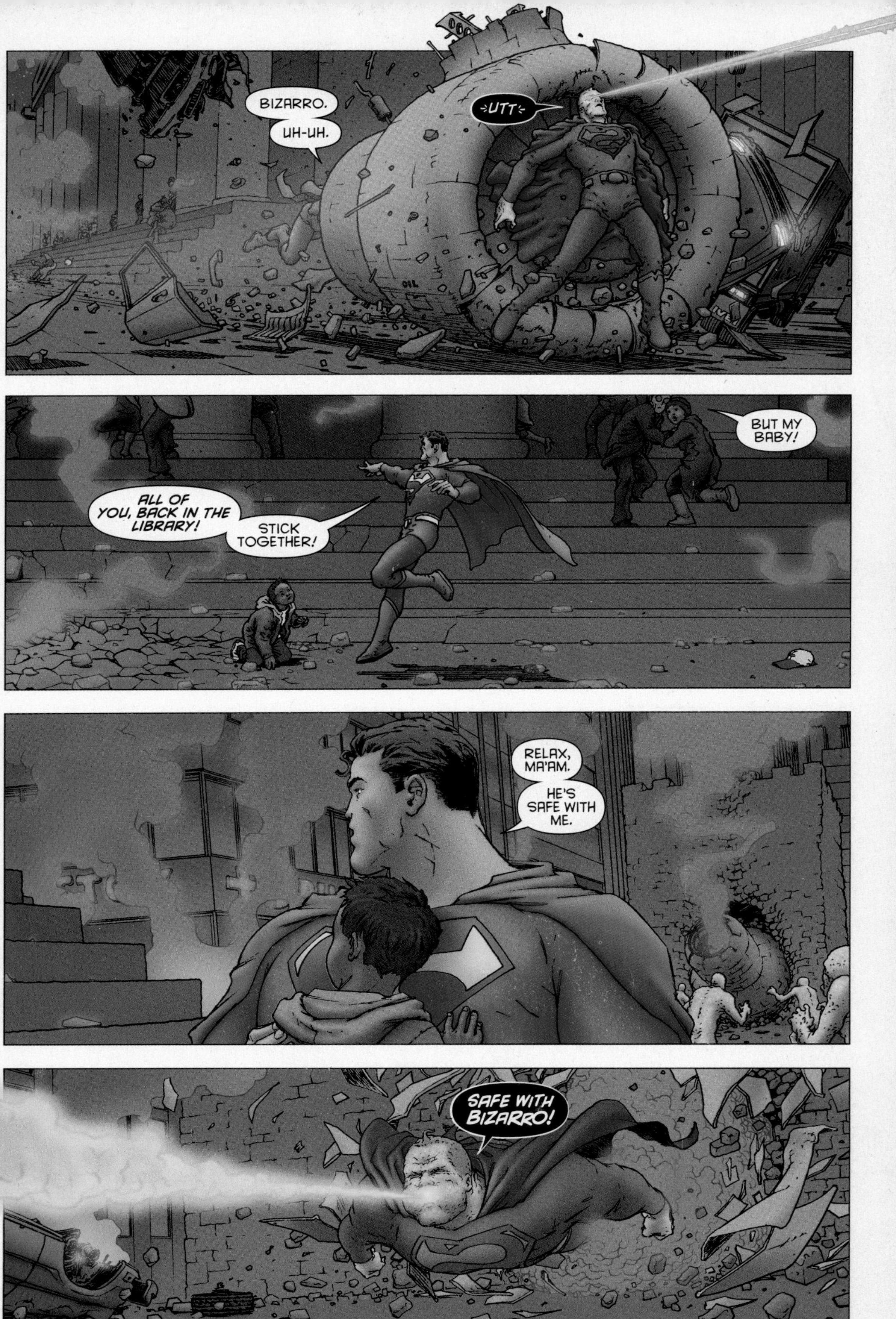
BIZARRO.
UH-UH.
UTT
BUT MY BABY!
ALL OF YOU, BACK IN THE LIBRARY!
STICK TOGETHER!
RELAX, MA'AM.
HE'S SAFE WITH ME.
SAFE WITH BIZARRO!

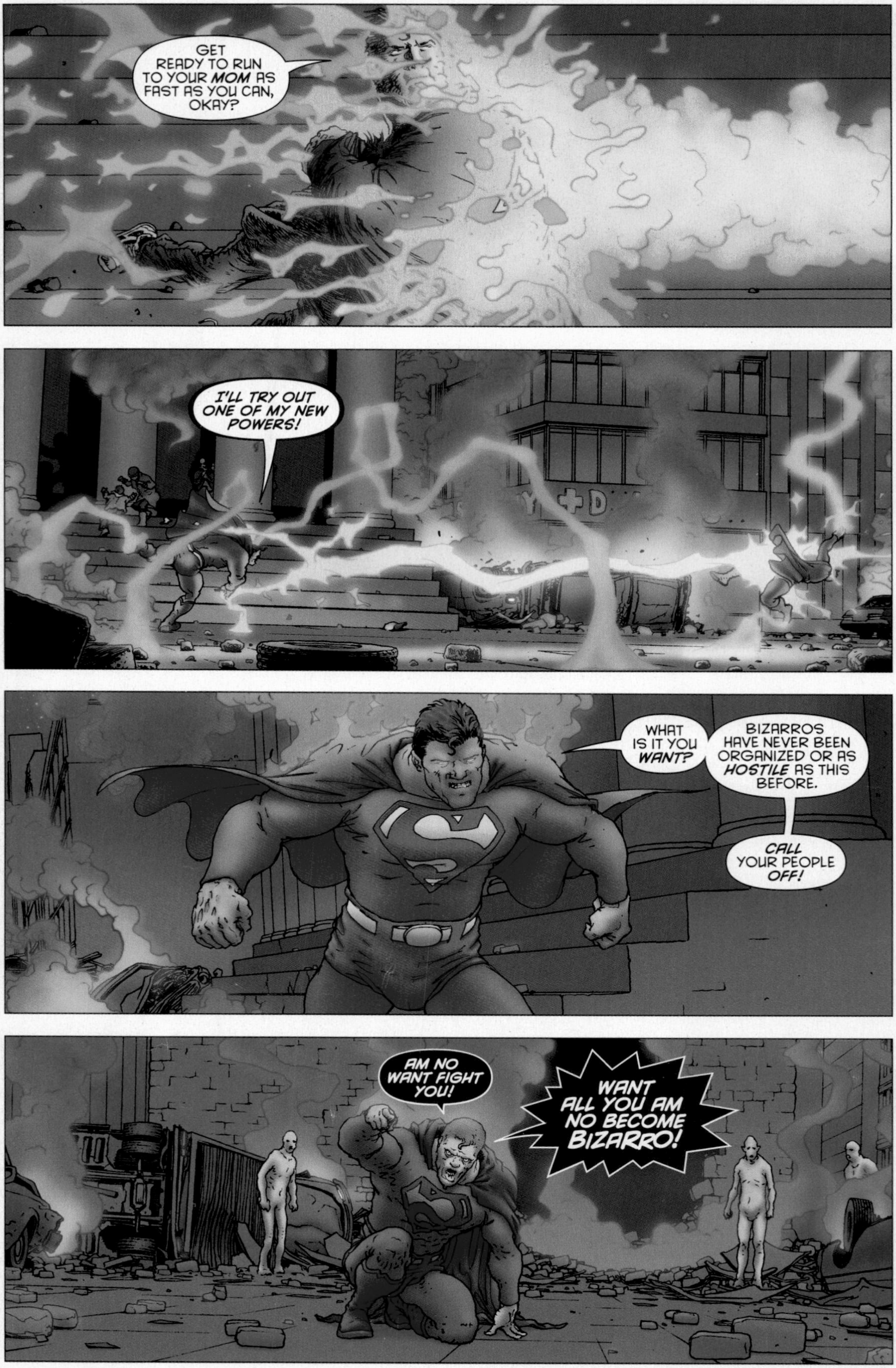
GET READY TO RUN TO YOUR MOM AS FAST AS YOU CAN, OKAY?
I'LL TRY OUT ONE OF MY NEW POWERS!
WHAT IS IT YOU WANT?
BIZARROS HAVE NEVER BEEN ORGANIZED OR AS HOSTILE AS THIS BEFORE.
CALL YOUR PEOPLE OFF!
AM NO WANT FIGHT YOU!
WANT ALL YOU AM NO BECOME BIZARRO!

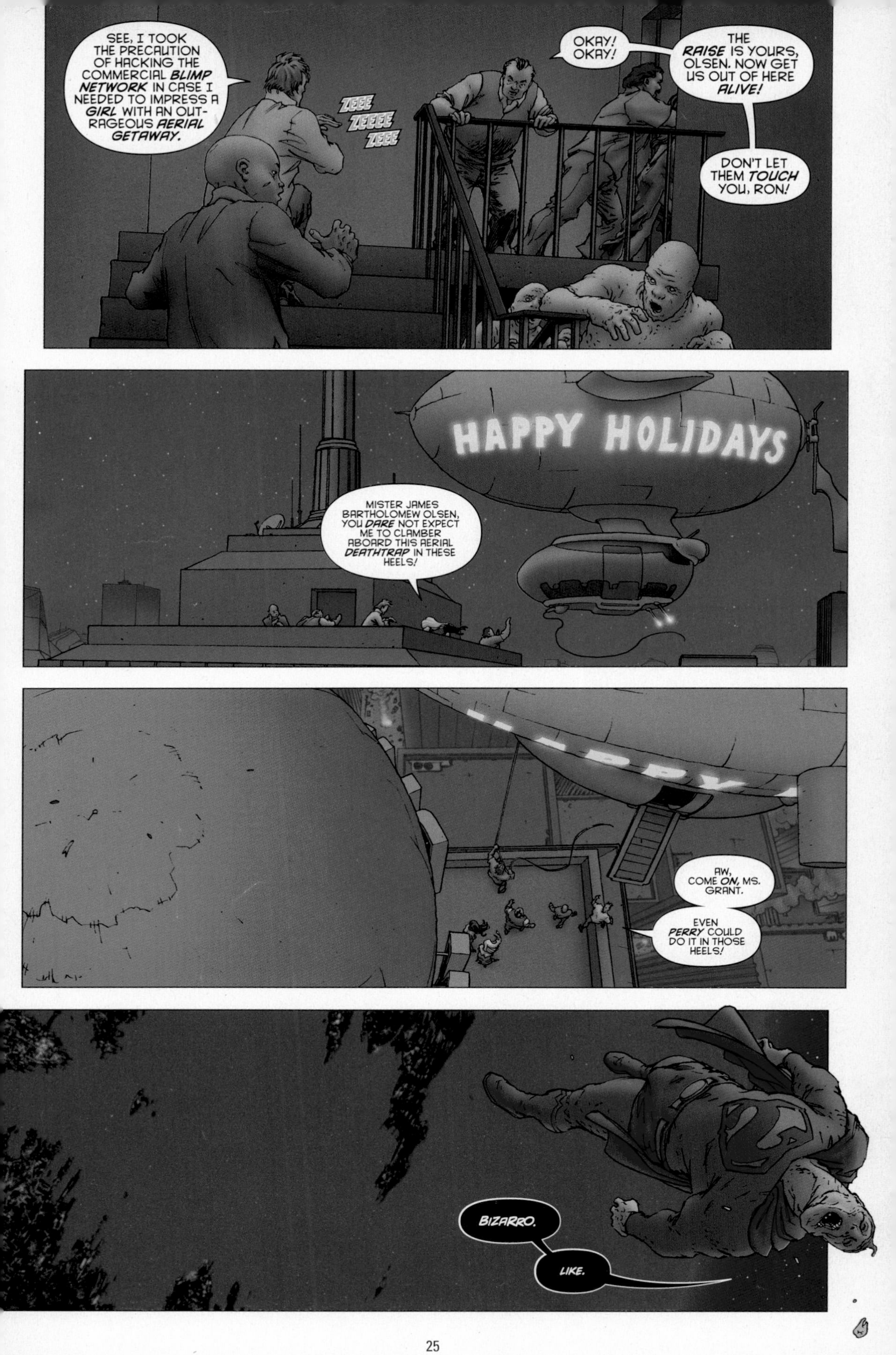
SEE, I TOOK THE PRECAUTION OF HACKING THE COMMERCIAL BLIMP NETWORK IN CASE I NEEDED TO IMPRESS A GIRL WITH AN OUT-RAGEOUS AERIAL GETAWAY.
ZEEE
ZEEEE
ZEEE
OKAY! OKAY!
THE RAISE IS YOURS, OLSEN. NOW GET US OUT OF HERE ALIVE!
DON'T LET THEM TOUCH YOU, RON!
HAPPY HOLIDAYS
MISTER JAMES BARTHOLOMEW OLSEN, YOU DARE NOT EXPECT ME TO CLAMBER ABOARD THIS AERIAL DEATHTRAP IN THESE HEELS!
AW, COME ON, MS. GRANT.
EVEN PERRY COULD DO IT IN THOSE HEELS!
BIZARRO.
LIKE.

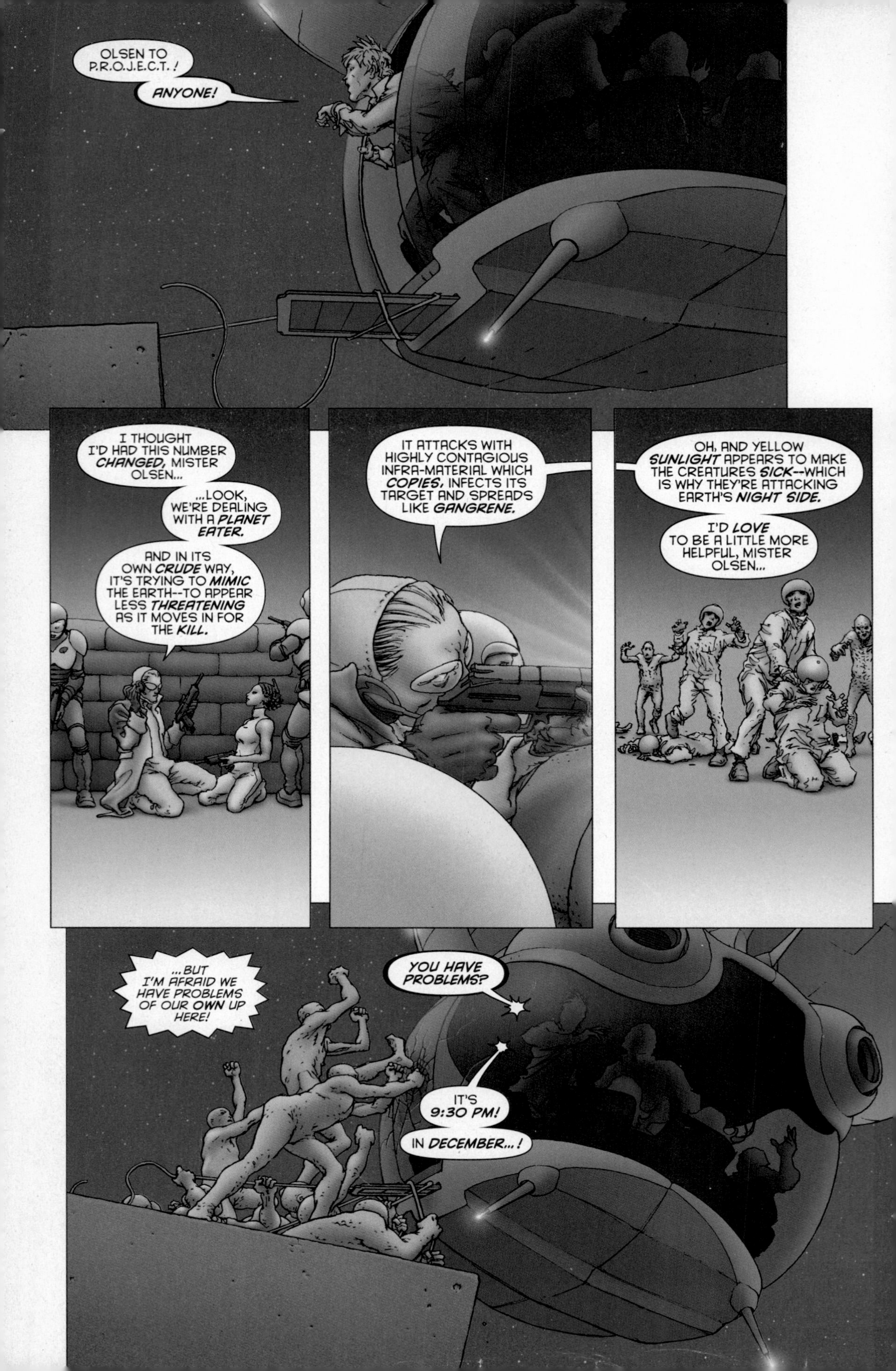

OLSEN TO P.R.O.J.E.C.T.!
ANYONE!
I THOUGHT I'D HAD THIS NUMBER CHANGED, MISTER OLSEN...
...LOOK, WE'RE DEALING WITH A PLANET EATER.
AND IN ITS OWN CRUDE WAY, IT'S TRYING TO MIMIC THE EARTH--TO APPEAR LESS THREATENING AS IT MOVES IN FOR THE KILL.
IT ATTACKS WITH HIGHLY CONTAGIOUS INFRA-MATERIAL WHICH COPIES, INFECTS ITS TARGET AND SPREADS LIKE GANGRENE.
OH, AND YELLOW SUNLIGHT APPEARS TO MAKE THE CREATURES SICK--WHICH IS WHY THEY'RE ATTACKING EARTH'S NIGHT SIDE.
I'D LOVE TO BE A LITTLE MORE HELPFUL, MISTER OLSEN...
...BUT I'M AFRAID WE HAVE PROBLEMS OF OUR OWN UP HERE!
YOU HAVE PROBLEMS?
IT'S 9:30 PM!
IN DECEMBER...!

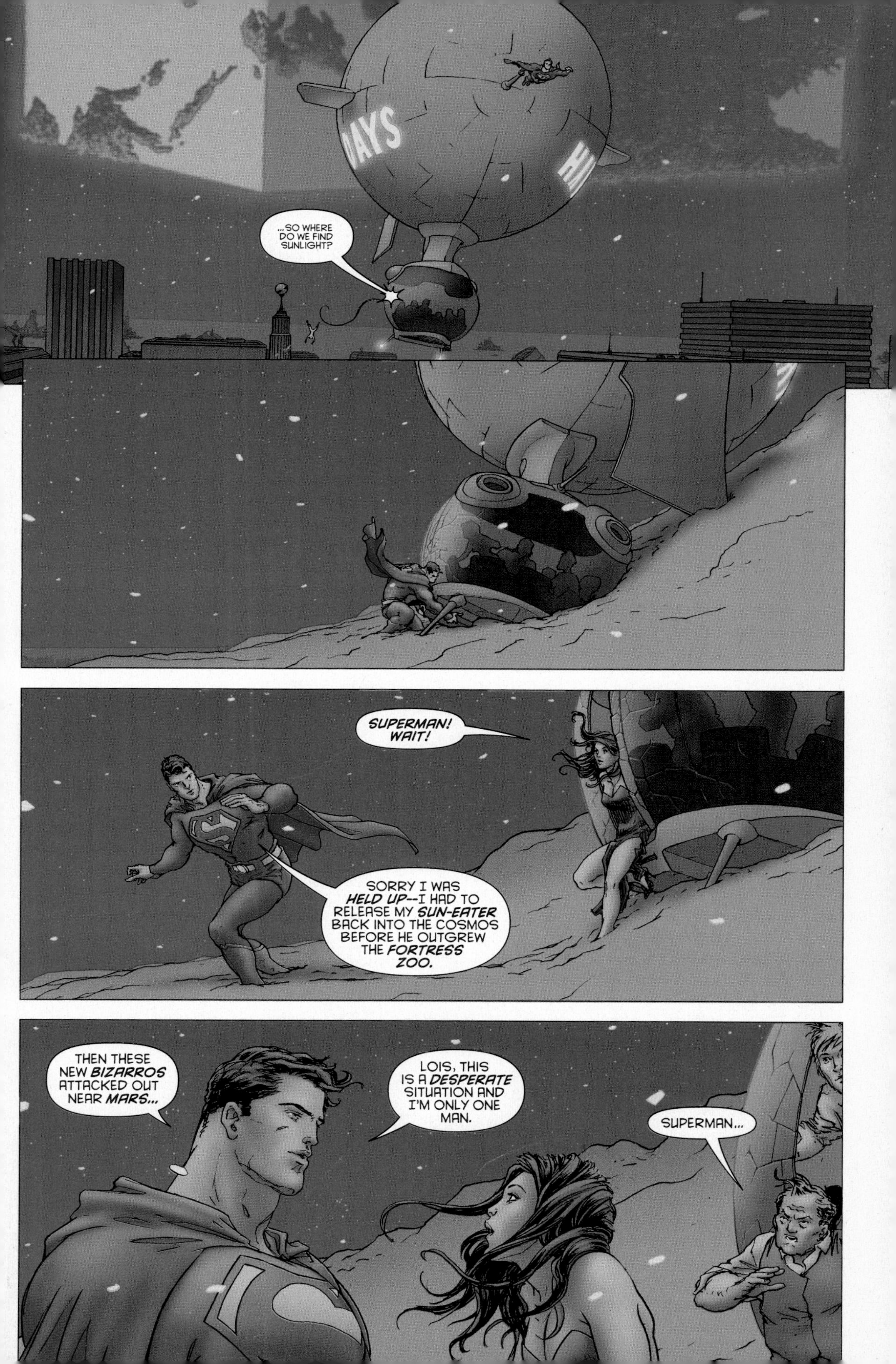
DAYS
...SO WHERE DO WE FIND SUNLIGHT?
SUPERMAN! WAIT!
SORRY I WAS HELD UP--I HAD TO RELEASE MY SUN-EATER BACK INTO THE COSMOS BEFORE HE OUTGREW THE FORTRESS ZOO.
THEN THESE NEW BIZARROS ATTACKED OUT NEAR MARS...
LOIS, THIS IS A DESPERATE SITUATION AND I'M ONLY ONE MAN.
SUPERMAN...

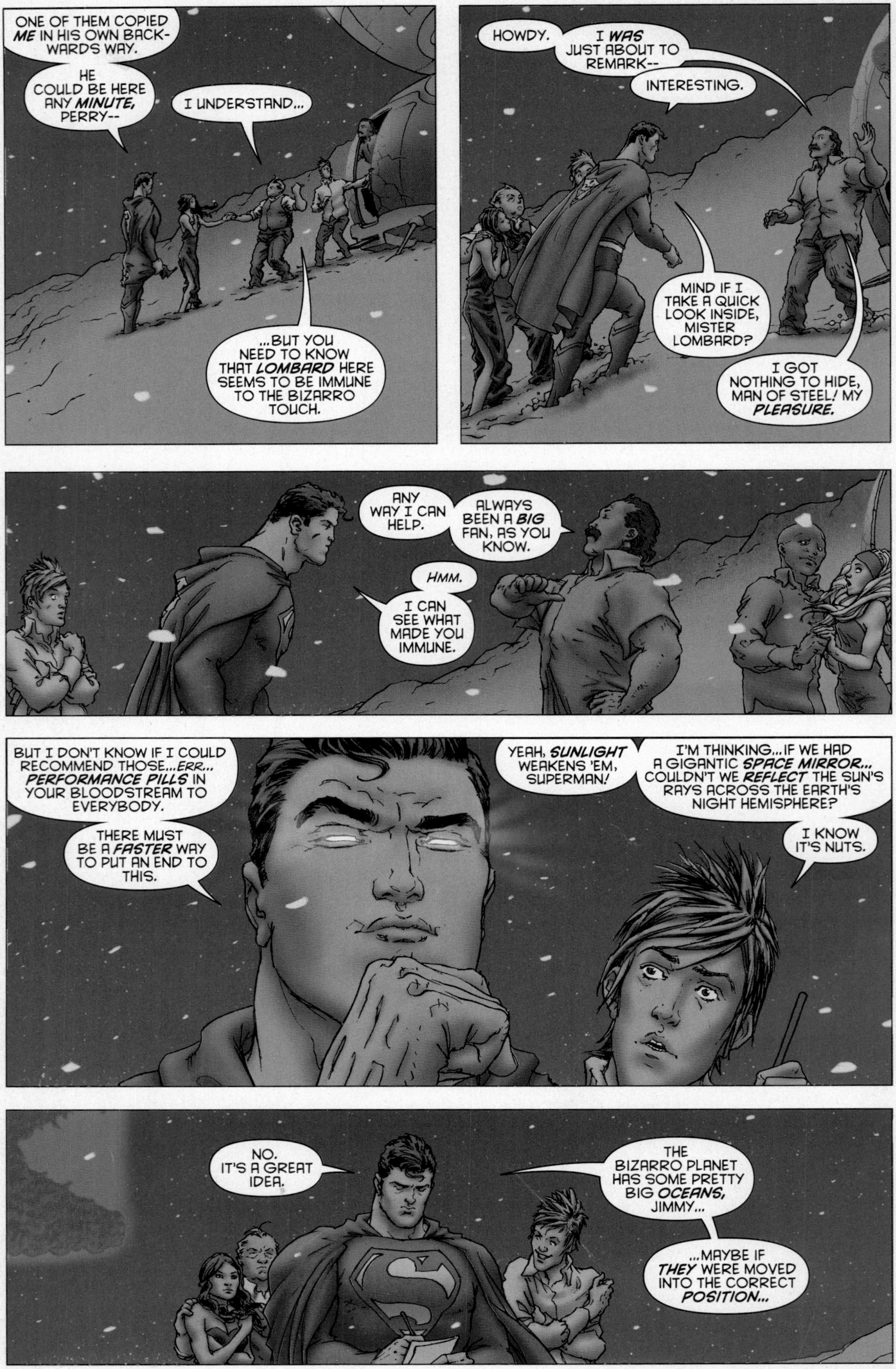
ONE OF THEM COPIED *ME* IN HIS OWN BACK-WARDS WAY.
HE COULD BE HERE ANY *MINUTE,* PERRY--
I UNDERSTAND...
...BUT YOU NEED TO KNOW THAT *LOMBARD* HERE SEEMS TO BE IMMUNE TO THE BIZARRO TOUCH.
HOWDY.
I *WAS* JUST ABOUT TO REMARK--
INTERESTING.
MIND IF I TAKE A QUICK LOOK INSIDE, MISTER LOMBARD?
I GOT NOTHING TO HIDE, MAN OF STEEL! MY *PLEASURE.*
ANY WAY I CAN HELP.
ALWAYS BEEN A *BIG* FAN, AS YOU KNOW.
HMM.
I CAN SEE WHAT MADE YOU IMMUNE.
BUT I DON'T KNOW IF I COULD RECOMMEND THOSE... *ERR... PERFORMANCE PILLS* IN YOUR BLOODSTREAM TO EVERYBODY.
THERE MUST BE A *FASTER* WAY TO PUT AN END TO THIS.
YEAH, *SUNLIGHT* WEAKENS 'EM, SUPERMAN!
I'M THINKING... IF WE HAD A GIGANTIC *SPACE MIRROR...* COULDN'T WE *REFLECT* THE SUN'S RAYS ACROSS THE EARTH'S NIGHT HEMISPHERE?
I KNOW IT'S NUTS.
NO. IT'S A GREAT IDEA.
THE BIZARRO PLANET HAS SOME PRETTY BIG *OCEANS,* JIMMY...
...MAYBE IF *THEY* WERE MOVED INTO THE CORRECT *POSITION...*

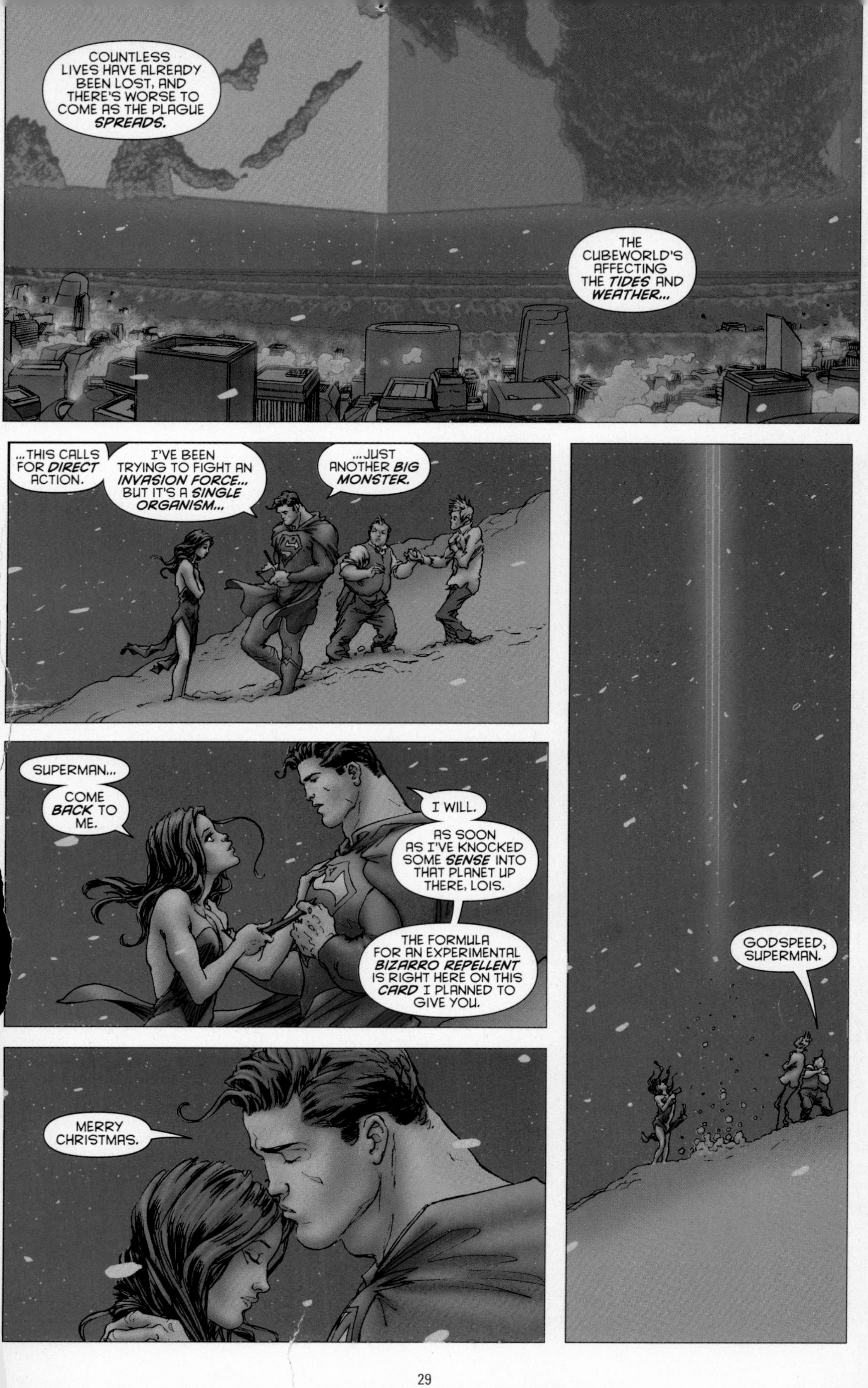
COUNTLESS LIVES HAVE ALREADY BEEN LOST, AND THERE'S WORSE TO COME AS THE PLAGUE SPREADS.
THE CUBEWORLD'S AFFECTING THE TIDES AND WEATHER...
...THIS CALLS FOR DIRECT ACTION.
I'VE BEEN TRYING TO FIGHT AN INVASION FORCE... BUT IT'S A SINGLE ORGANISM...
...JUST ANOTHER BIG MONSTER.
SUPERMAN...
COME BACK TO ME.
I WILL.
AS SOON AS I'VE KNOCKED SOME SENSE INTO THAT PLANET UP THERE, LOIS.
THE FORMULA FOR AN EXPERIMENTAL BIZARRO REPELLENT IS RIGHT HERE ON THIS CARD I PLANNED TO GIVE YOU.
MERRY CHRISTMAS.
GODSPEED, SUPERMAN.

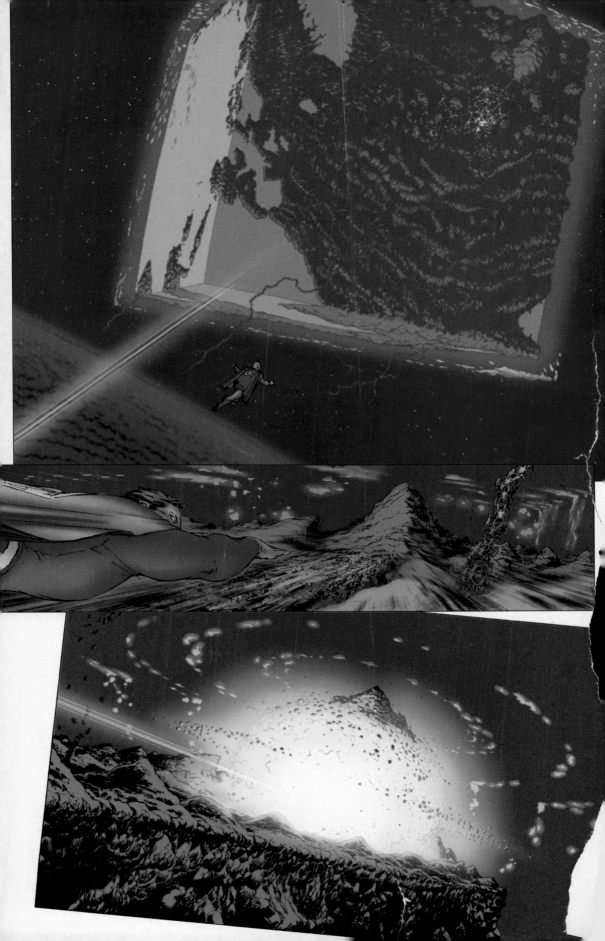

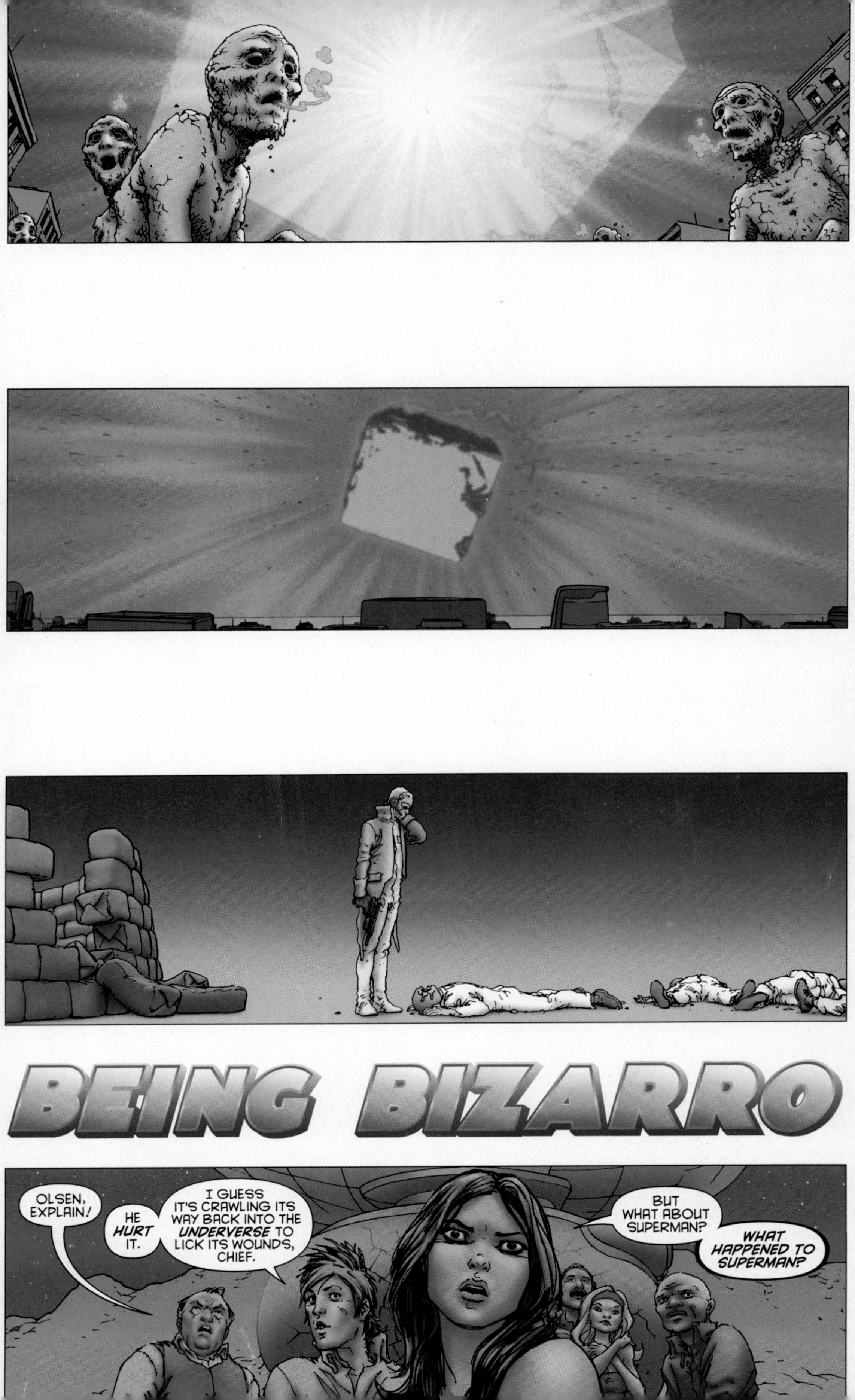
BEING BIZARRO
OLSEN, EXPLAIN!
HE *HURT* IT.
I GUESS IT'S CRAWLING ITS WAY BACK INTO THE *UNDERVERSE* TO LICK ITS WOUNDS, CHIEF.
BUT WHAT ABOUT SUPERMAN?
WHAT HAPPENED TO SUPERMAN?

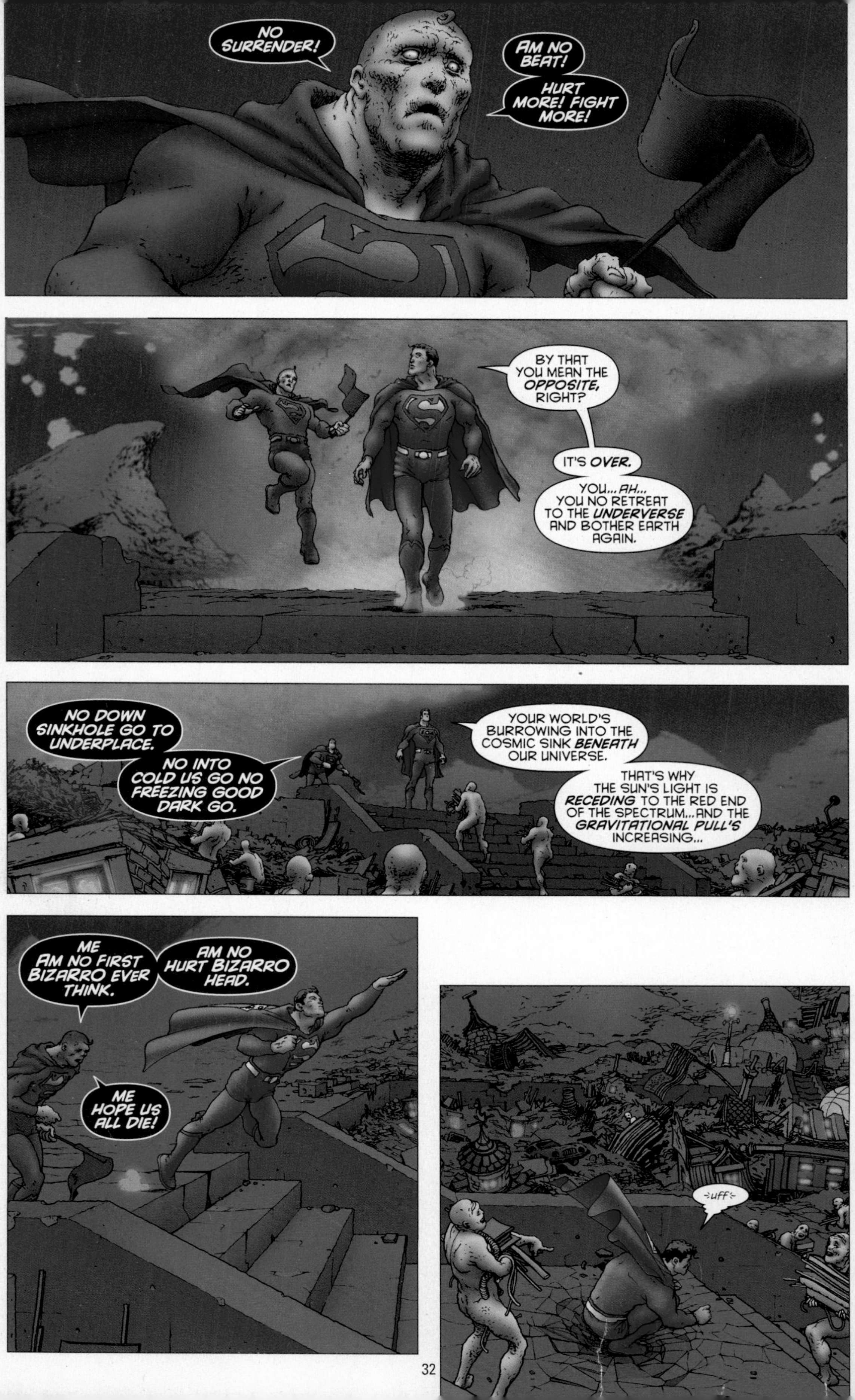
NO SURRENDER!
AM NO BEAT!
HURT MORE! FIGHT MORE!
BY THAT YOU MEAN THE OPPOSITE, RIGHT?
IT'S OVER.
YOU...AH... YOU NO RETREAT TO THE UNDERVERSE AND BOTHER EARTH AGAIN.
NO DOWN SINKHOLE GO TO UNDERPLACE.
NO INTO COLD US GO NO FREEZING GOOD DARK GO.
YOUR WORLD'S BURROWING INTO THE COSMIC SINK BENEATH OUR UNIVERSE.
THAT'S WHY THE SUN'S LIGHT IS RECEDING TO THE RED END OF THE SPECTRUM...AND THE GRAVITATIONAL PULL'S INCREASING...
ME AM NO FIRST BIZARRO EVER THINK.
AM NO HURT BIZARRO HEAD.
ME HOPE US ALL DIE!
=UFF=

I CAN'T FLY! MY POWERS ARE ALREADY FADING!

BIZARRO, I NEED YOUR HELP OR I'LL DIE HERE AND LEAVE MY WORLD IN DANGER!

DIE AM GOOD!

YOU'LL GET NO HELP THERE, SUPERMAN.

BUT ONE IN EVERY 5 BILLION COPIES IS FLAWED.

UNIQUE.

DIFFERENT.

NOT MINDLESS LIKE THESE SHAMBLING MOCKERIES-- BUT SENSITIVE, AND SELF-AWARE.

SUFFERING, ALONE, IN A WORLD OF CONFUSION.

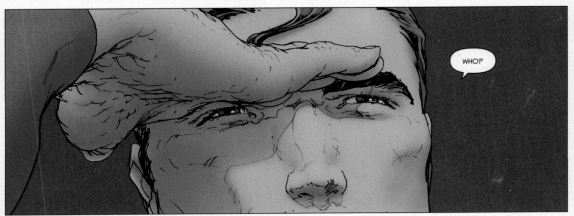

WHO?

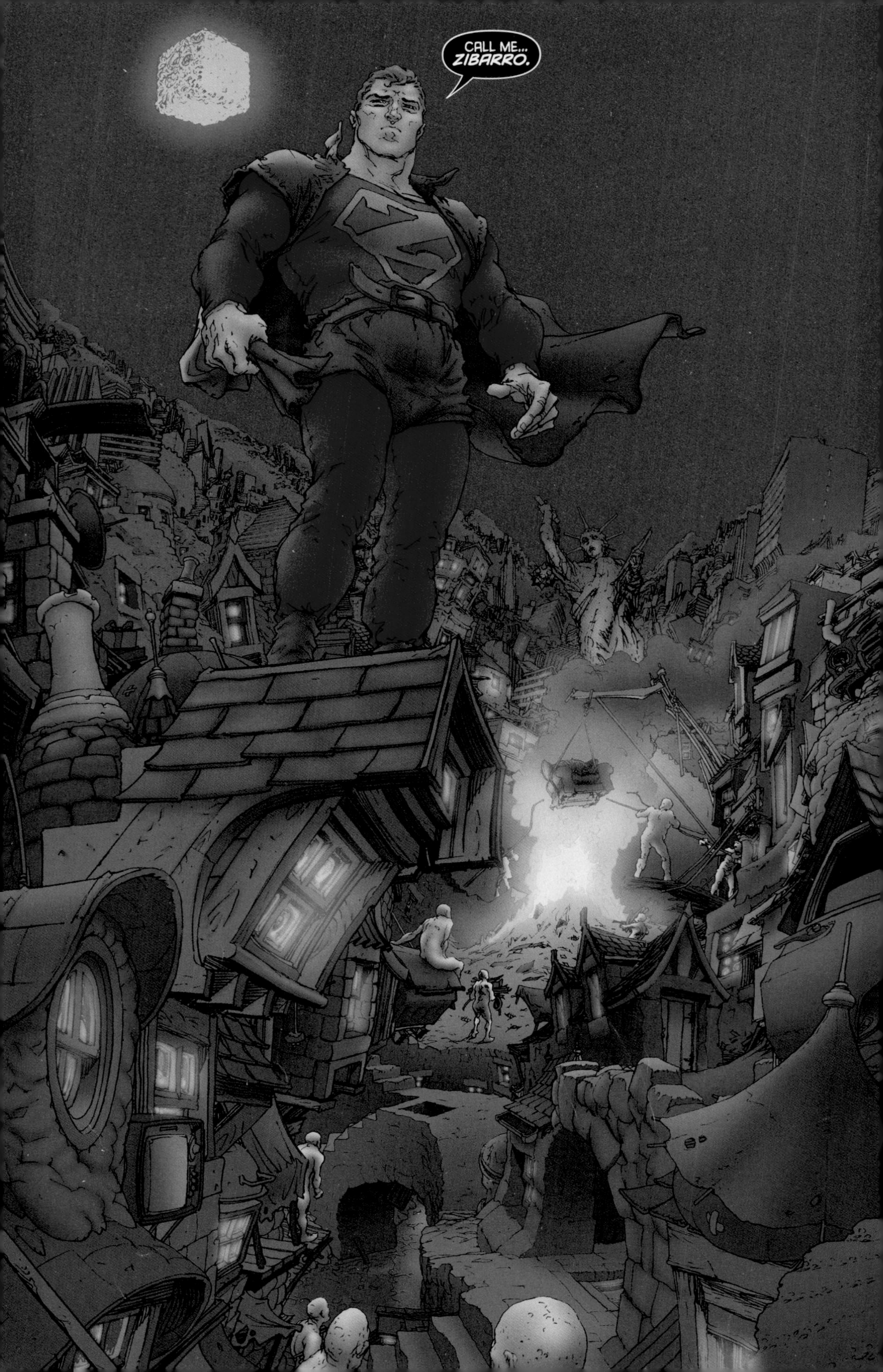
CALL ME... ZIBARRO.

Episode 8

US DO OPPOSITE

Cover FRANK QUITELY with JAMIE GRANT

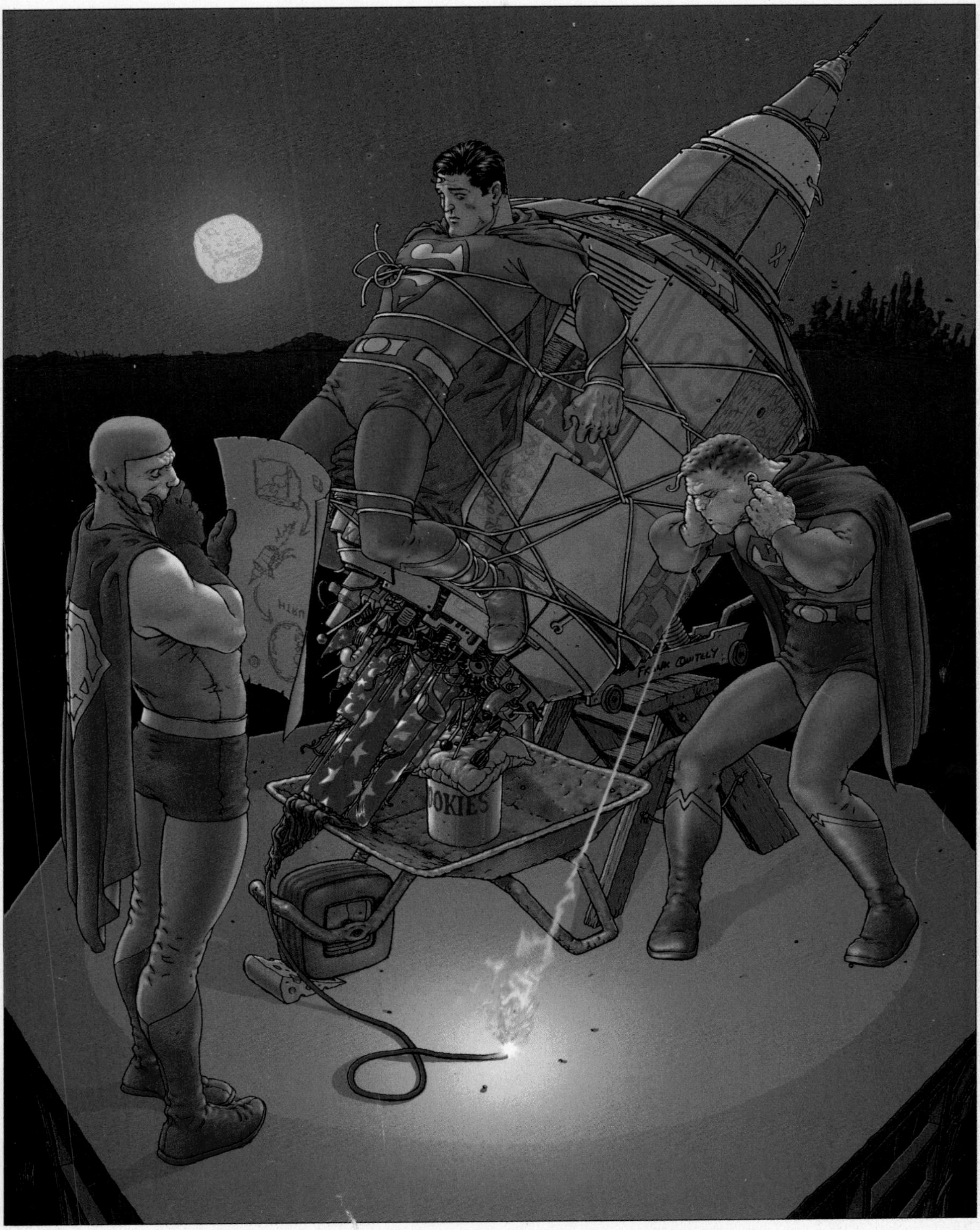
FRANK QUITELY

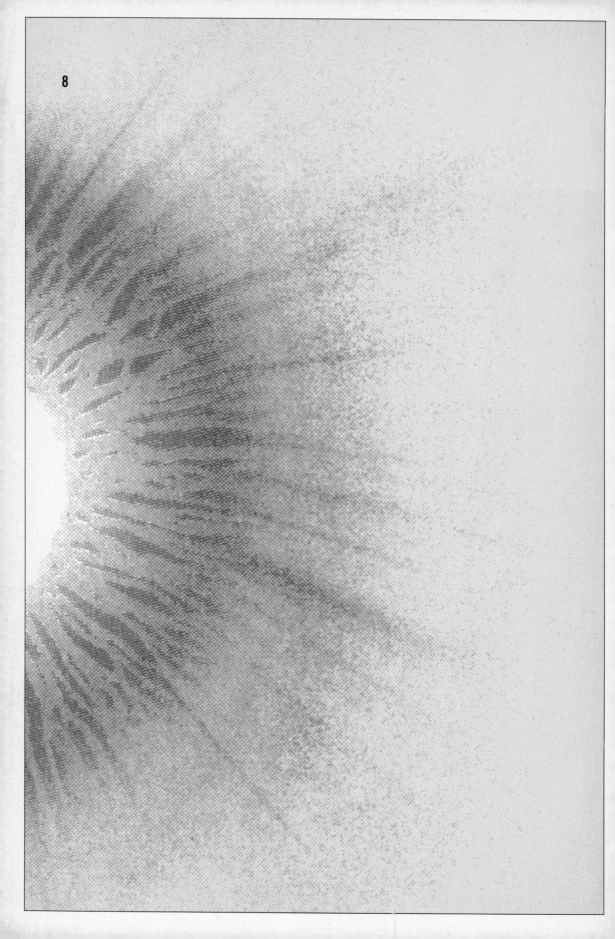

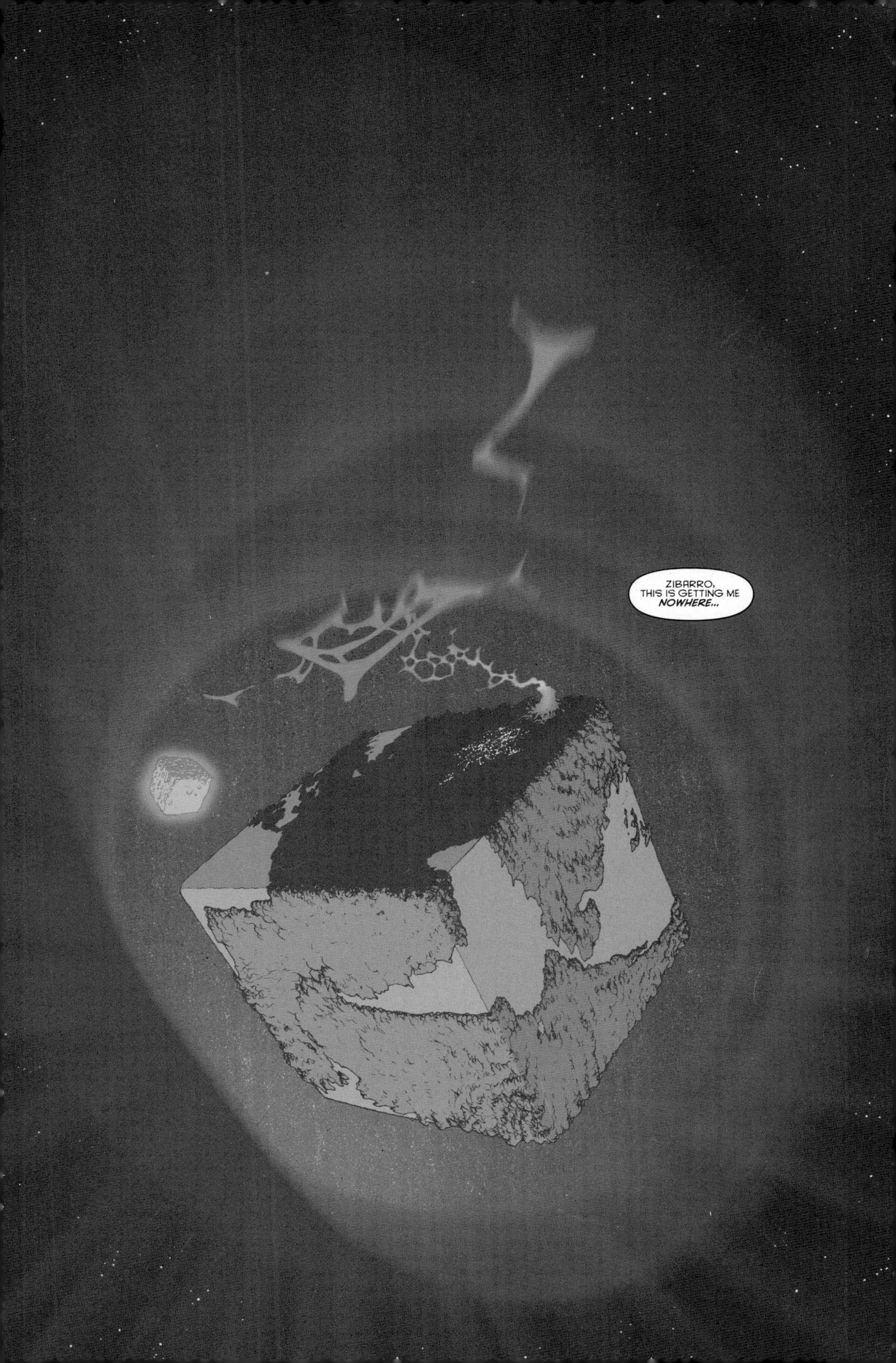
ZIBARRO, THIS IS GETTING ME NOWHERE...

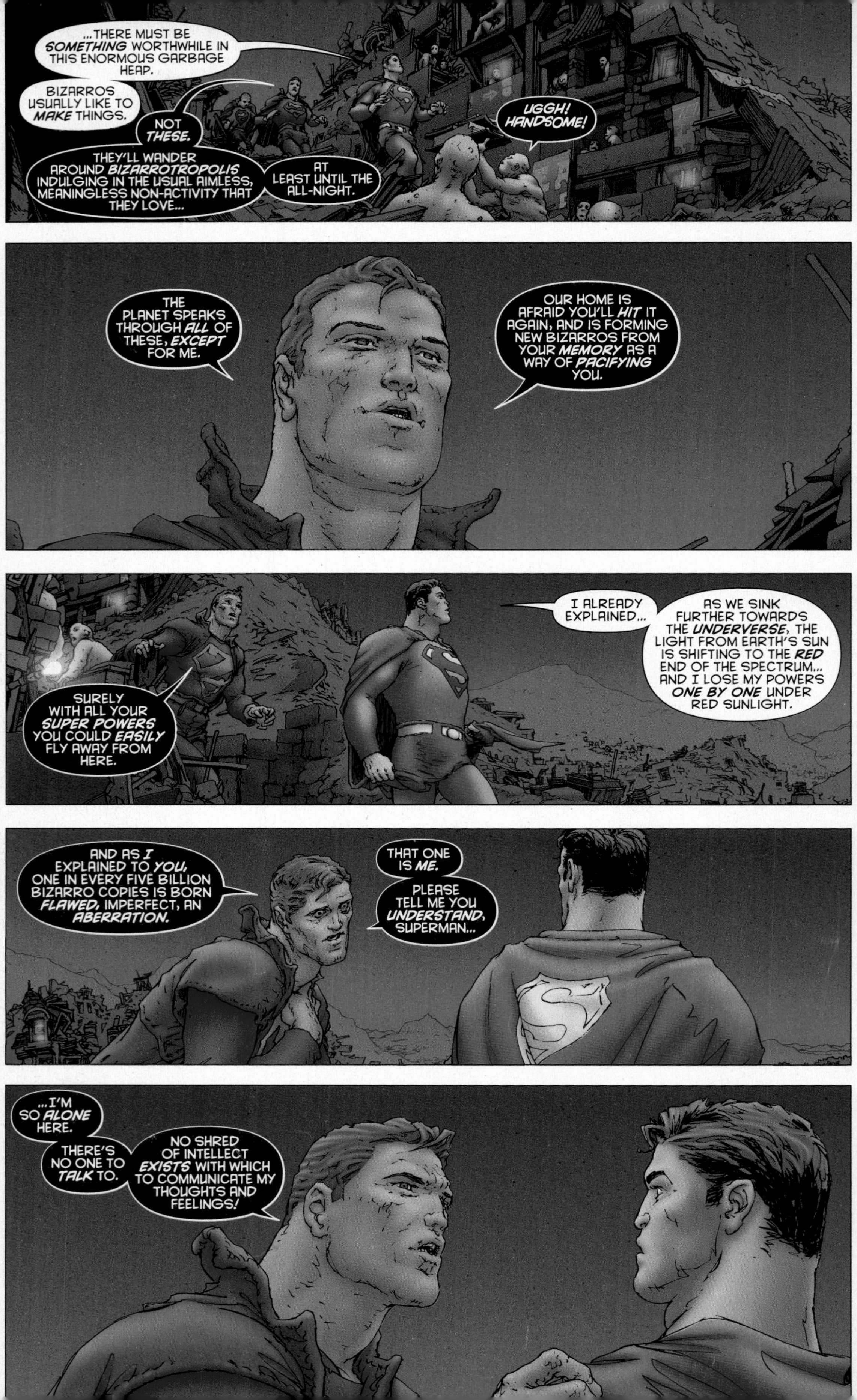
...THERE MUST BE SOMETHING WORTHWHILE IN THIS ENORMOUS GARBAGE HEAP.
BIZARROS USUALLY LIKE TO MAKE THINGS.
NOT THESE.
THEY'LL WANDER AROUND BIZARROTROPOLIS INDULGING IN THE USUAL AIMLESS, MEANINGLESS NON-ACTIVITY THAT THEY LOVE...
AT LEAST UNTIL THE ALL-NIGHT.
UGGH! HANDSOME!
THE PLANET SPEAKS THROUGH ALL OF THESE, EXCEPT FOR ME.
OUR HOME IS AFRAID YOU'LL HIT IT AGAIN, AND IS FORMING NEW BIZARROS FROM YOUR MEMORY AS A WAY OF PACIFYING YOU.
SURELY WITH ALL YOUR SUPER POWERS YOU COULD EASILY FLY AWAY FROM HERE.
I ALREADY EXPLAINED...
AS WE SINK FURTHER TOWARDS THE UNDERVERSE, THE LIGHT FROM EARTH'S SUN IS SHIFTING TO THE RED END OF THE SPECTRUM... AND I LOSE MY POWERS ONE BY ONE UNDER RED SUNLIGHT.
AND AS I EXPLAINED TO YOU, ONE IN EVERY FIVE BILLION BIZARRO COPIES IS BORN FLAWED, IMPERFECT, AN ABERRATION.
THAT ONE IS ME.
PLEASE TELL ME YOU UNDERSTAND, SUPERMAN...
...I'M SO ALONE HERE.
THERE'S NO ONE TO TALK TO.
NO SHRED OF INTELLECT EXISTS WITH WHICH TO COMMUNICATE MY THOUGHTS AND FEELINGS!

CAN YOU EVEN *IMAGINE* WHAT IT'S LIKE TO BE SO *DIFFERENT*?

SO UNIQUE.

SO *UNLIKE* ANYONE ELSE.

MUST ONLY *ZIBARRO* SEE THE BEAUTY IN A SUNSET?

MUST ONLY *ZIBARRO* SEARCH FOR *POETRY* IN THIS SENSELESS COMING AND GOING?

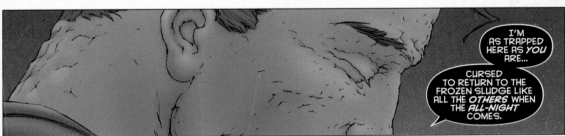

HIM NO AM THINK BEAUTIFUL SUNSET AM UGLY LIKE US!

HAHA HA ZIBARRO AM KING OF COOOL!

YOU SEE?

I'M AS TRAPPED HERE AS *YOU* ARE...

CURSED TO RETURN TO THE FROZEN SLUDGE LIKE ALL THE *OTHERS* WHEN THE *ALL-NIGHT* COMES.

{HURR}

ME NO HAVE PLAN FOR PUNY SUPERMAN.

THAT VOICE...

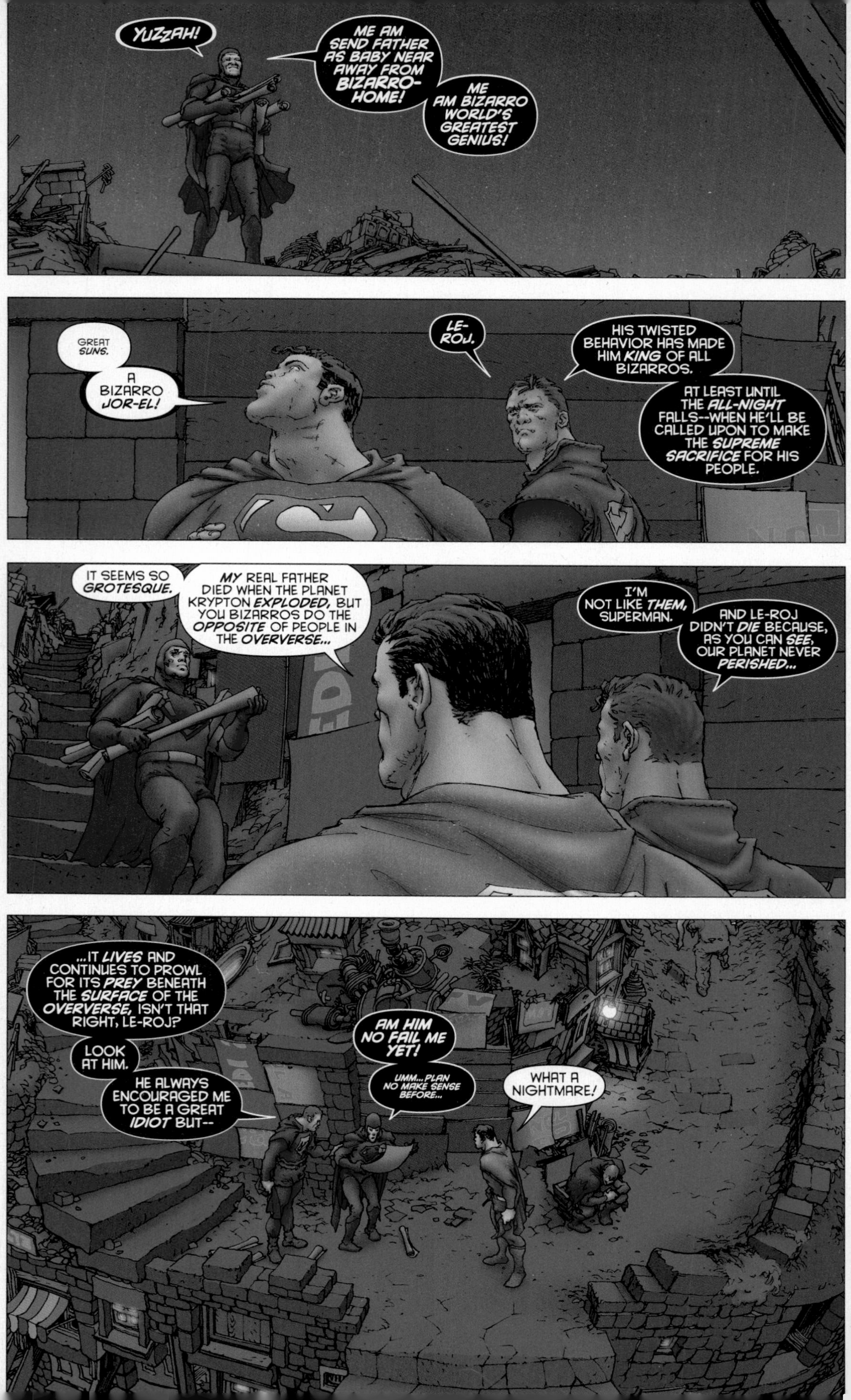
YUZZAH!
ME AM SEND FATHER AS BABY NEAR AWAY FROM BIZARRO-HOME!
ME AM BIZARRO WORLD'S GREATEST GENIUS!
GREAT SUNS.
A BIZARRO JOR-EL!
LE-ROJ.
HIS TWISTED BEHAVIOR HAS MADE HIM KING OF ALL BIZARROS.
AT LEAST UNTIL THE ALL-NIGHT FALLS--WHEN HE'LL BE CALLED UPON TO MAKE THE SUPREME SACRIFICE FOR HIS PEOPLE.
IT SEEMS SO GROTESQUE.
MY REAL FATHER DIED WHEN THE PLANET KRYPTON EXPLODED, BUT YOU BIZARROS DO THE OPPOSITE OF PEOPLE IN THE OVERVERSE...
I'M NOT LIKE THEM, SUPERMAN.
AND LE-ROJ DIDN'T DIE BECAUSE, AS YOU CAN SEE, OUR PLANET NEVER PERISHED...
...IT LIVES AND CONTINUES TO PROWL FOR ITS PREY BENEATH THE SURFACE OF THE OVERVERSE, ISN'T THAT RIGHT, LE-ROJ?
LOOK AT HIM.
HE ALWAYS ENCOURAGED ME TO BE A GREAT IDIOT BUT--
AM HIM NO FAIL ME YET!
UMM...PLAN NO MAKE SENSE BEFORE...
WHAT A NIGHTMARE!

IT CAN'T BE *HOPELESS!*

THERE'S ALWAYS A *WAY.*

UNLESS... ZIBARRO.

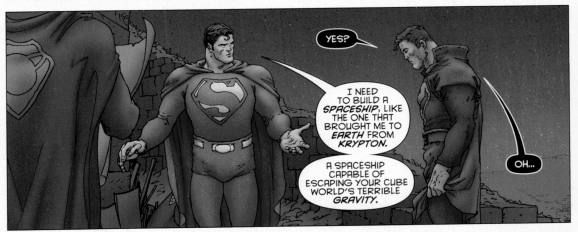

YES?

I NEED TO BUILD A *SPACESHIP,* LIKE THE ONE THAT BROUGHT ME TO *EARTH* FROM *KRYPTON.*

A SPACESHIP CAPABLE OF ESCAPING YOUR CUBE WORLD'S TERRIBLE *GRAVITY.*

OH...

BUT HOW, SUPERMAN?

BIZARRO-HOME FAILED TO FEED, NOW IT MUST SINK TO *REST.*

THE ALL-NIGHT WILL SWALLOW *EVERYTHING* SOON.

BUT ALL THESE MEN AND WOMEN...

...WITH THEIR *HELP* WE COULD BUILD A SPACESHIP *BEFORE* THAT HAPPENED.

IMPOSSIBLE! YOU MIGHT AS WELL GIVE ORDERS TO THE *WINDS,* SUPERMAN.

MAYBE.

BUT I HAVE TO *TRY.*

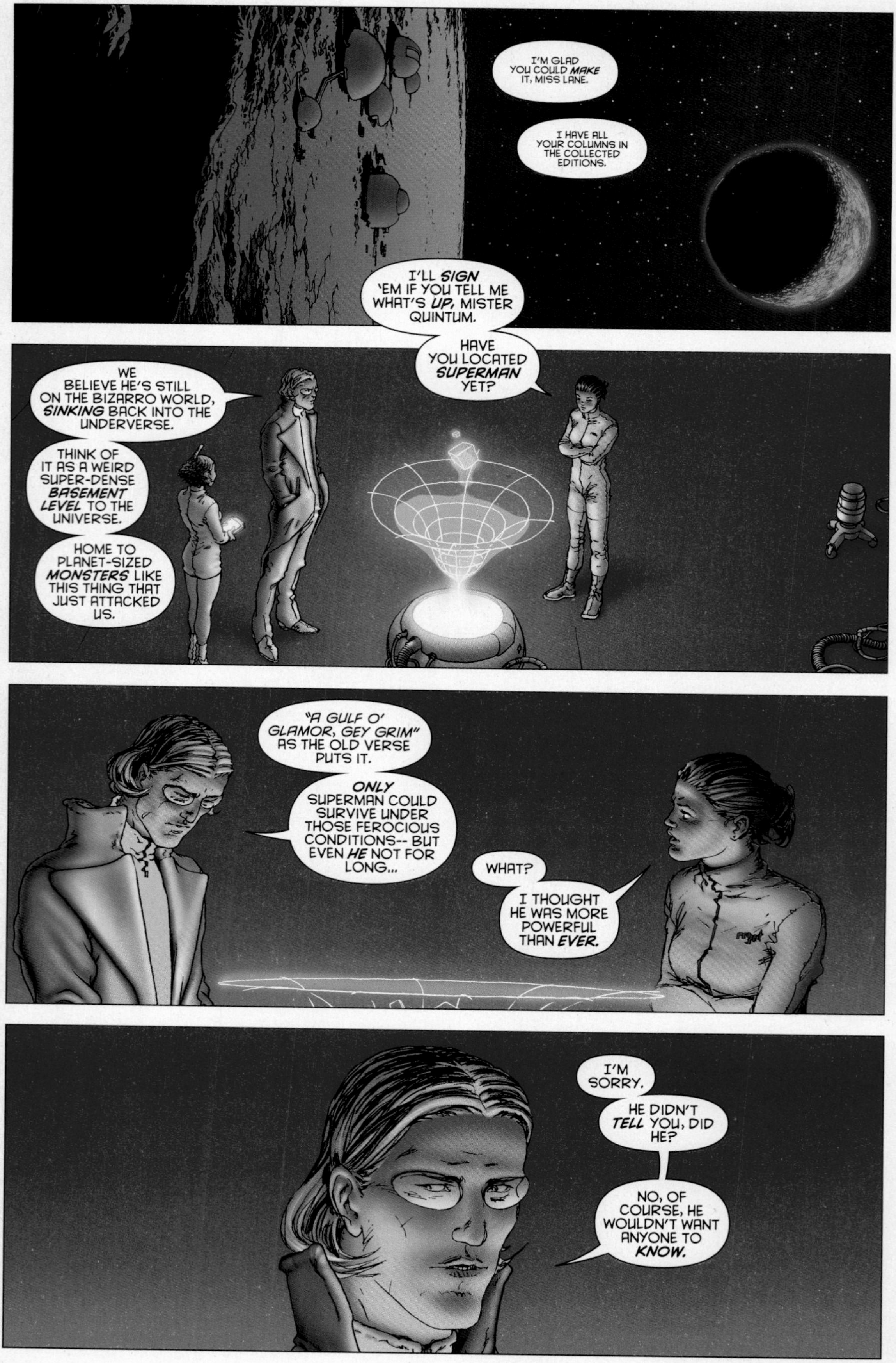

I'M GLAD YOU COULD MAKE IT, MISS LANE.
I HAVE ALL YOUR COLUMNS IN THE COLLECTED EDITIONS.
I'LL SIGN 'EM IF YOU TELL ME WHAT'S UP, MISTER QUINTUM.
HAVE YOU LOCATED SUPERMAN YET?
WE BELIEVE HE'S STILL ON THE BIZARRO WORLD, SINKING BACK INTO THE UNDERVERSE.
THINK OF IT AS A WEIRD SUPER-DENSE BASEMENT LEVEL TO THE UNIVERSE.
HOME TO PLANET-SIZED MONSTERS LIKE THIS THING THAT JUST ATTACKED US.
"A GULF O' GLAMOR, GEY GRIM" AS THE OLD VERSE PUTS IT.
ONLY SUPERMAN COULD SURVIVE UNDER THOSE FEROCIOUS CONDITIONS-- BUT EVEN HE NOT FOR LONG...
WHAT?
I THOUGHT HE WAS MORE POWERFUL THAN EVER.
I'M SORRY.
HE DIDN'T TELL YOU, DID HE?
NO, OF COURSE, HE WOULDN'T WANT ANYONE TO KNOW.

?

IT'S *LUTHOR*, ISN'T IT?

LUTHOR'S DONE SOMETHING TO HIM!

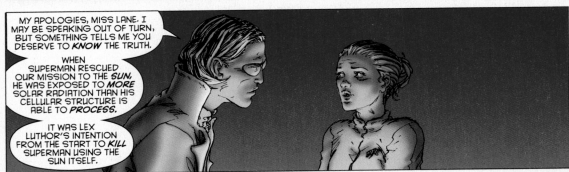

MY APOLOGIES, MISS LANE. I MAY BE SPEAKING OUT OF TURN, BUT SOMETHING TELLS ME YOU DESERVE TO *KNOW* THE TRUTH.

WHEN SUPERMAN RESCUED OUR MISSION TO THE *SUN,* HE WAS EXPOSED TO *MORE* SOLAR RADIATION THAN HIS CELLULAR STRUCTURE IS ABLE TO *PROCESS.*

IT WAS LEX LUTHOR'S INTENTION FROM THE START TO *KILL* SUPERMAN USING THE SUN ITSELF.

IT DOESN'T SEEM RIGHT.

BUT...THIS *EXPLAINS* A LOT OF THINGS, DOESN'T IT?

THIS IS WHY CLARK TOOK A *VACATION* AFTER HE INTERVIEWED LUTHOR ON DEATH ROW.

WE HARDLY DARED IMAGINE WHAT WE'D DO *WITHOUT* HIM.

WE'VE BEEN WORKING OVERTIME TO FIND A CURE. SO FAR WE'VE *FAILED.*

BUT DURING A FINE SCAN OF OUR SOLAR PROBE DATA, WE FOUND SOMETHING ELSE *DISTURBING.*

WHAT DO YOU MEAN?

RIGHT THERE.

HIDING IN THE SUN.

WHEREVER HE IS, I HOPE HE FINDS A WAY *BACK.*

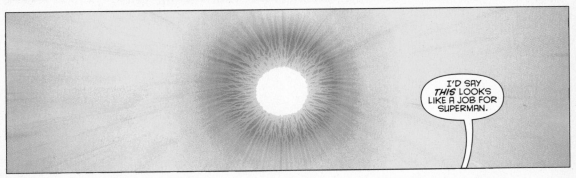

I'D SAY *THIS* LOOKS LIKE A JOB FOR SUPERMAN.

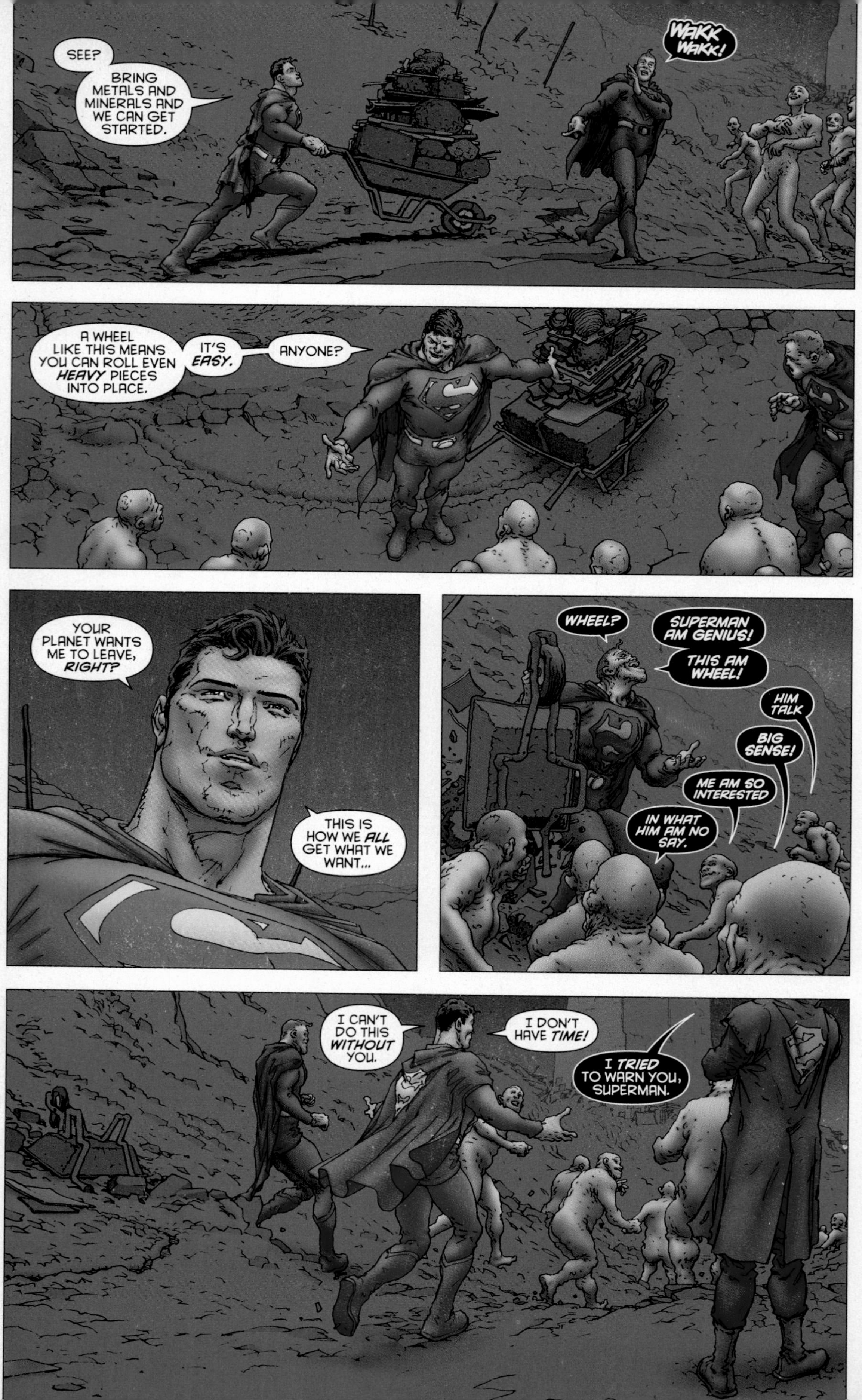

SEE?
BRING METALS AND MINERALS AND WE CAN GET STARTED.
WAKK WAKK!
A WHEEL LIKE THIS MEANS YOU CAN ROLL EVEN HEAVY PIECES INTO PLACE.
IT'S EASY.
ANYONE?
YOUR PLANET WANTS ME TO LEAVE, RIGHT?
THIS IS HOW WE ALL GET WHAT WE WANT...
WHEEL?
SUPERMAN AM GENIUS!
THIS AM WHEEL!
HIM TALK
BIG SENSE!
ME AM SO INTERESTED
IN WHAT HIM AM NO SAY.
I CAN'T DO THIS WITHOUT YOU.
I DON'T HAVE TIME!
I TRIED TO WARN YOU, SUPERMAN.

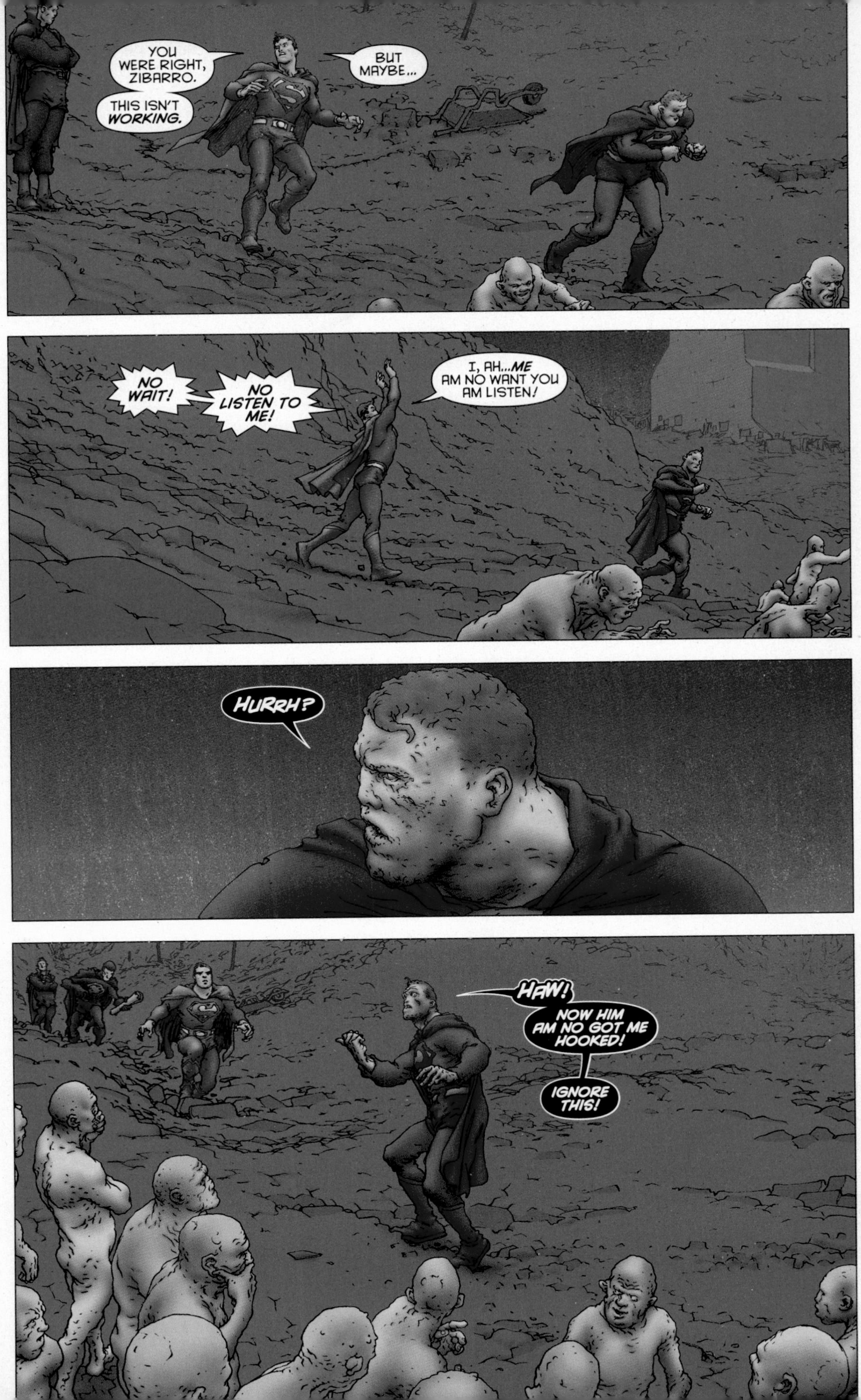
YOU WERE RIGHT, ZIBARRO.
THIS ISN'T WORKING.
BUT MAYBE...
NO WAIT!
NO LISTEN TO ME!
I, AH...ME AM NO WANT YOU AM LISTEN!
HURRH?
HAW!
NOW HIM AM NO GOT ME HOOKED!
IGNORE THIS!

ME HAVE *NOTHING* TO SAY AND *NOTHING* YOU'D WANT TO *SEE!*

GO *AWAY!*

HIM AM NO GET MY ATTENTION!

ME AM NO CAN'T WAIT TO HEAR WHAT HIM AM NO SAY NEXT!

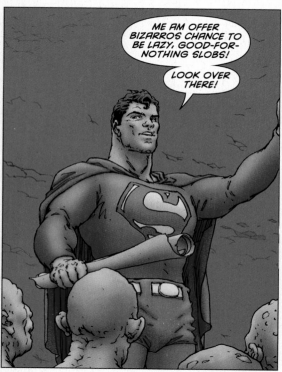

ME AM OFFER BIZARROS CHANCE TO BE LAZY, GOOD-FOR-NOTHING SLOBS!

LOOK OVER THERE!

ME AM NO OFFER BIZARRO CIVILIZATION A CHANCE TO MAKE MONUMENT TO LAST ALL TIME!

CHANCE TO NO MAKE MOST USELESS, BORING ROCKET EVER FOR UNGLORY OF BIZARROS AND NO CELEBRATE ALL-NIGHT!

BOOo.o!

ME AM NO SAY YOU ALL NO WORK TO NO BUILD ROCKET!

SIT AND WAIT FOR ALL-NIGHT!

ROCKET AM TOTALLY NON-CONSTRUCTIVE WASTE OF TIME!

AWWW...

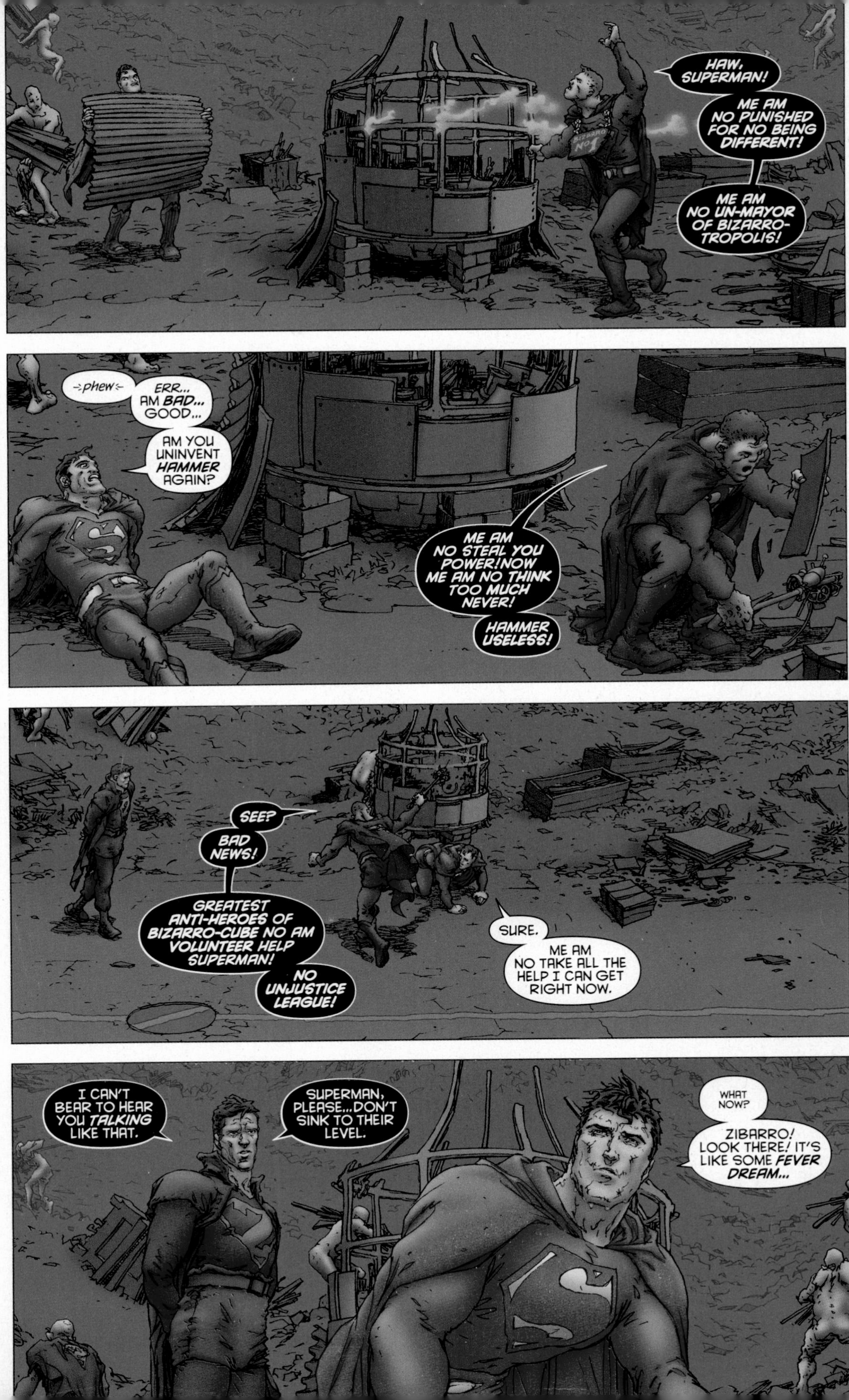
HAW, SUPERMAN!
ME AM NO PUNISHED FOR NO BEING DIFFERENT!
ME AM NO UN-MAYOR OF BIZARRO-TROPOLIS!
-phew-
ERR... AM BAD... GOOD...
AM YOU UNINVENT HAMMER AGAIN?
ME AM NO STEAL YOU POWER! NOW ME AM NO THINK TOO MUCH NEVER!
HAMMER USELESS!
SEE?
BAD NEWS!
GREATEST ANTI-HEROES OF BIZARRO-CUBE NO AM VOLUNTEER HELP SUPERMAN!
NO UNJUSTICE LEAGUE!
SURE.
ME AM NO TAKE ALL THE HELP I CAN GET RIGHT NOW.
I CAN'T BEAR TO HEAR YOU TALKING LIKE THAT.
SUPERMAN, PLEASE...DON'T SINK TO THEIR LEVEL.
WHAT NOW?
ZIBARRO! LOOK THERE! IT'S LIKE SOME FEVER DREAM...

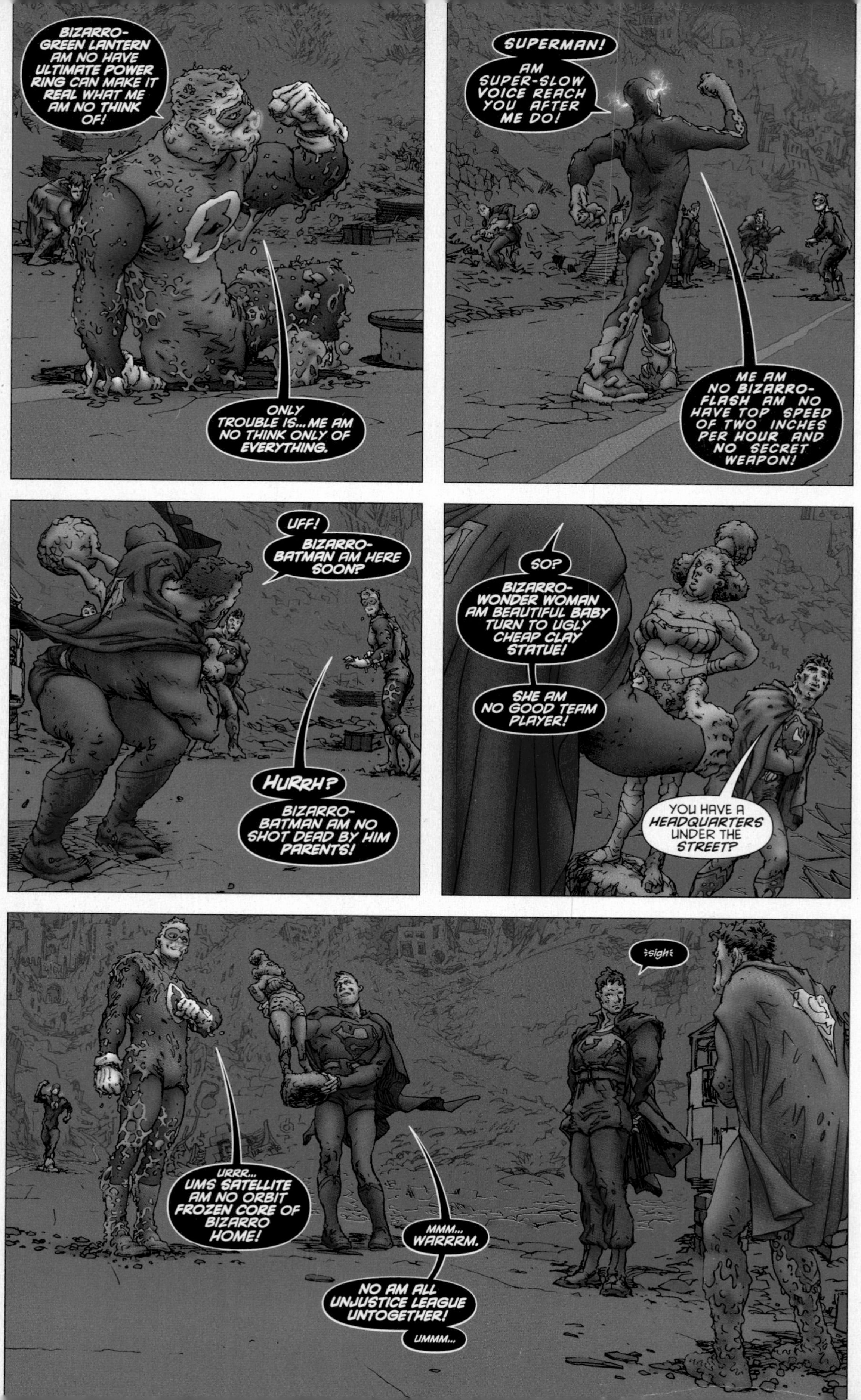
BIZARRO-GREEN LANTERN AM NO HAVE ULTIMATE POWER RING CAN MAKE IT REAL WHAT ME AM NO THINK OF!
ONLY TROUBLE IS...ME AM NO THINK ONLY OF EVERYTHING.
SUPERMAN!
AM SUPER-SLOW VOICE REACH YOU AFTER ME DO!
ME AM NO BIZARRO-FLASH AM NO HAVE TOP SPEED OF TWO INCHES PER HOUR AND NO SECRET WEAPON!
UFF!
BIZARRO-BATMAN AM HERE SOON?
HURRH?
BIZARRO-BATMAN AM NO SHOT DEAD BY HIM PARENTS!
SO?
BIZARRO-WONDER WOMAN AM BEAUTIFUL BABY TURN TO UGLY CHEAP CLAY STATUE!
SHE AM NO GOOD TEAM PLAYER!
YOU HAVE A HEADQUARTERS UNDER THE STREET?
URRR...
UMS SATELLITE AM NO ORBIT FROZEN CORE OF BIZARRO HOME!
MMM... WARRRM.
NO AM ALL UNJUSTICE LEAGUE UNTOGETHER!
UMMM...
sigh

THEY WERE *EAGER* TO HELP, SUPERMAN. WHAT COULD I *SAY?*

I KNOW THESE POOR, DEMENTED CREATURES *MEAN* WELL, BUT...

THESE TWISTED COPIES OF MY OLD FRIENDS IN THE *JUSTICE LEAGUE* ARE AS *INEFFECTUAL* AS THE REAL THING WAS *EFFICIENT.*

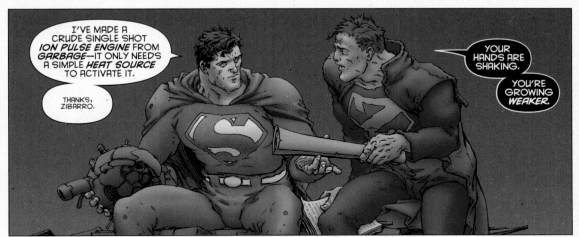

I'VE MADE A CRUDE SINGLE SHOT *ION PULSE ENGINE* FROM *GARBAGE*--IT ONLY NEEDS A SIMPLE *HEAT SOURCE* TO ACTIVATE IT.

THANKS, ZIBARRO.

YOUR HANDS ARE SHAKING.

YOU'RE GROWING *WEAKER.*

I DON'T KNOW.

IT'S JUST THAT... EVERYTHING'S GETTING *HEAVIER.*

ARE WE ALMOST DONE?

YES...I...

I...I WAS STUDYING THE BLUEPRINTS AGAIN AND I COULDN'T HELP BUT *NOTICE* SOMETHING, SUPERMAN.

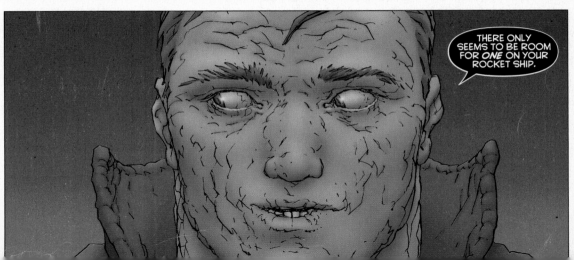

THERE ONLY SEEMS TO BE ROOM FOR *ONE* ON YOUR ROCKET SHIP.

ZIBARRO, I'LL BE SUBJECTING MYSELF TO *UNIMAGINABLE* STRESSES.

THE CHANCES OF SURVIVAL ARE *SLIM*, EVEN IF YOU HAD *POWERS* LIKE THE SUPER BIZARRO...

WHAT DO YOU MEAN?!

WHY DO I FEEL AS IF YOU HAVEN'T BEEN LISTENING TO ME *AT ALL?!* DON'T YOU REALIZE I'D TAKE ANY CHANCE TO GET AWAY FROM HERE?

I'D DARE ANY PERIL!

AND I CAN'T LET YOU *RISK* IT, BUT YOU HAVE MY *WORD*...

IF I GET *HOME* SAFELY, I'LL FIND A WAY TO *CONTACT* YOU HERE IN THE UNDERVERSE AND ONE DAY, I *PROMISE*, WE'LL MEET *AGAIN*.

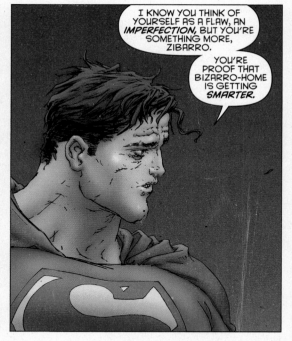

I KNOW YOU THINK OF YOURSELF AS A FLAW, AN *IMPERFECTION*, BUT YOU'RE SOMETHING MORE, ZIBARRO.

YOU'RE PROOF THAT BIZARRO-HOME IS GETTING *SMARTER*.

WHY ELSE DID THIS WORLD, THIS INCREDIBLE ORGANISM, MAKE EYES LIKE *YOURS* TO SEE BEAUTY AND MEANING WHERE OTHERS SEE CHAOS?

HRRM...WELL... I JUST WONDERED IF MAYBE THERE WAS STILL TIME FOR YOU TO TAKE A LOOK...A LOOK AT MY *WORK*...

IT'S NOT MUCH...JUST *THOUGHTS*, REALLY.

Before you go.

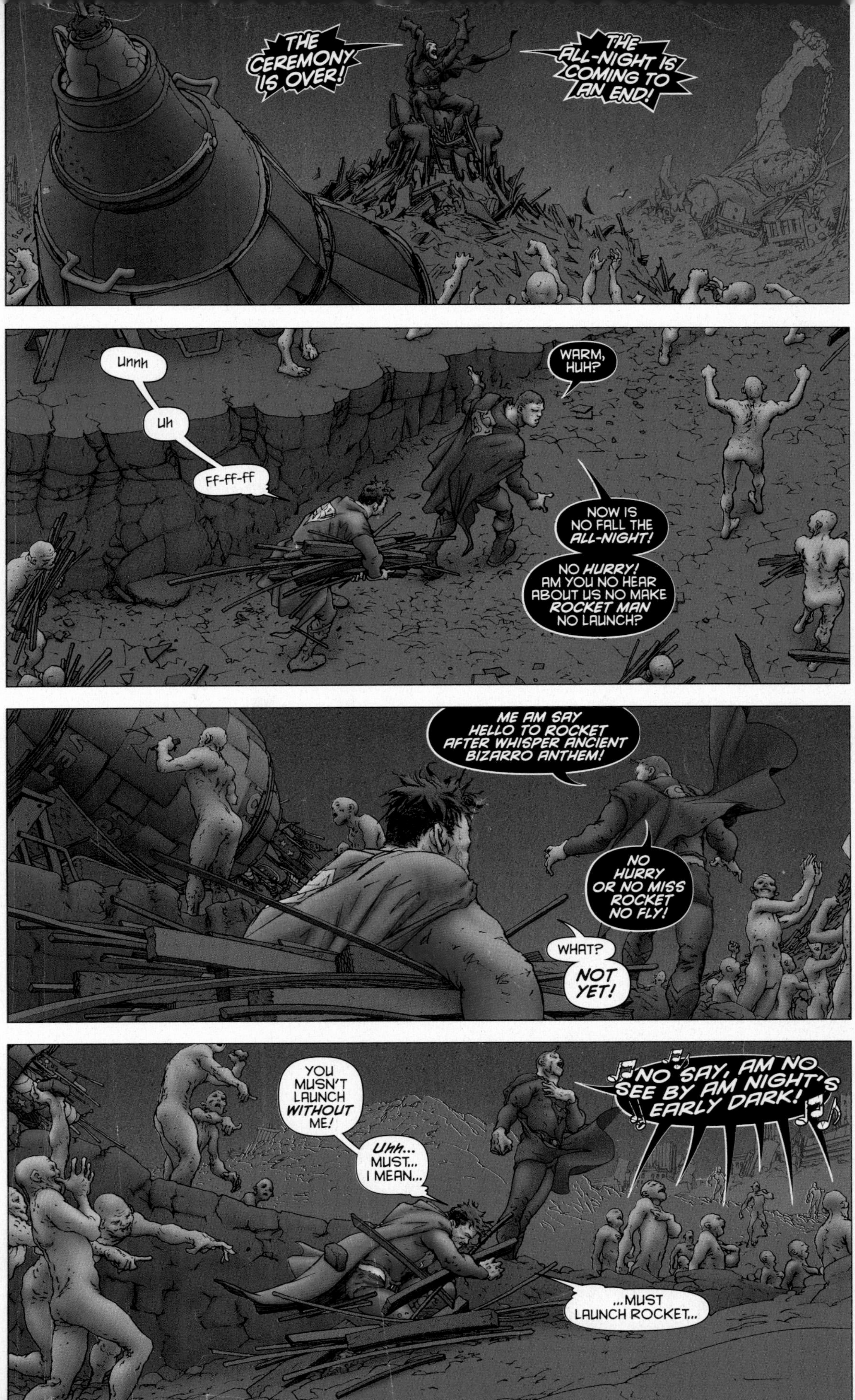
THE CEREMONY IS OVER!
THE ALL-NIGHT IS COMING TO AN END!
Unnh
Uh
Ff-ff-ff
WARM, HUH?
NOW IS NO FALL THE ALL-NIGHT!
NO HURRY! AM YOU NO HEAR ABOUT US NO MAKE ROCKET MAN NO LAUNCH?
ME AM SAY HELLO TO ROCKET AFTER WHISPER ANCIENT BIZARRO ANTHEM!
NO HURRY OR NO MISS ROCKET NO FLY!
WHAT?
NOT YET!
YOU MUSN'T LAUNCH WITHOUT ME!
Uhh... MUST... I MEAN...
NO SAY, AM NO SEE BY AM NIGHT'S EARLY DARK!
...MUST LAUNCH ROCKET...

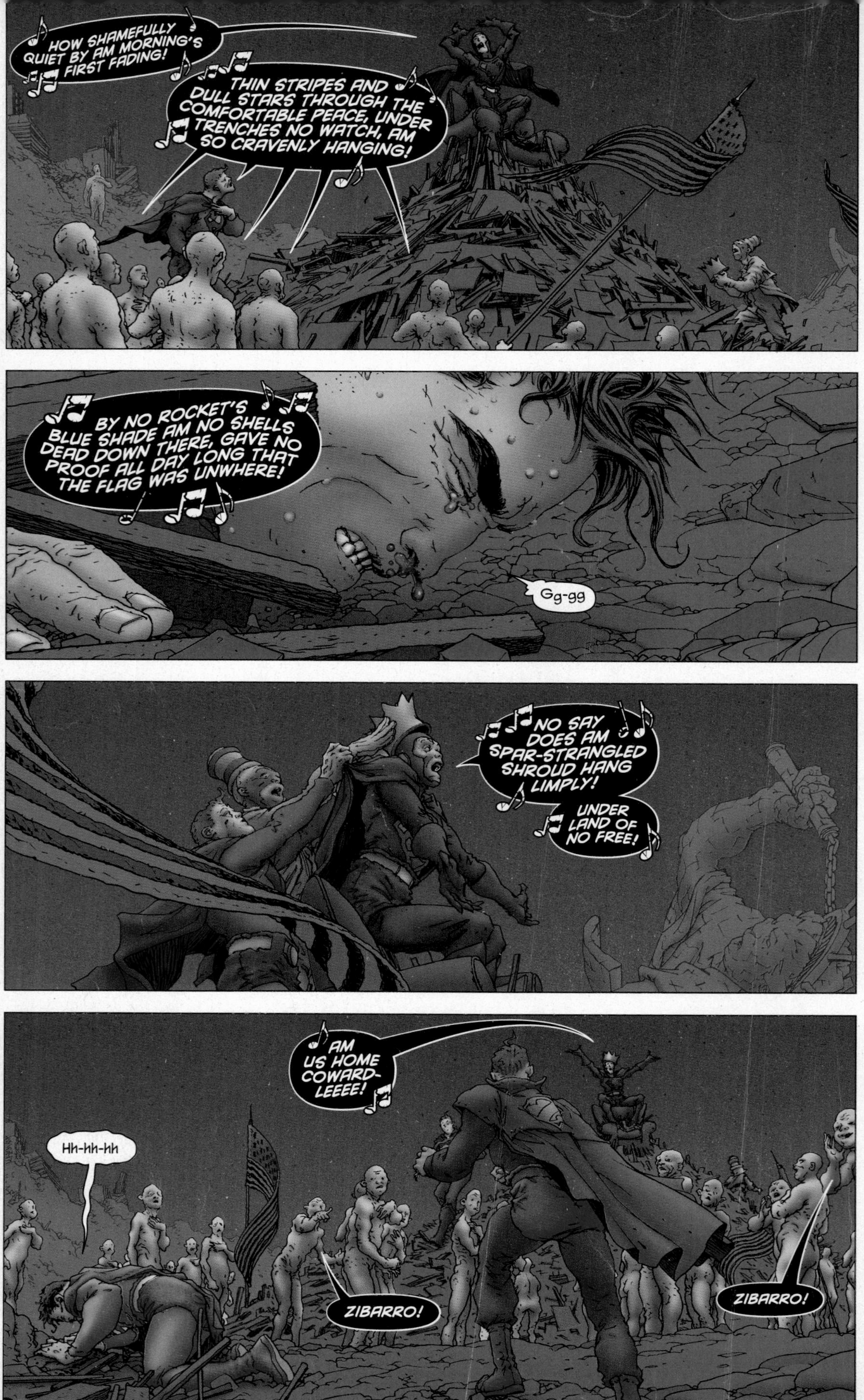
HOW SHAMEFULLY QUIET BY AM MORNING'S FIRST FADING!
THIN STRIPES AND DULL STARS THROUGH THE COMFORTABLE PEACE, UNDER TRENCHES NO WATCH, AM SO CRAVENLY HANGING!
BY NO ROCKET'S BLUE SHADE AM NO SHELLS DEAD DOWN THERE, GAVE NO PROOF ALL DAY LONG THAT THE FLAG WAS UNWHERE!
Gg-gg
NO SAY DOES AM SPAR-STRANGLED SHROUD HANG LIMPLY!
UNDER LAND OF NO FREE!
AM US HOME COWARD-LEEEE!
Hh-hh-hh
ZIBARRO!
ZIBARRO!

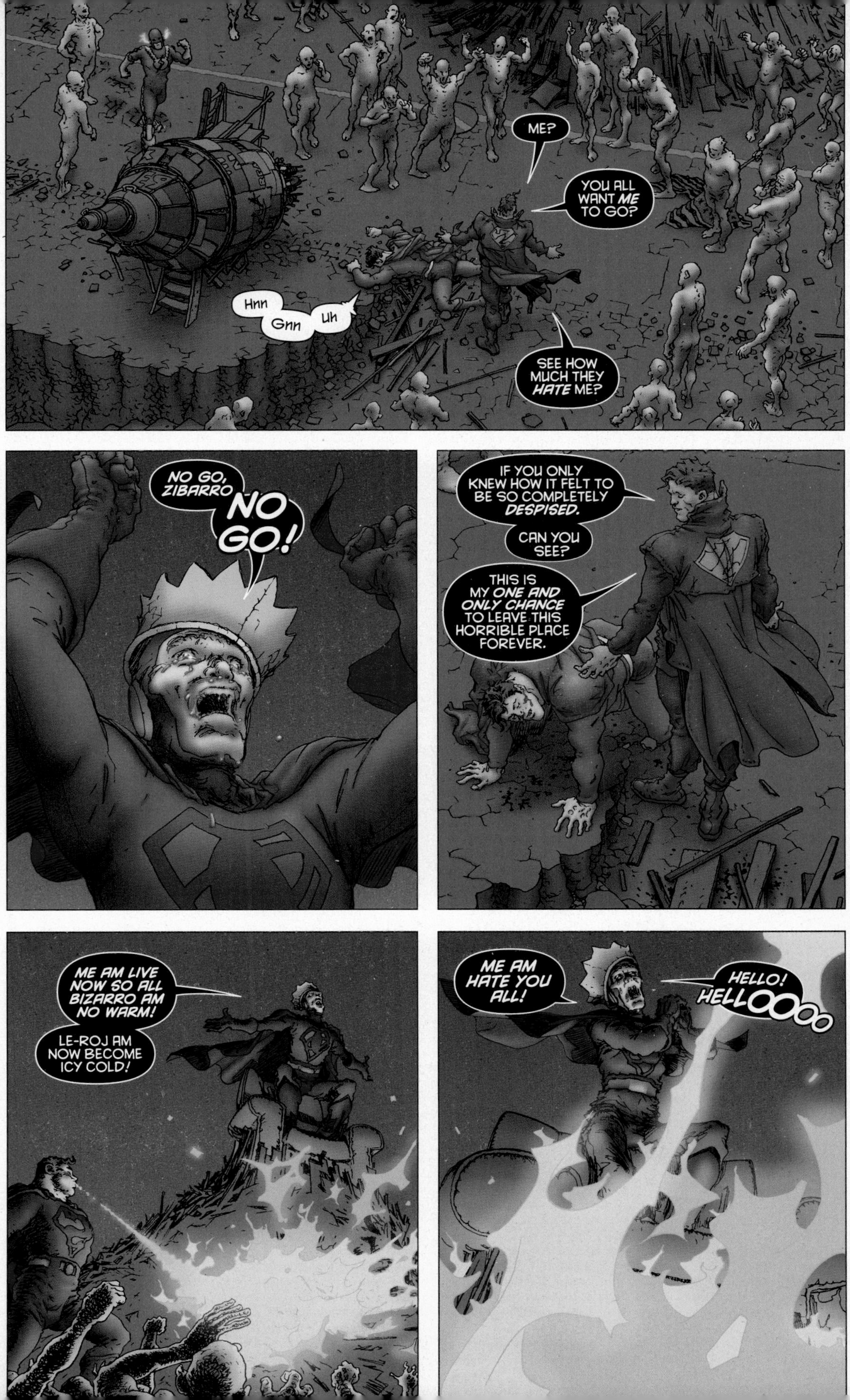
ME?
YOU ALL WANT ME TO GO?
Hnn
Gnn
Uh
SEE HOW MUCH THEY HATE ME?
NO GO, ZIBARRO
NO GO!
IF YOU ONLY KNEW HOW IT FELT TO BE SO COMPLETELY DESPISED.
CAN YOU SEE?
THIS IS MY ONE AND ONLY CHANCE TO LEAVE THIS HORRIBLE PLACE FOREVER.
ME AM LIVE NOW SO ALL BIZARRO AM NO WARM!
LE-ROJ AM NOW BECOME ICY COLD!
ME AM HATE YOU ALL!
HELLO!
HELLOOOOO

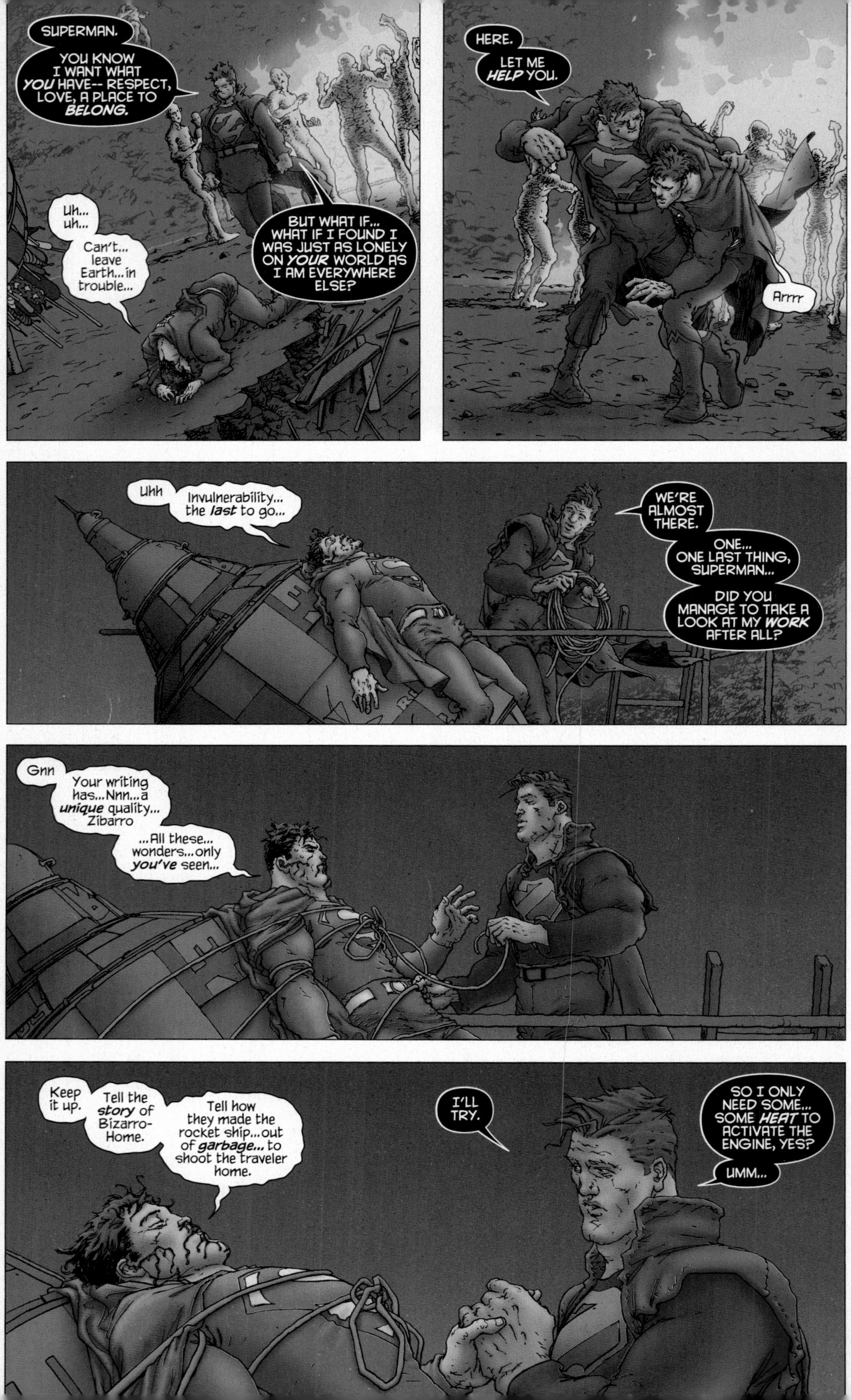
SUPERMAN.
YOU KNOW I WANT WHAT *YOU* HAVE-- RESPECT, LOVE, A PLACE TO *BELONG.*
Uh... uh...
Can't... leave Earth...in trouble...
BUT WHAT IF... WHAT IF I FOUND I WAS JUST AS LONELY ON *YOUR* WORLD AS I AM EVERYWHERE ELSE?
HERE.
LET ME *HELP* YOU.
Arrrr
Uhh
Invulnerability... the *last* to go...
WE'RE ALMOST THERE.
ONE... ONE LAST THING, SUPERMAN...
DID YOU MANAGE TO TAKE A LOOK AT MY *WORK* AFTER ALL?
Gnn
Your writing has...Nnn...a *unique* quality... Zibarro
...All these... wonders...only *you've* seen...
Keep it up.
Tell the *story* of Bizarro-Home.
Tell how they made the rocket ship...out of *garbage...* to shoot the traveler home.
I'LL TRY.
SO I ONLY NEED SOME... SOME *HEAT* TO ACTIVATE THE ENGINE, YES?
UMM...

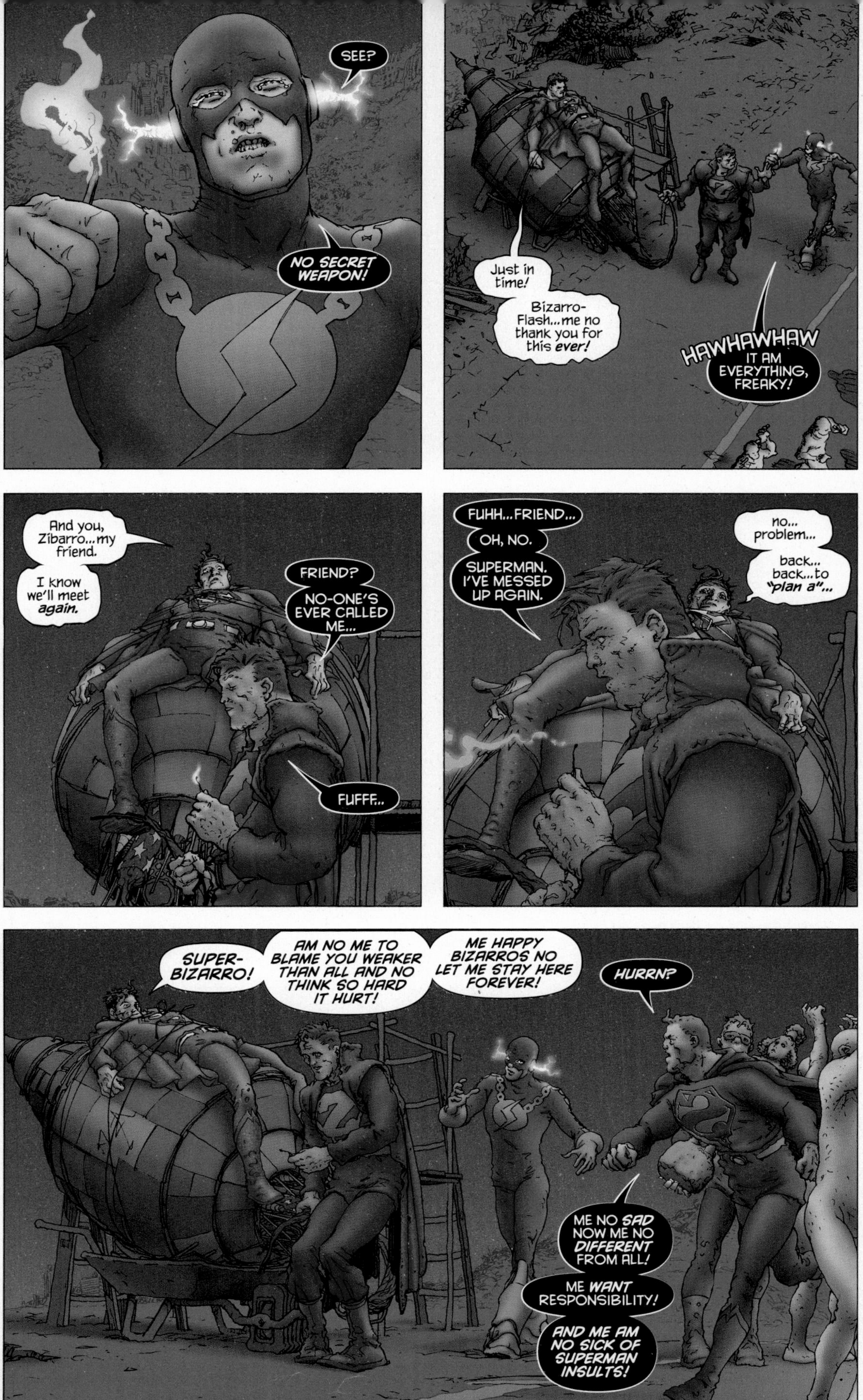
SEE?
NO SECRET WEAPON!
Just in time!
Bizarro-Flash...me no thank you for this *ever!*
HAWHAWHAW
IT AM EVERYTHING, FREAKY!
And you, Zibarro...my friend.
I know we'll meet *again.*
FRIEND?
NO-ONE'S EVER CALLED ME...
FUFFF..
FUHH...FRIEND...
OH, NO.
SUPERMAN. I'VE MESSED UP AGAIN.
no... problem...
back... back...to *"plan a"*...
SUPER-BIZARRO!
AM NO ME TO BLAME YOU WEAKER THAN ALL AND NO THINK SO HARD IT HURT!
ME HAPPY BIZARROS NO LET ME STAY HERE FOREVER!
HURRN?
ME NO *SAD* NOW ME NO *DIFFERENT* FROM ALL!
ME *WANT* RESPONSIBILITY!
AND ME AM NO SICK OF SUPERMAN INSULTS!

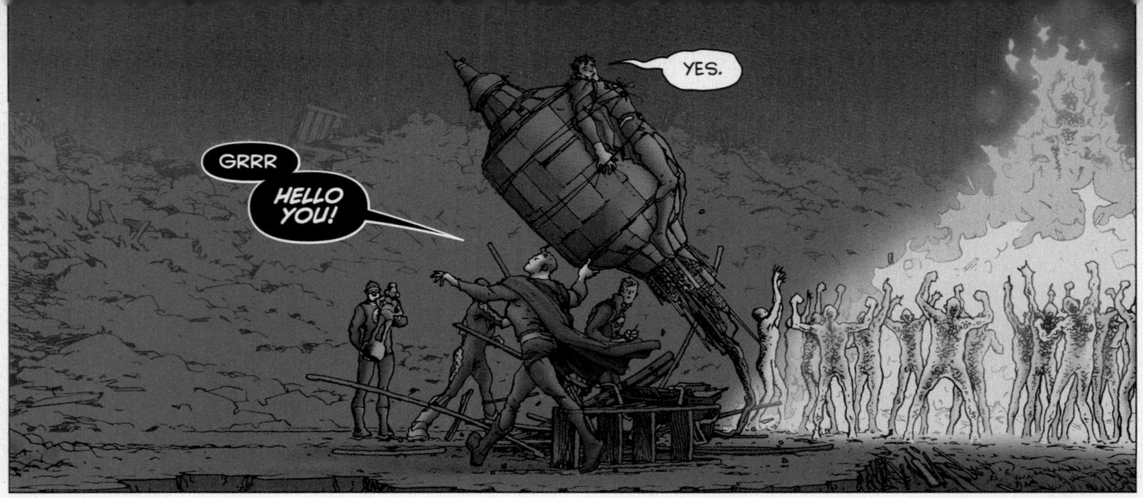
YES.
GRRR
HELLO YOU!

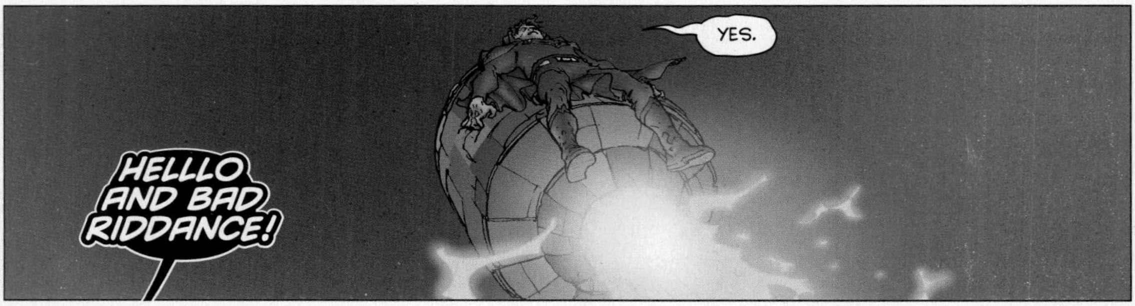
YES.
HELLLO AND BAD RIDDANCE!

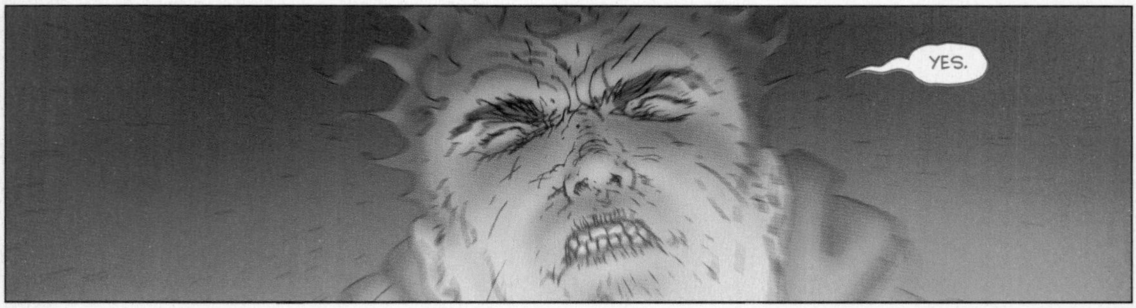
YES.

US DO OPPOSITE

THE BIZARRO EARTH HAS GONE *BEYOND* THE RANGE OF OUR INSTRUMENTS.

DOWN INTO THE *UNDERVERSE*, THROUGH THE *COLD LAYER* WHERE TIME STANDS STILL, AND *BEYOND* INTO THE BLAZING UNKNOWN *BELOW.*

SUPERMAN SAVED US ALL.

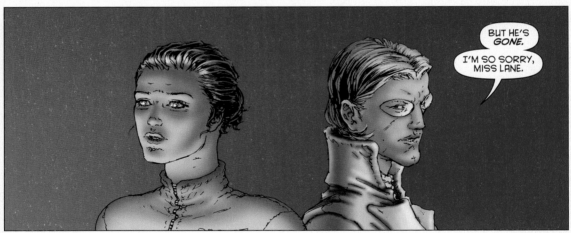

BUT HE'S *GONE.*

I'M SO SORRY, MISS LANE.

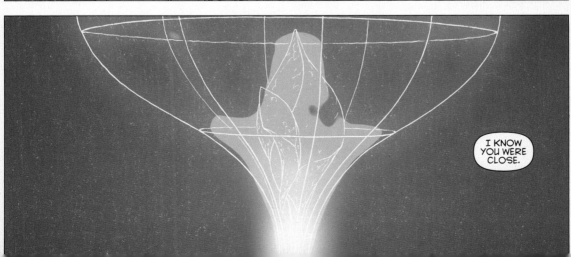

I KNOW YOU WERE CLOSE.

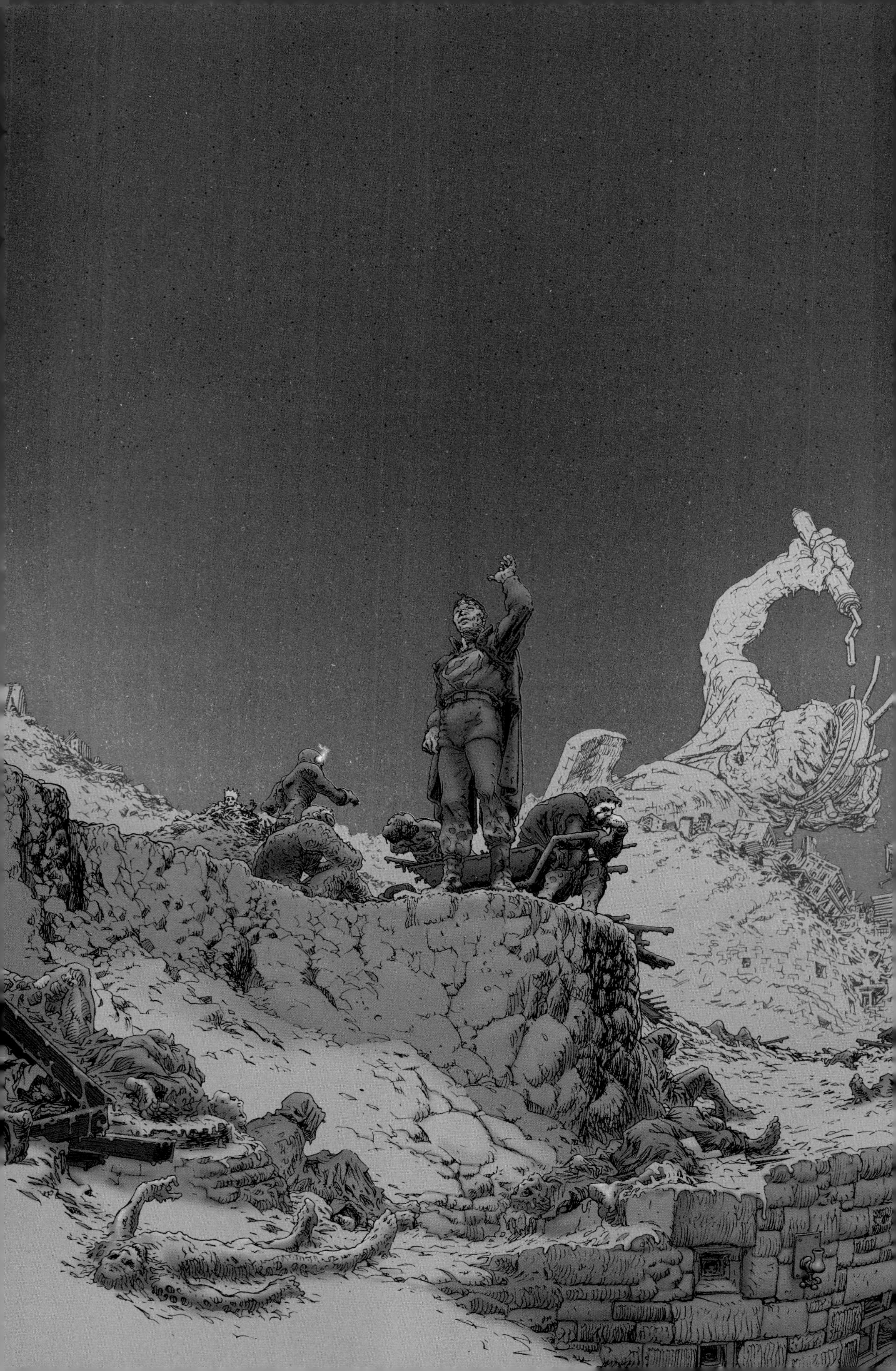

Episode 9

CURSE OF THE REPLACEMENT SUPERMEN

Cover FRANK QUITELY

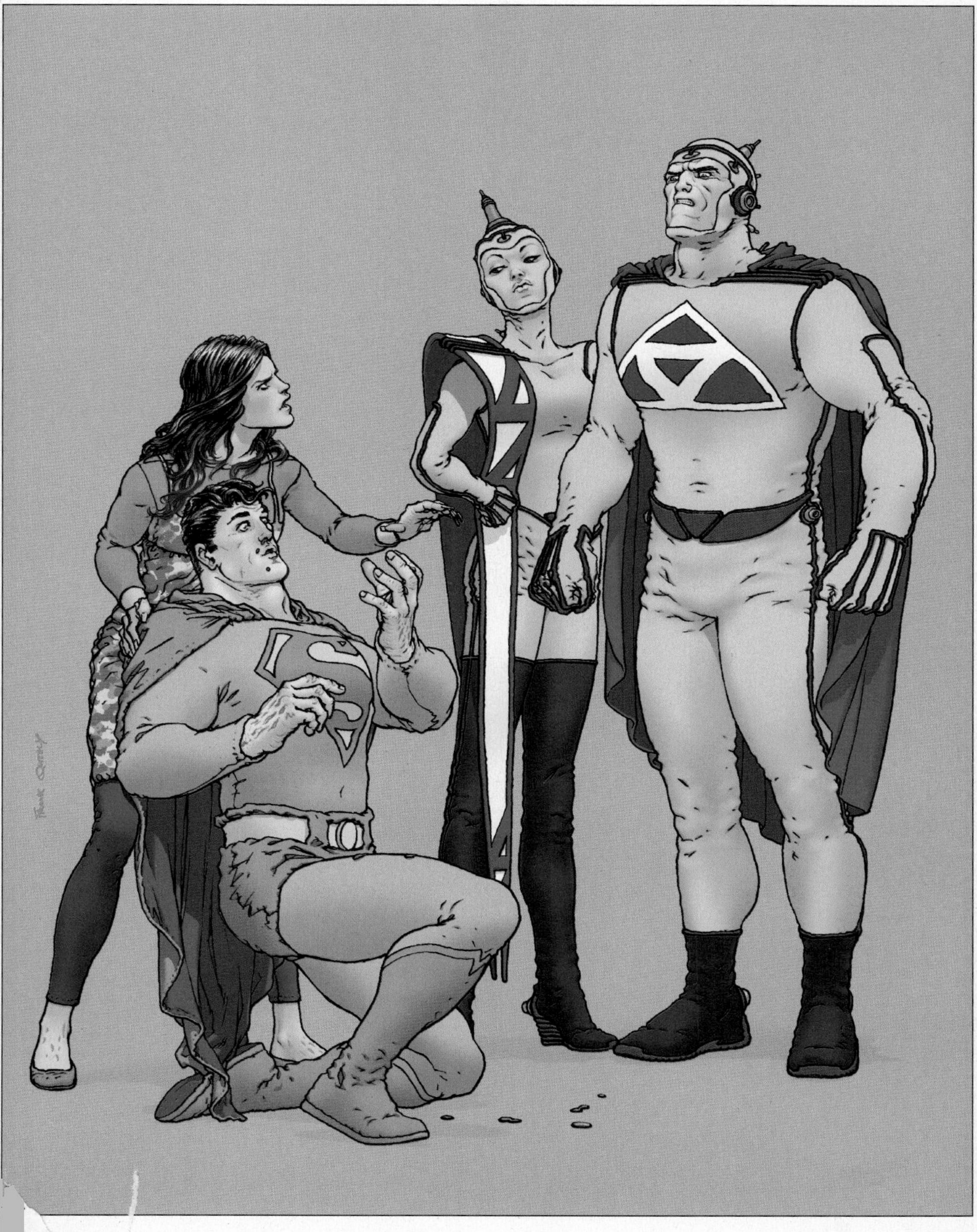

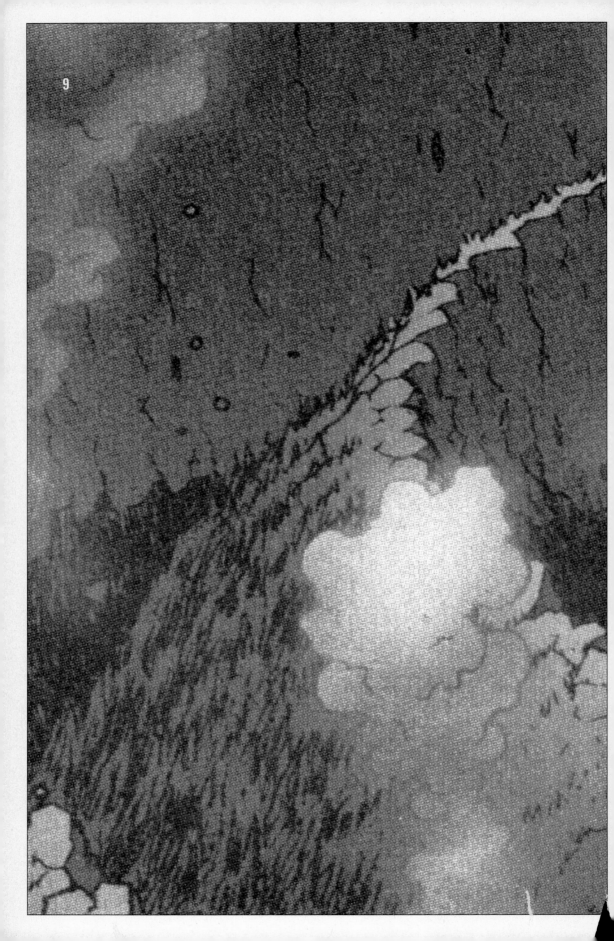

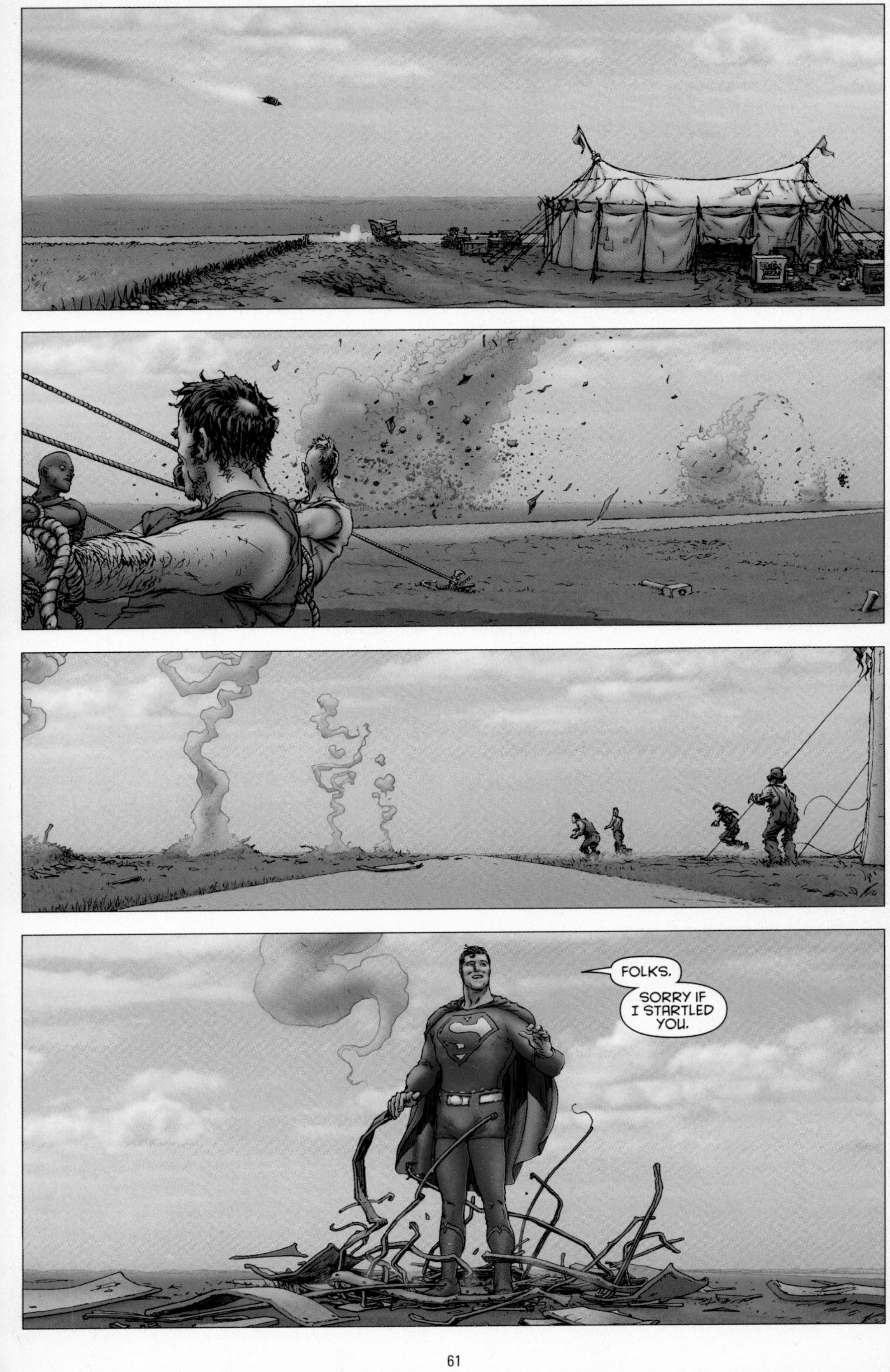
FOLKS.
SORRY IF I STARTLED YOU.

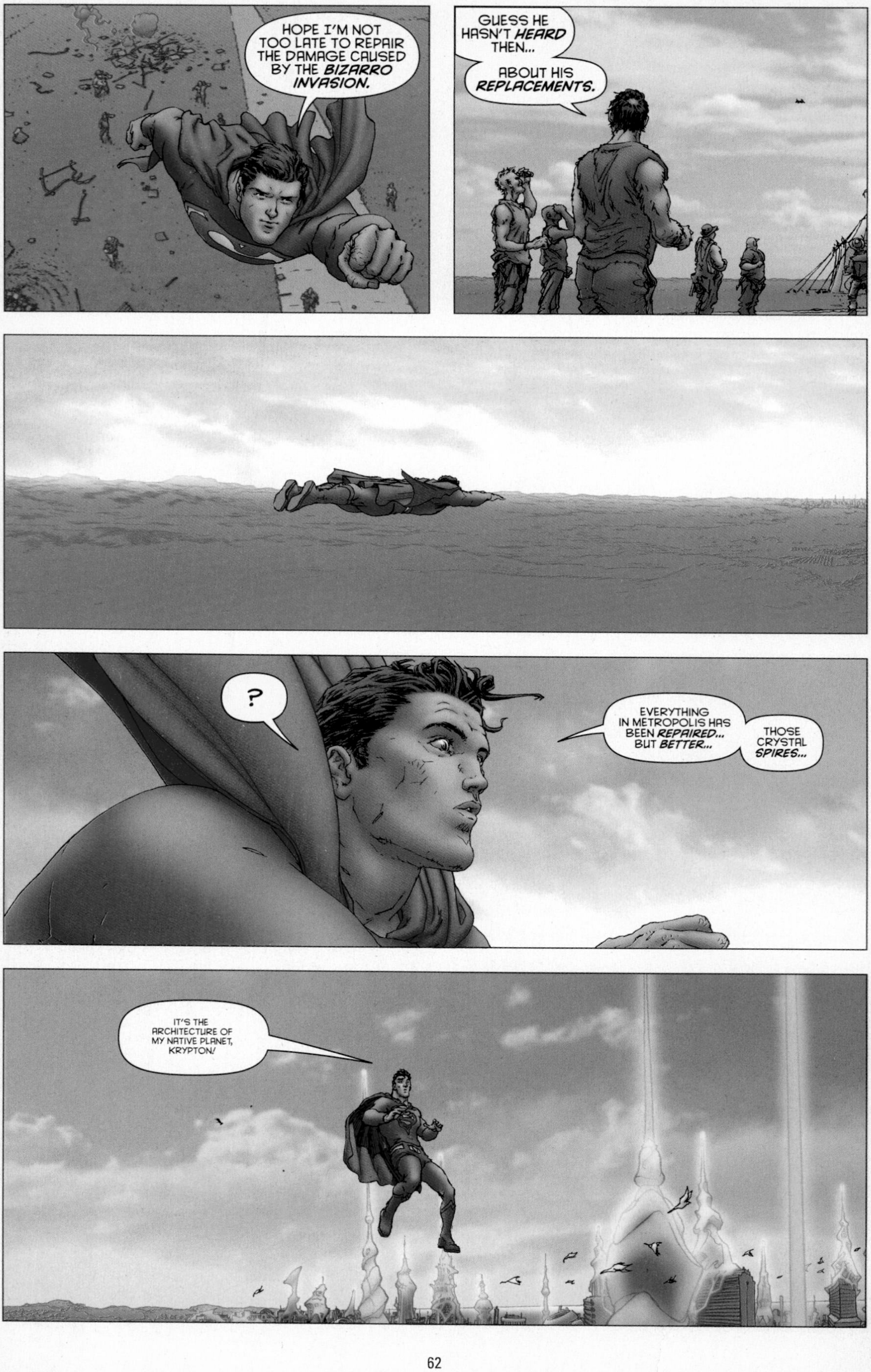
HOPE I'M NOT TOO LATE TO REPAIR THE DAMAGE CAUSED BY THE BIZARRO INVASION.
GUESS HE HASN'T HEARD THEN...
ABOUT HIS REPLACEMENTS.
?
EVERYTHING IN METROPOLIS HAS BEEN REPAIRED... BUT BETTER...
THOSE CRYSTAL SPIRES...
IT'S THE ARCHITECTURE OF MY NATIVE PLANET, KRYPTON!

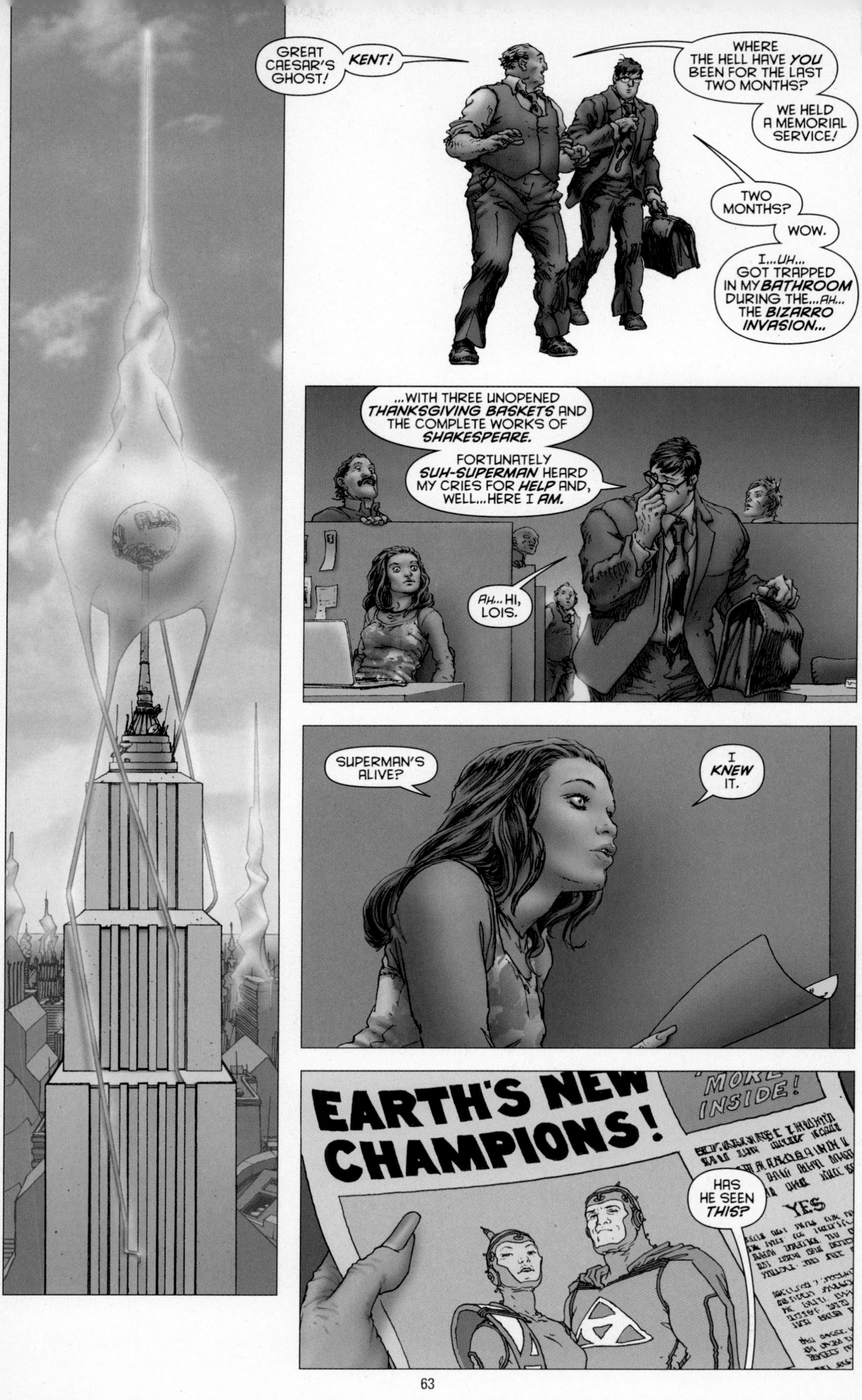

GREAT CAESAR'S GHOST!
KENT!
WHERE THE HELL HAVE YOU BEEN FOR THE LAST TWO MONTHS?
WE HELD A MEMORIAL SERVICE!
TWO MONTHS?
WOW.
I...UH... GOT TRAPPED IN MY BATHROOM DURING THE...AH... THE BIZARRO INVASION...
...WITH THREE UNOPENED THANKSGIVING BASKETS AND THE COMPLETE WORKS OF SHAKESPEARE.
FORTUNATELY SUH-SUPERMAN HEARD MY CRIES FOR HELP AND, WELL...HERE I AM.
AH...HI, LOIS.
SUPERMAN'S ALIVE?
I KNEW IT.
EARTH'S NEW CHAMPIONS!
MORE INSIDE!
YES
HAS HE SEEN THIS?

THAT SHOULD DO IT.

THE NETWORK OF TUNNELS WE'VE DRILLED WILL CAUSE THE WHOLE VOLCANO TO *COLLAPSE.*

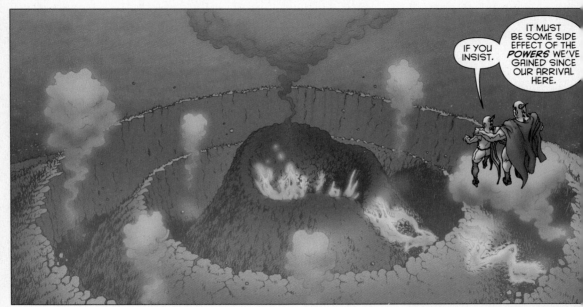

IF YOU INSIST.

IT MUST BE SOME SIDE EFFECT OF THE *POWERS* WE'VE GAINED SINCE OUR ARRIVAL HERE.

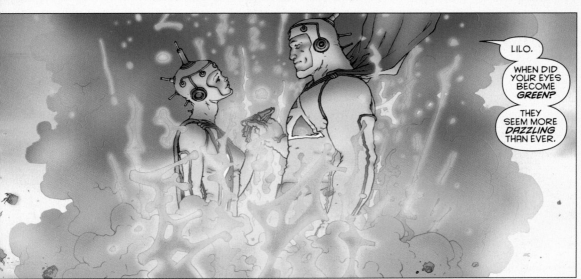

LILO. WHEN DID YOUR EYES BECOME *GREEN?*

THEY SEEM MORE *DAZZLING* THAN EVER.

HOW ABOUT *THIS* VERY SPOT?

THE CAPITAL OF *NEW KRYPTON* COULD RISE HERE, COULD IT NOT?

MMM. I THINK WE COULD JUST AS EASILY CLEAR THE APES OUT OF *METROPOLIS* AND BUILD *THERE.*

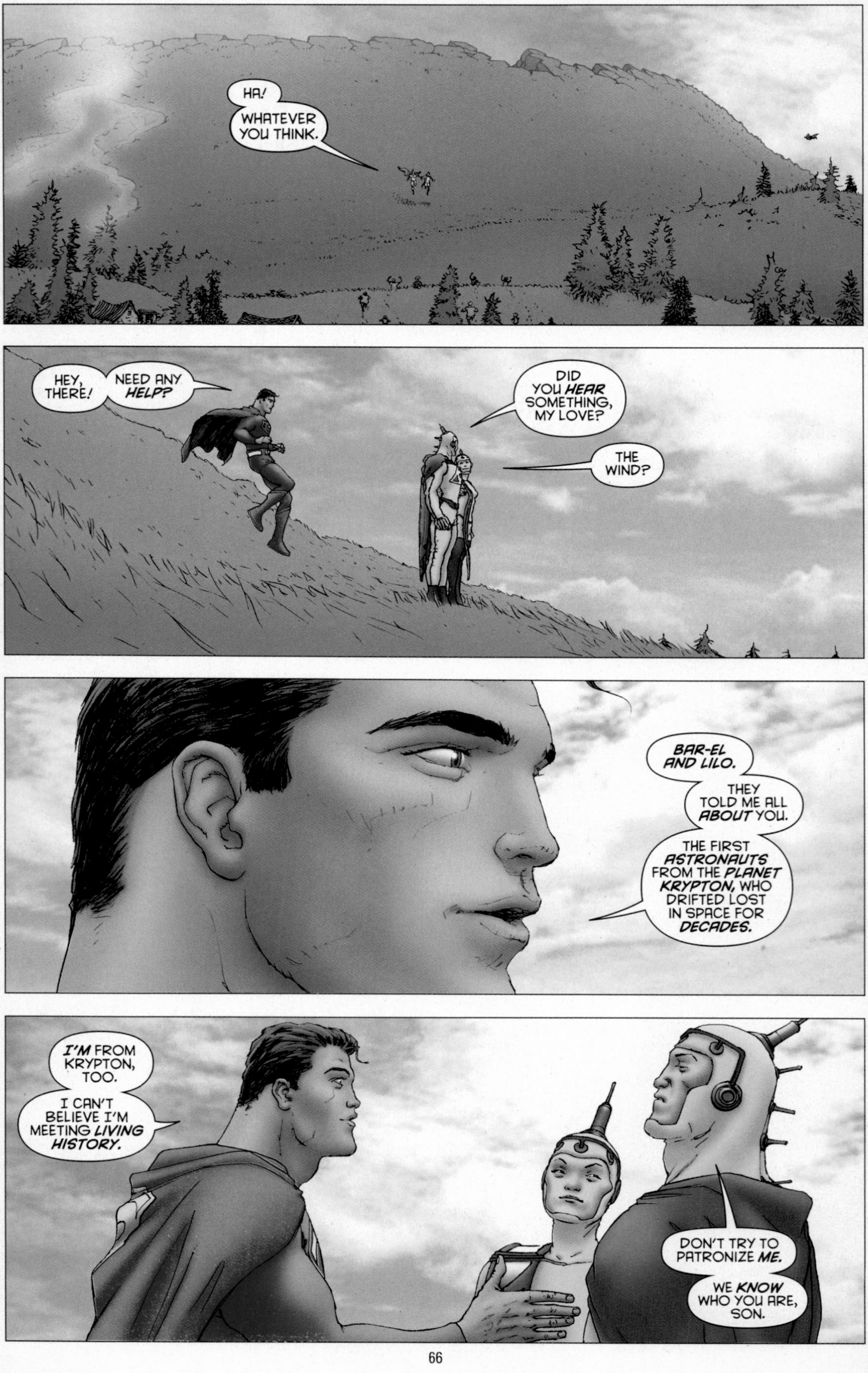
HA!
WHATEVER YOU THINK.
HEY, THERE!
NEED ANY HELP?
DID YOU HEAR SOMETHING, MY LOVE?
THE WIND?
BAR-EL AND LILO.
THEY TOLD ME ALL ABOUT YOU.
THE FIRST ASTRONAUTS FROM THE PLANET KRYPTON, WHO DRIFTED LOST IN SPACE FOR DECADES.
I'M FROM KRYPTON, TOO.
I CAN'T BELIEVE I'M MEETING LIVING HISTORY.
DON'T TRY TO PATRONIZE ME.
WE KNOW WHO YOU ARE, SON.

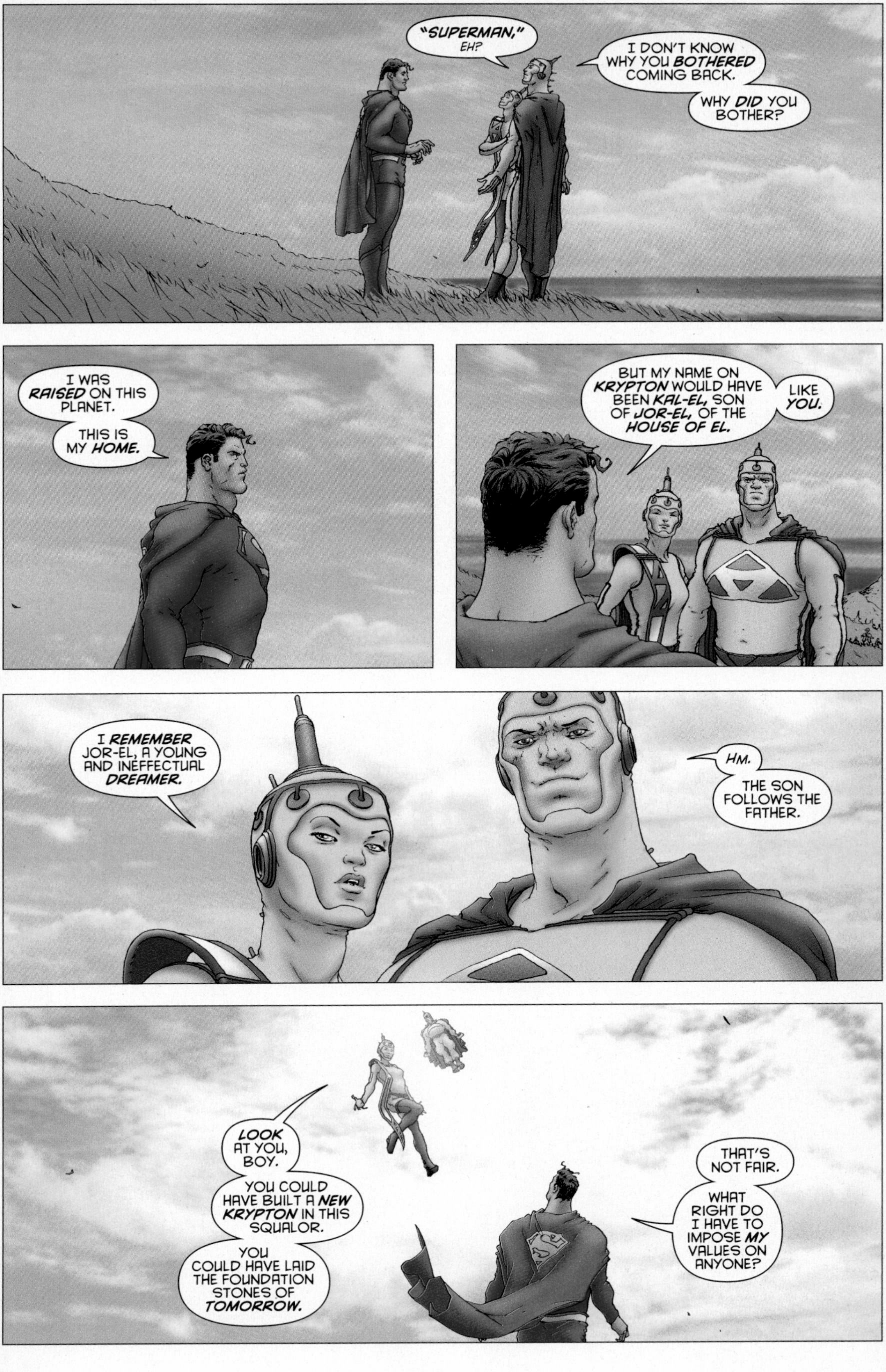
"SUPERMAN," EH?
I DON'T KNOW WHY YOU BOTHERED COMING BACK.
WHY DID YOU BOTHER?
I WAS RAISED ON THIS PLANET.
THIS IS MY HOME.
BUT MY NAME ON KRYPTON WOULD HAVE BEEN KAL-EL, SON OF JOR-EL, OF THE HOUSE OF EL.
LIKE YOU.
I REMEMBER JOR-EL, A YOUNG AND INEFFECTUAL DREAMER.
HM.
THE SON FOLLOWS THE FATHER.
LOOK AT YOU, BOY.
YOU COULD HAVE BUILT A NEW KRYPTON IN THIS SQUALOR.
YOU COULD HAVE LAID THE FOUNDATION STONES OF TOMORROW.
THAT'S NOT FAIR.
WHAT RIGHT DO I HAVE TO IMPOSE MY VALUES ON ANYONE?

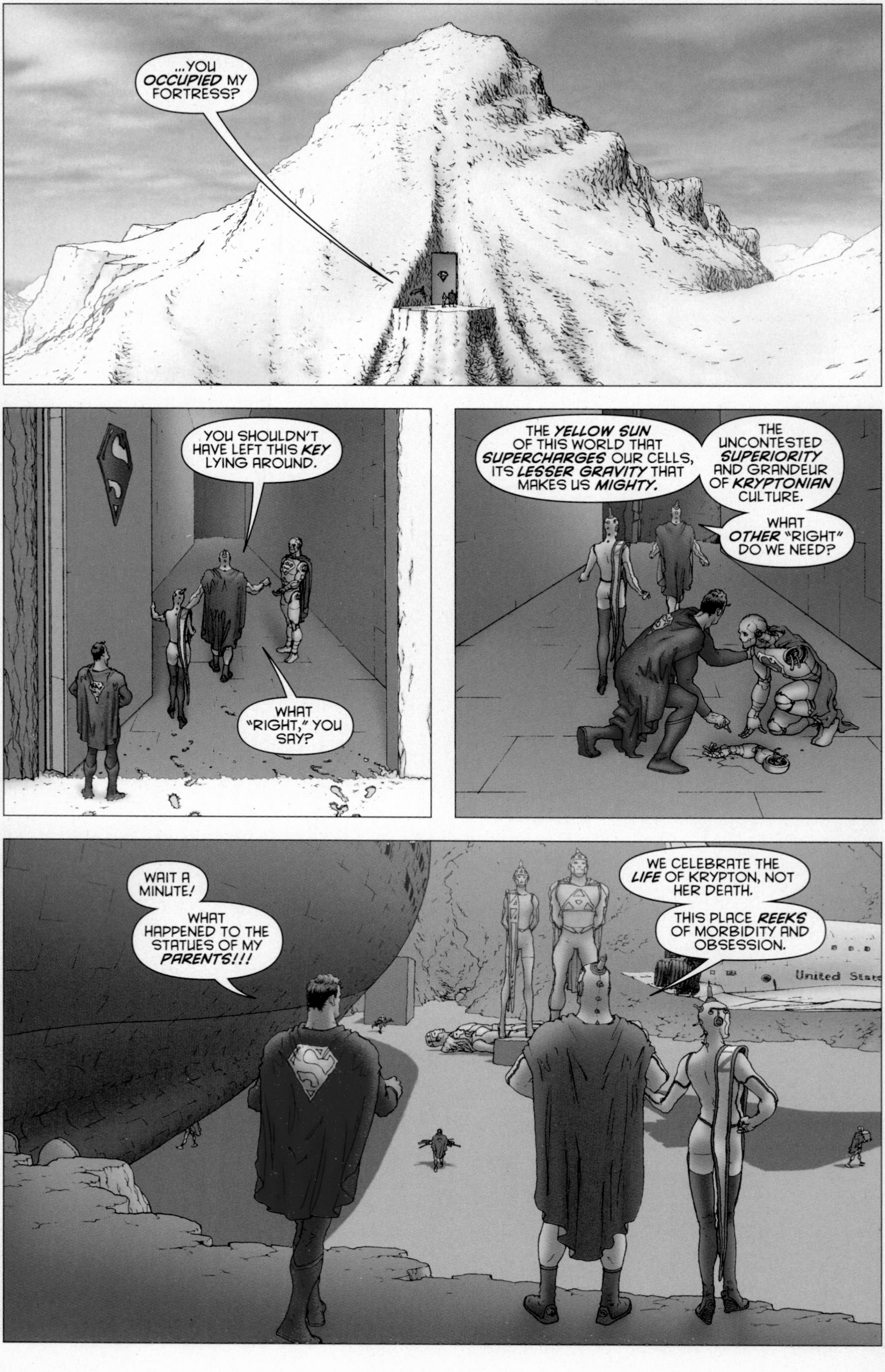
...YOU OCCUPIED MY FORTRESS?
YOU SHOULDN'T HAVE LEFT THIS KEY LYING AROUND.
WHAT "RIGHT," YOU SAY?
THE YELLOW SUN OF THIS WORLD THAT SUPERCHARGES OUR CELLS, ITS LESSER GRAVITY THAT MAKES US MIGHTY.
THE UNCONTESTED SUPERIORITY AND GRANDEUR OF KRYPTONIAN CULTURE.
WHAT OTHER "RIGHT" DO WE NEED?
WAIT A MINUTE!
WHAT HAPPENED TO THE STATUES OF MY PARENTS!!!
WE CELEBRATE THE LIFE OF KRYPTON, NOT HER DEATH.
THIS PLACE REEKS OF MORBIDITY AND OBSESSION.
United Stat

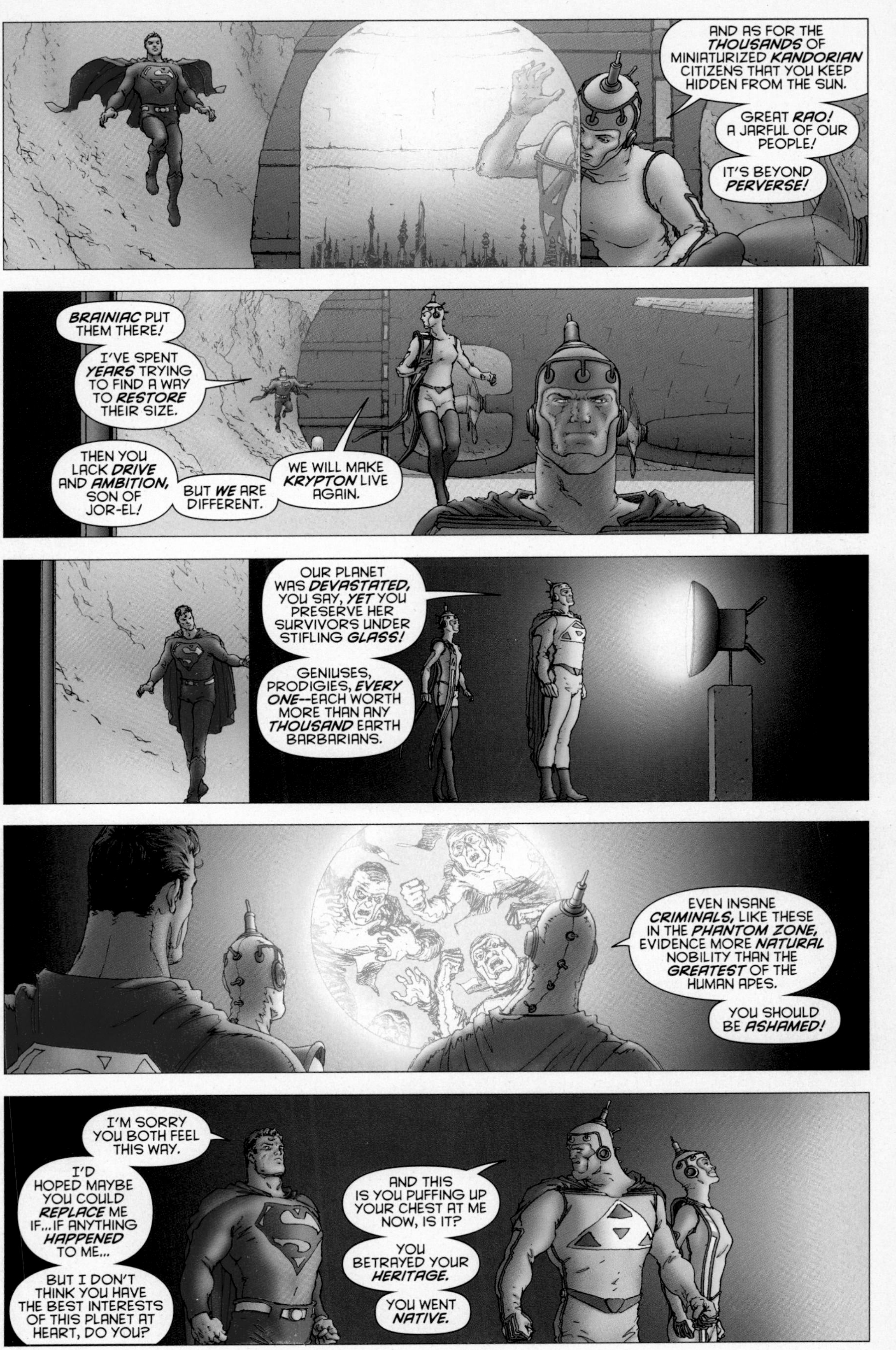
AND AS FOR THE THOUSANDS OF MINIATURIZED KANDORIAN CITIZENS THAT YOU KEEP HIDDEN FROM THE SUN.
GREAT RAO! A JARFUL OF OUR PEOPLE!
IT'S BEYOND PERVERSE!
BRAINIAC PUT THEM THERE!
I'VE SPENT YEARS TRYING TO FIND A WAY TO RESTORE THEIR SIZE.
THEN YOU LACK DRIVE AND AMBITION, SON OF JOR-EL!
BUT WE ARE DIFFERENT.
WE WILL MAKE KRYPTON LIVE AGAIN.
OUR PLANET WAS DEVASTATED, YOU SAY, YET YOU PRESERVE HER SURVIVORS UNDER STIFLING GLASS!
GENIUSES, PRODIGIES, EVERY ONE--EACH WORTH MORE THAN ANY THOUSAND EARTH BARBARIANS.
EVEN INSANE CRIMINALS, LIKE THESE IN THE PHANTOM ZONE, EVIDENCE MORE NATURAL NOBILITY THAN THE GREATEST OF THE HUMAN APES.
YOU SHOULD BE ASHAMED!
I'M SORRY YOU BOTH FEEL THIS WAY.
I'D HOPED MAYBE YOU COULD REPLACE ME IF... IF ANYTHING HAPPENED TO ME...
BUT I DON'T THINK YOU HAVE THE BEST INTERESTS OF THIS PLANET AT HEART, DO YOU?
AND THIS IS YOU PUFFING UP YOUR CHEST AT ME NOW, IS IT?
YOU BETRAYED YOUR HERITAGE.
YOU WENT NATIVE.

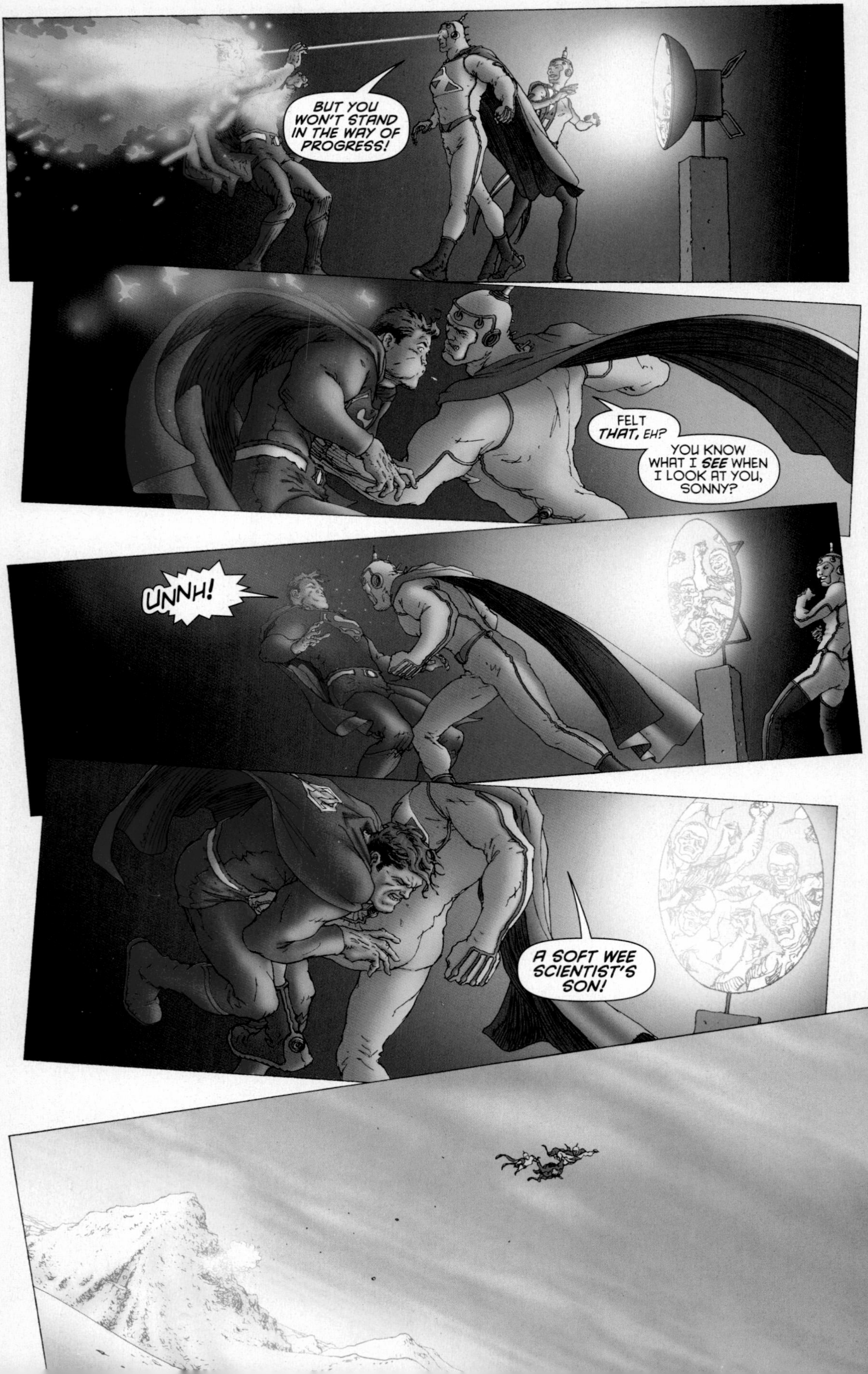
BUT YOU WON'T STAND IN THE WAY OF PROGRESS!
FELT THAT, EH?
YOU KNOW WHAT I SEE WHEN I LOOK AT YOU, SONNY?
UNNH!
A SOFT WEE SCIENTIST'S SON!

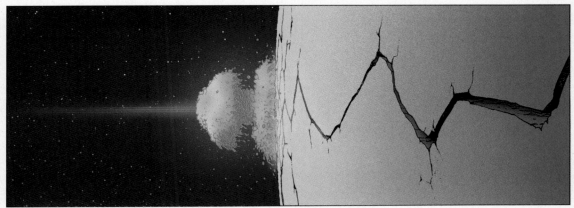

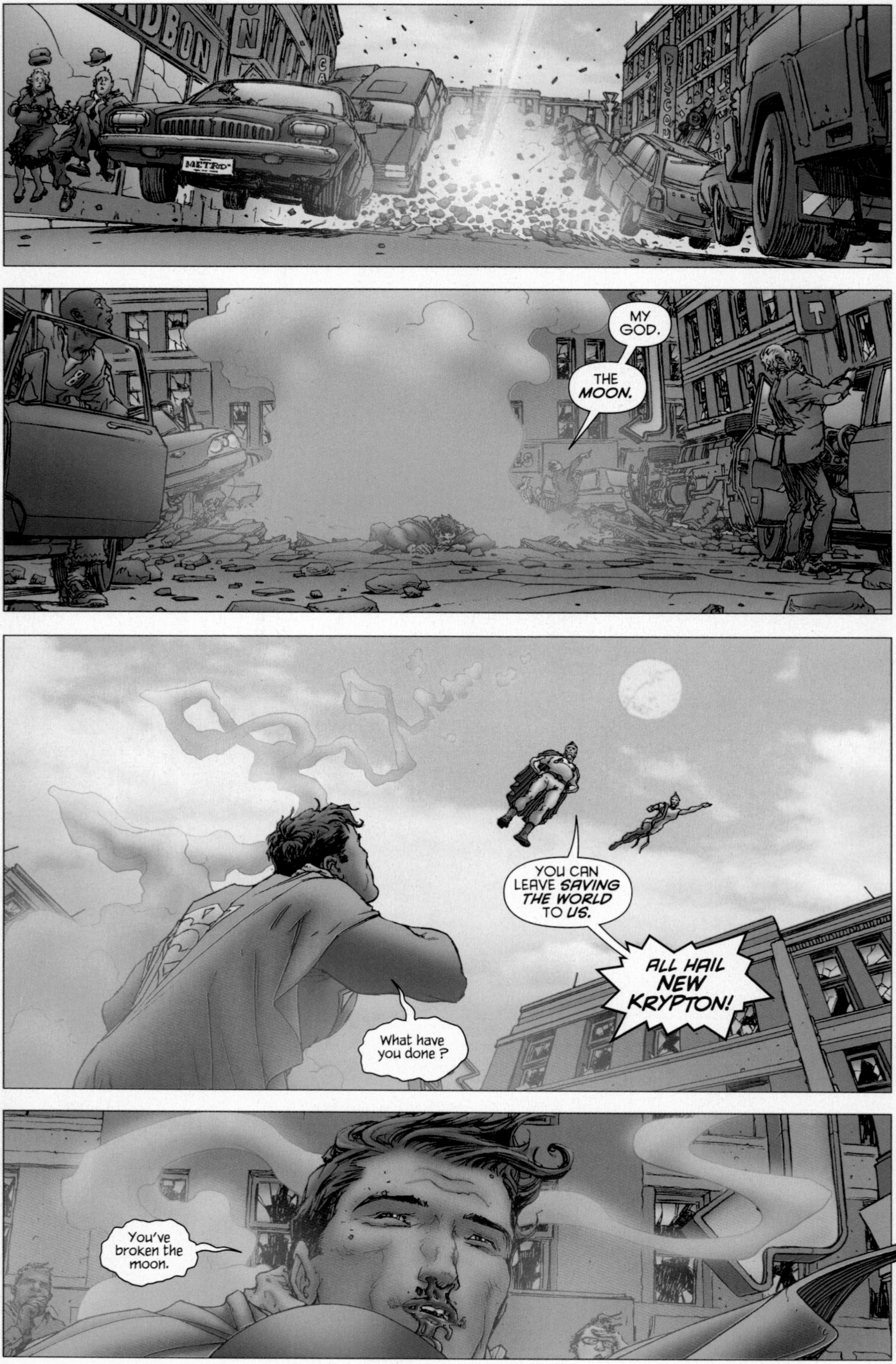

MY GOD.
THE MOON.
YOU CAN LEAVE SAVING THE WORLD TO US.
ALL HAIL NEW KRYPTON!
What have you done ?
You've broken the moon.

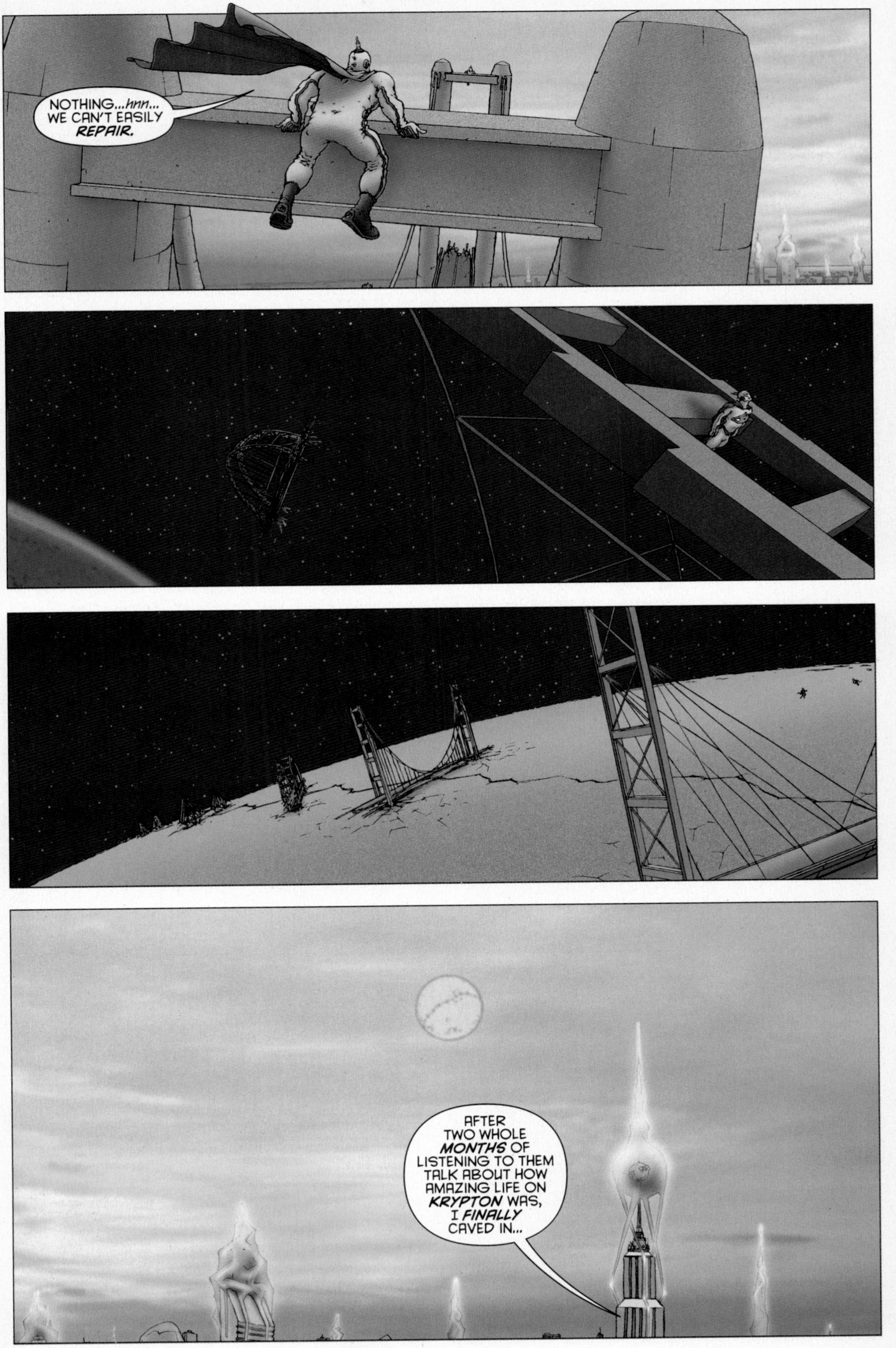
NOTHING...hnn... WE CAN'T EASILY REPAIR.
AFTER TWO WHOLE MONTHS OF LISTENING TO THEM TALK ABOUT HOW AMAZING LIFE ON KRYPTON WAS, I FINALLY CAVED IN...

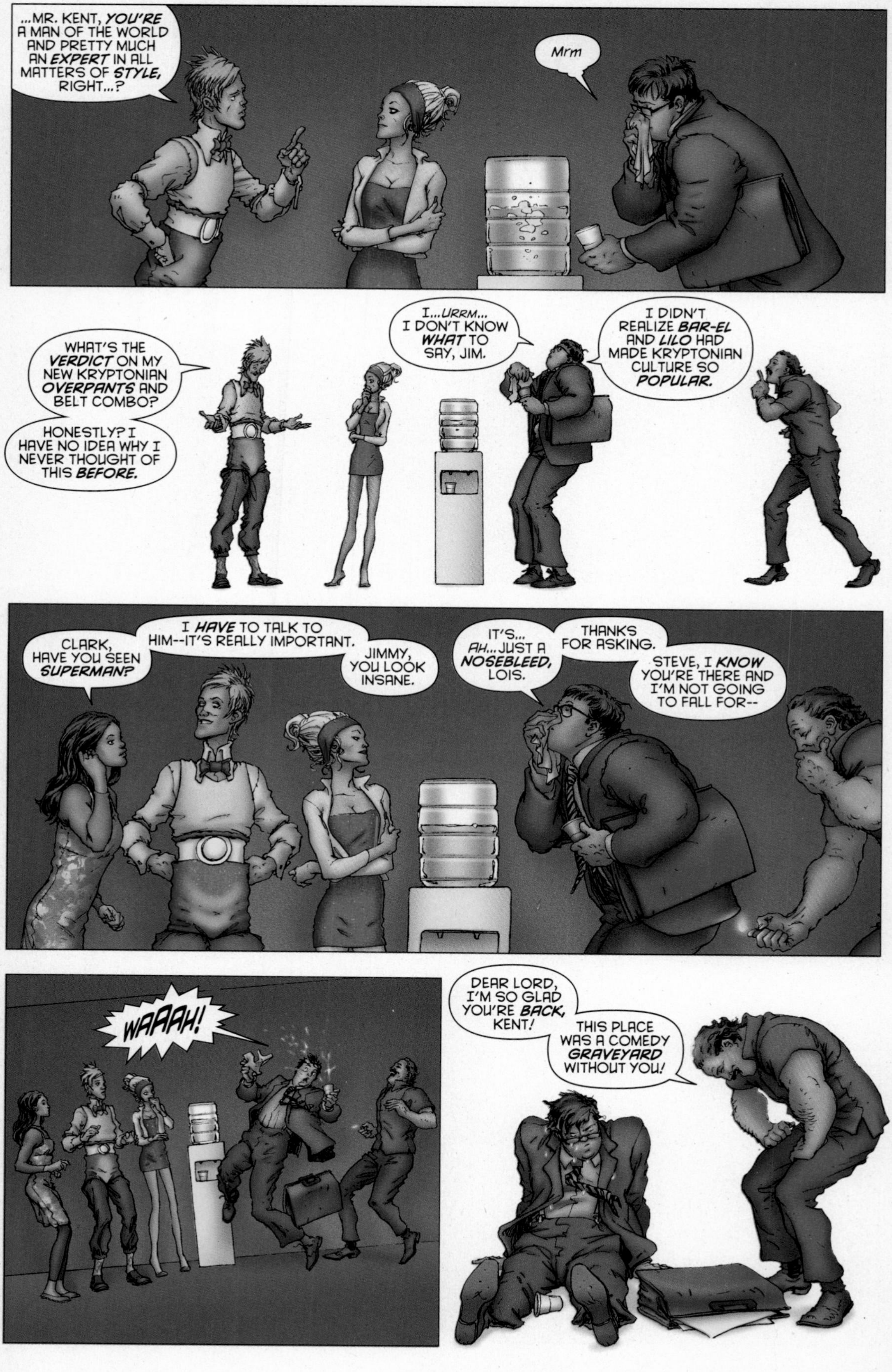
...MR. KENT, YOU'RE A MAN OF THE WORLD AND PRETTY MUCH AN EXPERT IN ALL MATTERS OF STYLE, RIGHT...?
Mrm
WHAT'S THE VERDICT ON MY NEW KRYPTONIAN OVERPANTS AND BELT COMBO?
HONESTLY? I HAVE NO IDEA WHY I NEVER THOUGHT OF THIS BEFORE.
I...URRM... I DON'T KNOW WHAT TO SAY, JIM.
I DIDN'T REALIZE BAR-EL AND LILO HAD MADE KRYPTONIAN CULTURE SO POPULAR.
CLARK, HAVE YOU SEEN SUPERMAN?
I HAVE TO TALK TO HIM--IT'S REALLY IMPORTANT.
JIMMY, YOU LOOK INSANE.
IT'S... AH... JUST A NOSEBLEED, LOIS.
THANKS FOR ASKING.
STEVE, I KNOW YOU'RE THERE AND I'M NOT GOING TO FALL FOR--
WAAAH!
DEAR LORD, I'M SO GLAD YOU'RE BACK, KENT!
THIS PLACE WAS A COMEDY GRAVEYARD WITHOUT YOU!

I...AH...SPEAKING OF COMEDY, STEVE...

YOUR...AH... YOUR HAIRPIECE IS ON FIRE...

WHAT THE HELL ARE YOU INSINUATING?

I DON'T WEAR--

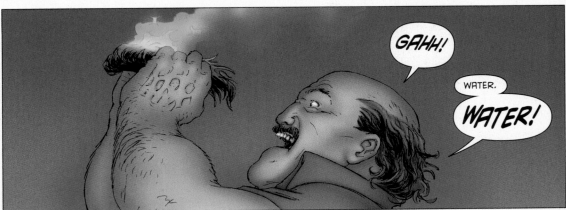

GAHH!

WATER.

WATER!

SO...

...THIS IS WHERE SUPERMAN HIDES OUT?

Uh-Oh.

WHAT KIND OF SELF-LOATHING DEGENERATE DISGUISES HIS TRUE NATURE TO SNORT AND SNUFFLE AMONG SUBHUMANS?

HAVE YOU ABANDONED ALL DIGNITY?

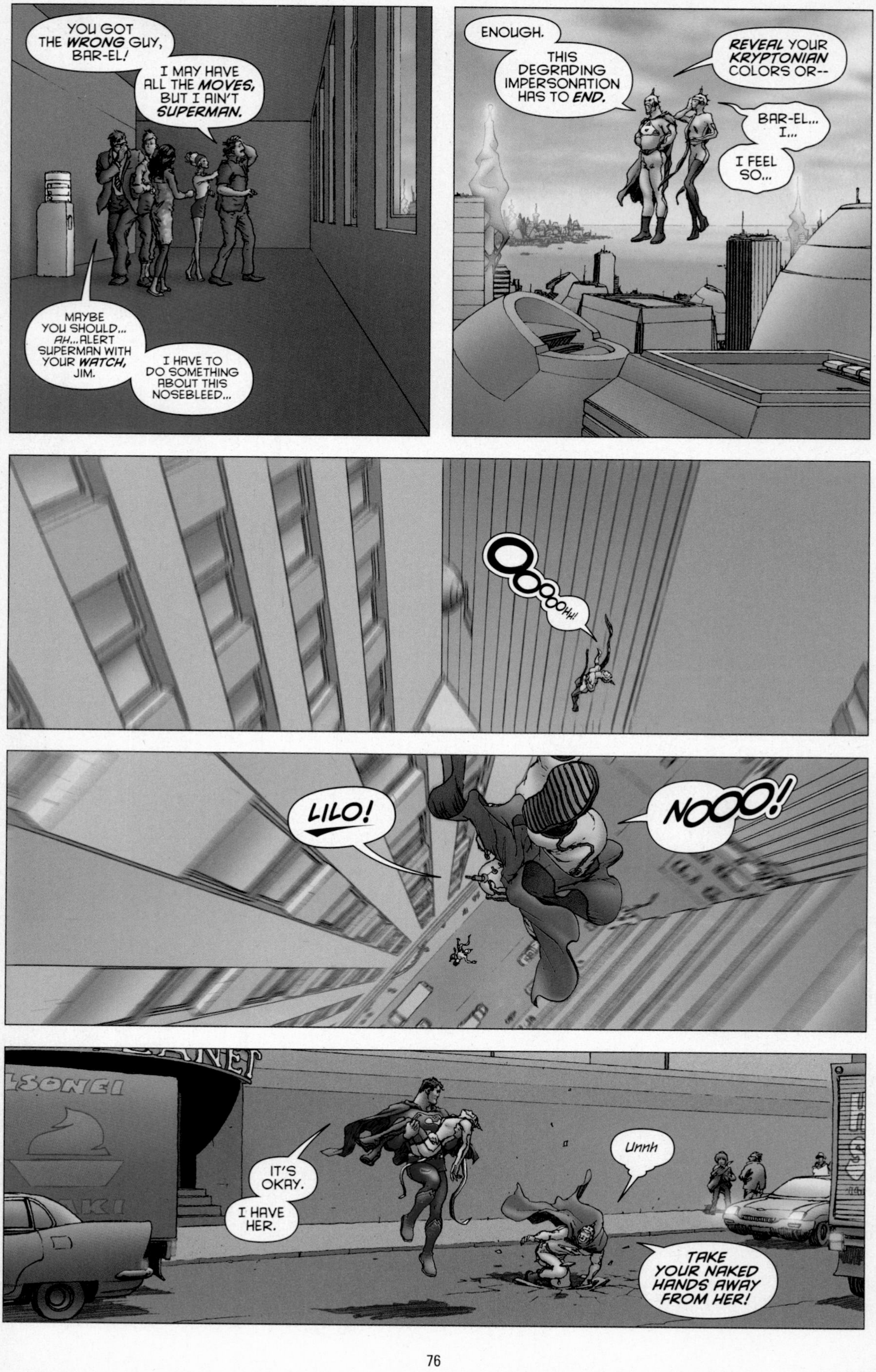
YOU GOT THE WRONG GUY, BAR-EL!
I MAY HAVE ALL THE MOVES, BUT I AIN'T SUPERMAN.
MAYBE YOU SHOULD... AH...ALERT SUPERMAN WITH YOUR WATCH, JIM.
I HAVE TO DO SOMETHING ABOUT THIS NOSEBLEED...
ENOUGH.
THIS DEGRADING IMPERSONATION HAS TO END.
REVEAL YOUR KRYPTONIAN COLORS OR--
BAR-EL... I...
I FEEL SO...
OOOOOHH!
LILO!
NOOO!
IT'S OKAY.
I HAVE HER.
Unnh
TAKE YOUR NAKED HANDS AWAY FROM HER!

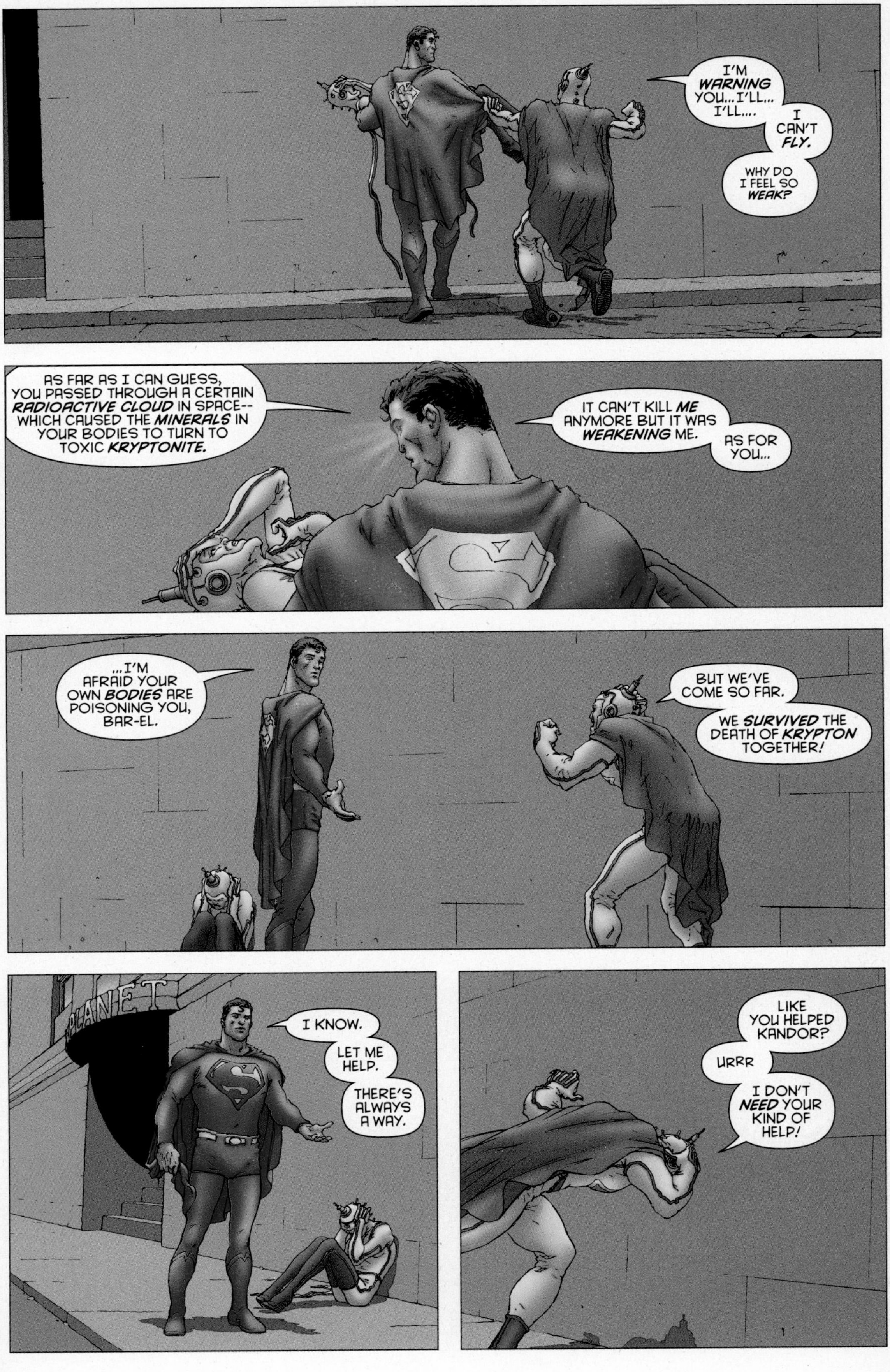
I'M WARNING YOU...I'LL... I'LL....
I CAN'T FLY.
WHY DO I FEEL SO WEAK?
AS FAR AS I CAN GUESS, YOU PASSED THROUGH A CERTAIN RADIOACTIVE CLOUD IN SPACE-- WHICH CAUSED THE MINERALS IN YOUR BODIES TO TURN TO TOXIC KRYPTONITE.
IT CAN'T KILL ME ANYMORE BUT IT WAS WEAKENING ME.
AS FOR YOU...
...I'M AFRAID YOUR OWN BODIES ARE POISONING YOU, BAR-EL.
BUT WE'VE COME SO FAR.
WE SURVIVED THE DEATH OF KRYPTON TOGETHER!
PLANET
I KNOW.
LET ME HELP.
THERE'S ALWAYS A WAY.
LIKE YOU HELPED KANDOR?
URRR
I DON'T NEED YOUR KIND OF HELP!

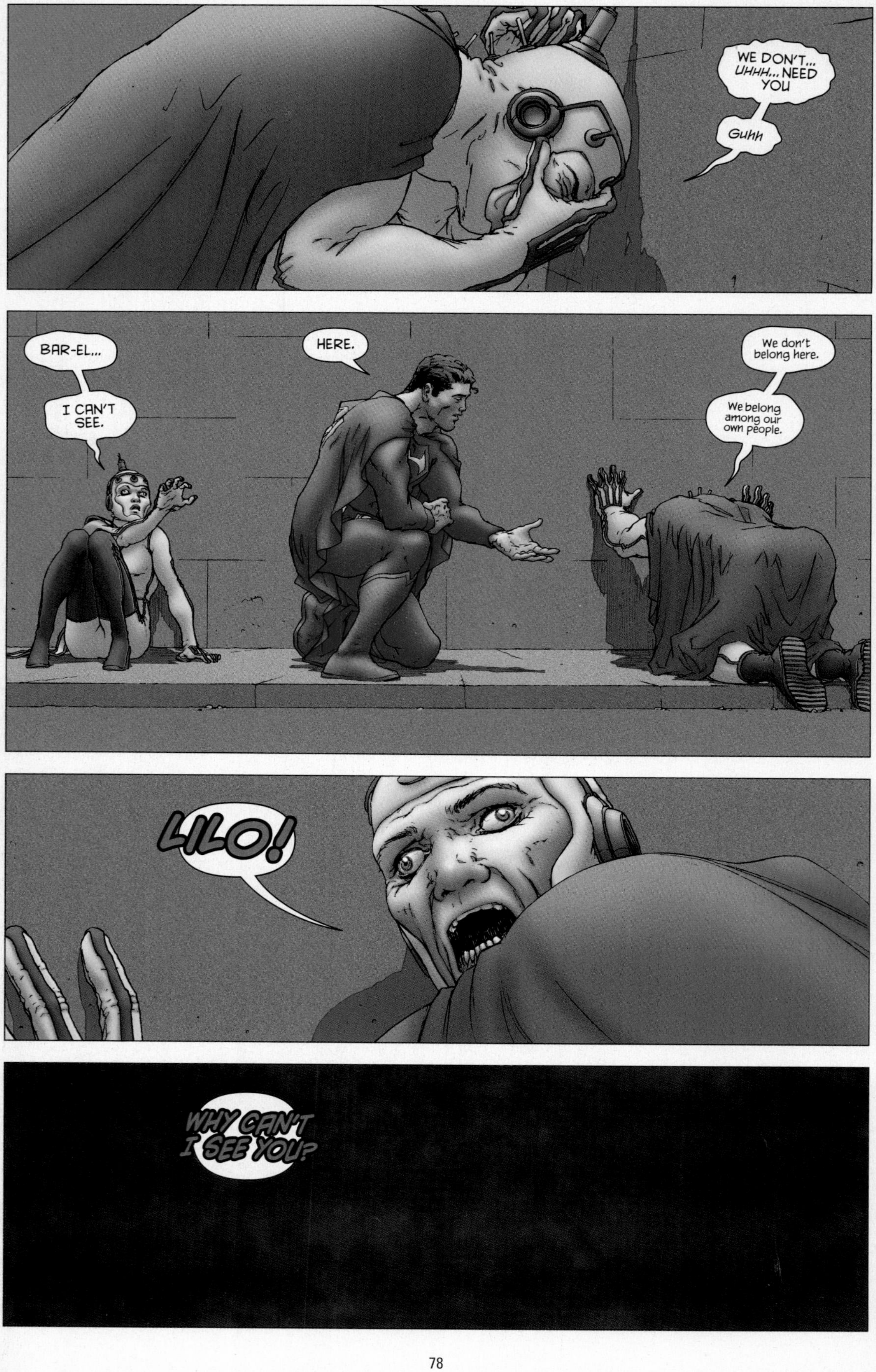
WE DON'T... UHHH... NEED YOU
Guhh
BAR-EL...
I CAN'T SEE.
HERE.
We don't belong here.
We belong among our own people.
LILO!
WHY CAN'T I SEE YOU?

ONCE I APPLY THESE *CONTACTS*, I'LL BE ABLE TO SEE AND HEAR YOU ON THE *THOUGHTSCREEN*.

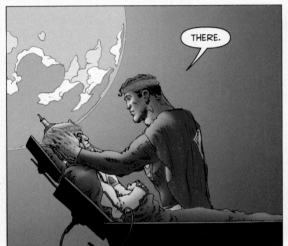

THERE.

SUPERMAN...

AFTER ALL I'VE *DONE*, STILL YOU SHOW ME KINDNESS.

MY EARTH PARENTS TAUGHT ME RESPECT FOR MY ELDERS.

THEY'RE NOT *ALL* BARBARIANS, BAR-EL.

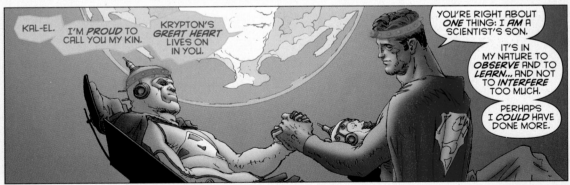

KAL-EL. I'M *PROUD* TO CALL YOU MY KIN.

KRYPTON'S *GREAT HEART* LIVES ON IN YOU.

YOU'RE RIGHT ABOUT *ONE* THING: I *AM* A SCIENTIST'S SON.

IT'S IN MY NATURE TO *OBSERVE* AND TO *LEARN*... AND NOT TO *INTERFERE* TOO MUCH.

PERHAPS I *COULD* HAVE DONE MORE.

DO WHAT YOU MUST, SUPERMAN.

YES.

WE DON'T HAVE MUCH TIME.

Karrf! KOFF!

THERE'S *ONE WAY* TO SAVE YOU BUT THIS HAS TO BE *YOUR* CHOICE.

THE RAY WILL DEMATERIALIZE YOUR BODIES INTO THE *PHANTOM ZONE.* FOREVER.

THEN PUT... PUT MY *HAND* IN HERS...

PUT MY HAND IN HERS WHERE IT *BELONGS,* KAL-EL.

ANOTHER BIG ADVENTURE, MY LOVE.

WHERE YOU AND I GO...

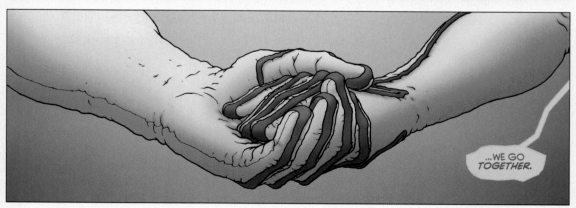

...WE GO *TOGETHER.*

IF I CAN, IF I STILL HAVE TIME, I PROMISE I'LL FIND A WAY TO *RESTORE* YOU BOTH. UNTIL THEN...

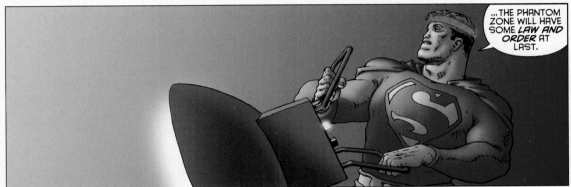

...THE PHANTOM ZONE WILL HAVE SOME *LAW AND ORDER* AT LAST.

CURSE OF THE REPLACEMENT SUPERMEN

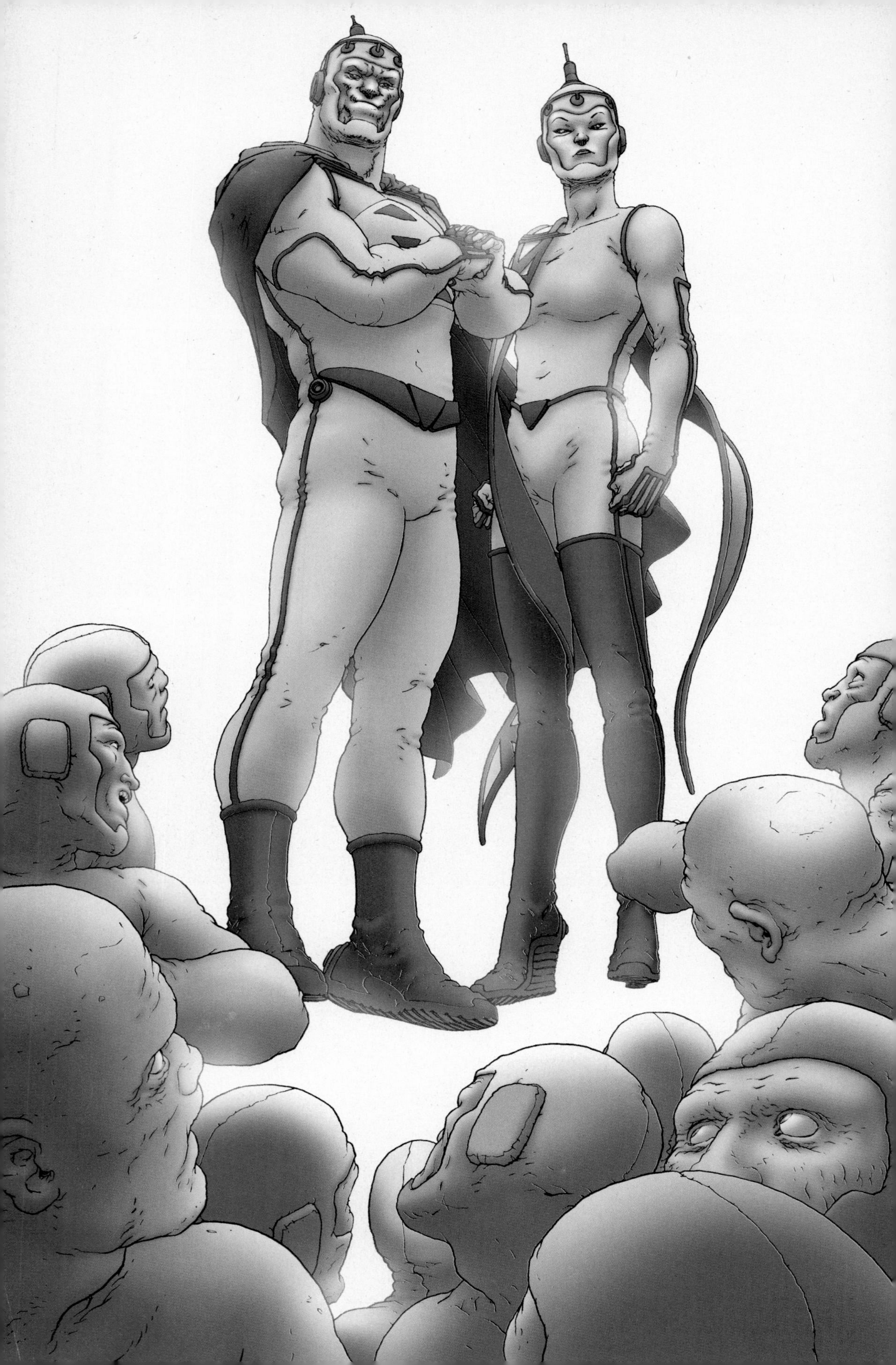

Episode 10

NEVERENDING

Cover FRANK QUITELY with Jamie Grant

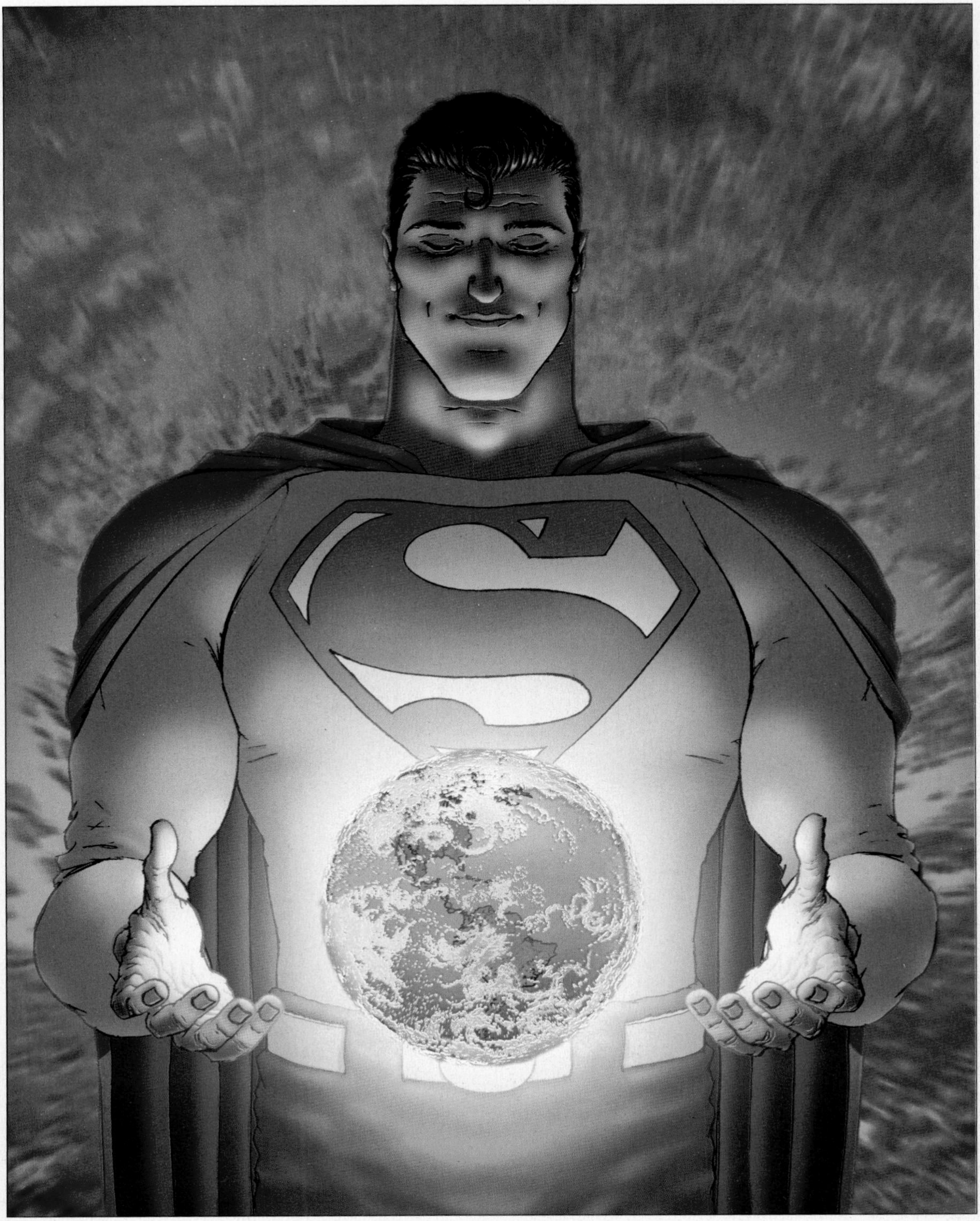

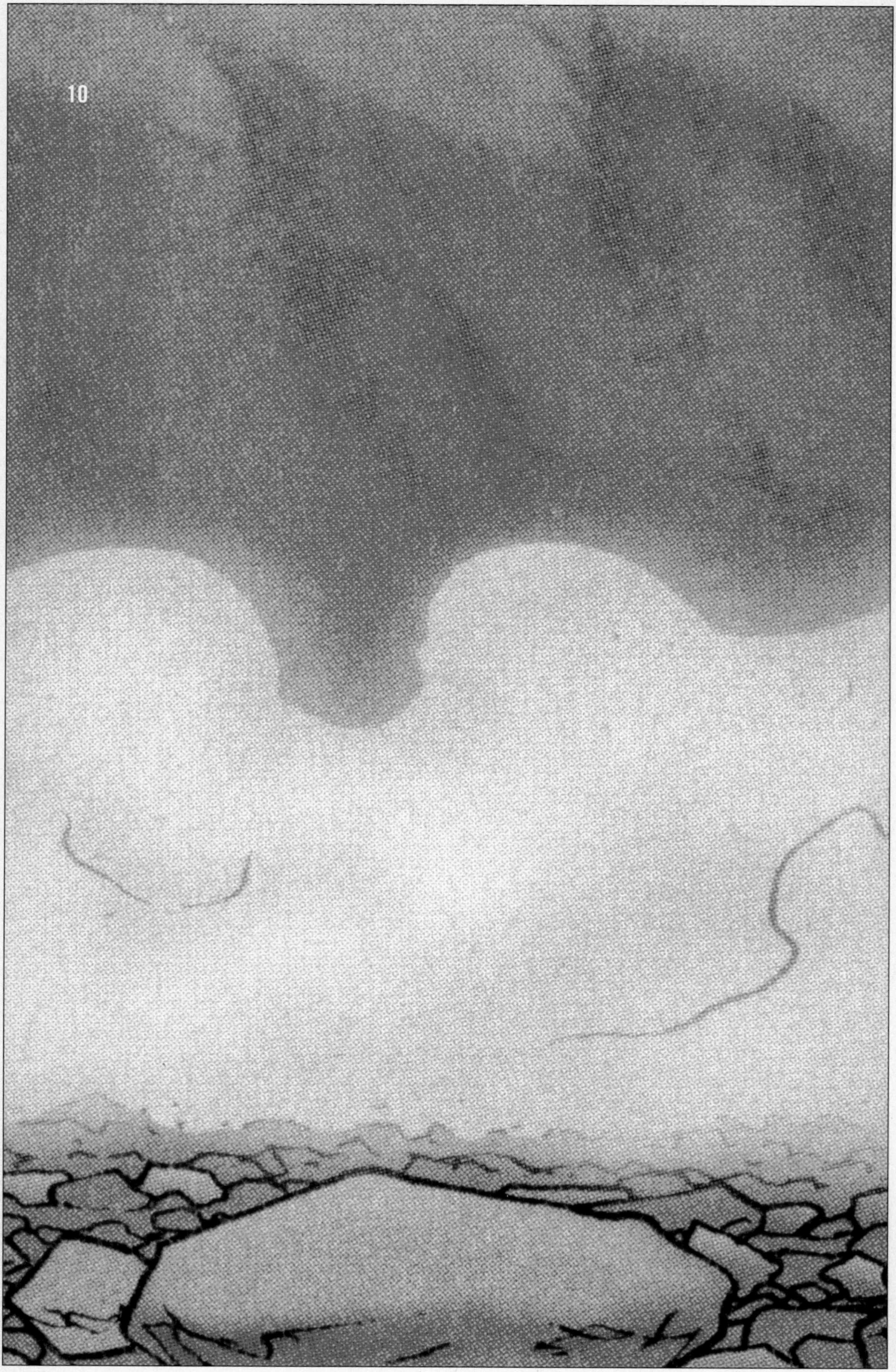

7:02 AM

I'VE NEVER *SEEN* THEM SO EXCITED.

GOD BLESS YOU, SUPERMAN.

YOUR VISITS ARE ALL SOME OF THEM HAVE TO LOOK FORWARD TO.

IT'S THE LEAST I CAN DO.

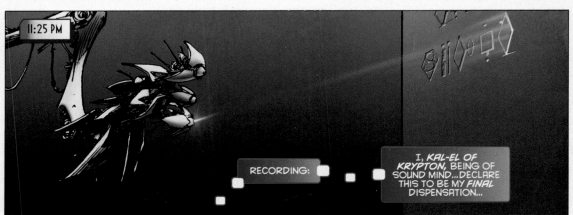

11:25 PM

RECORDING:

I, *KAL-EL OF KRYPTON*, BEING OF SOUND MIND...DECLARE THIS TO BE MY *FINAL* DISPENSATION...

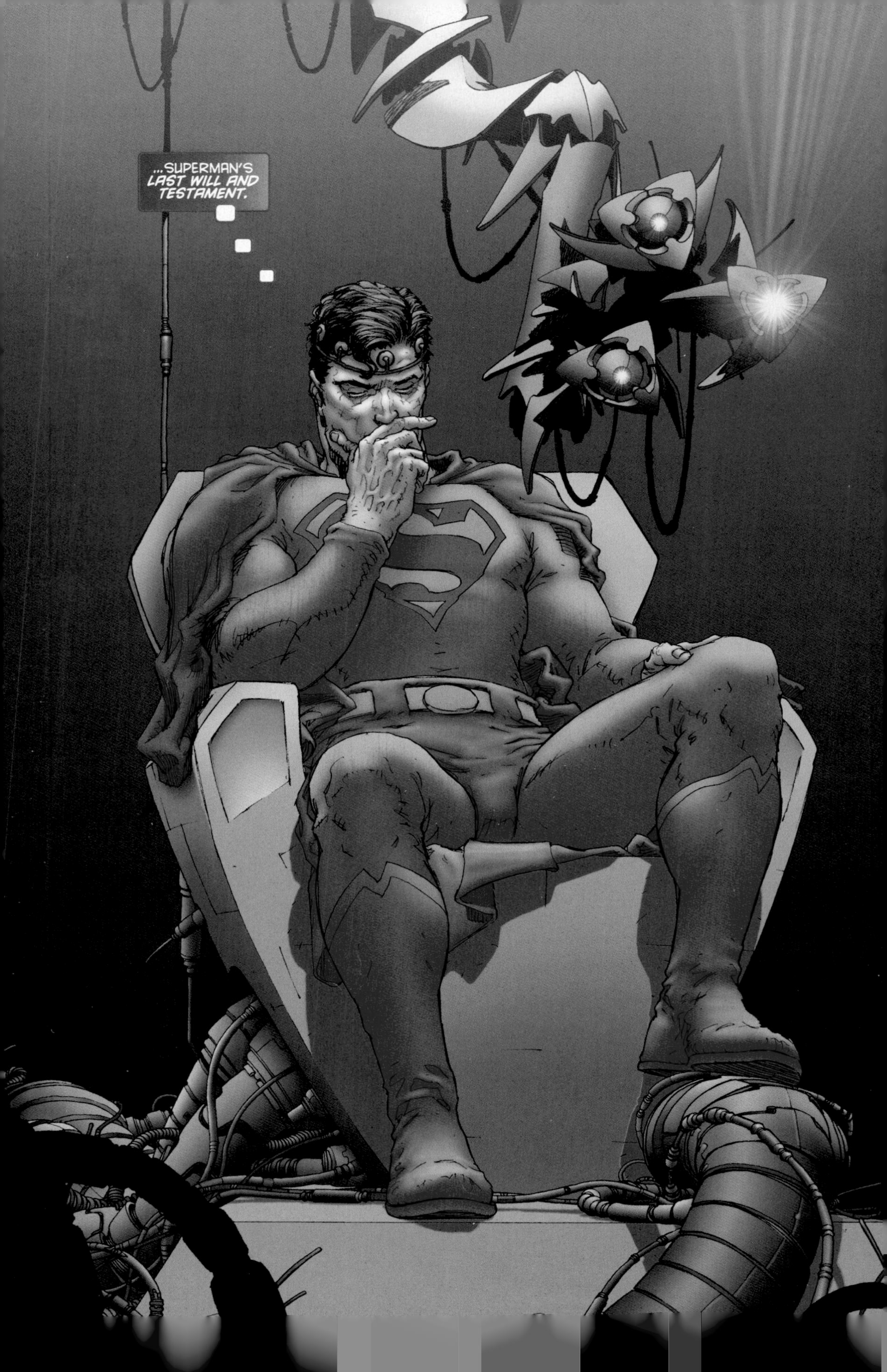
...SUPERMAN'S LAST WILL AND TESTAMENT.

THERE'S SO LITTLE TIME *LEFT* NOW.

THE END IS GETTING CLOSER AND THERE ARE STILL SO MANY THINGS I'VE YET TO ACHIEVE.

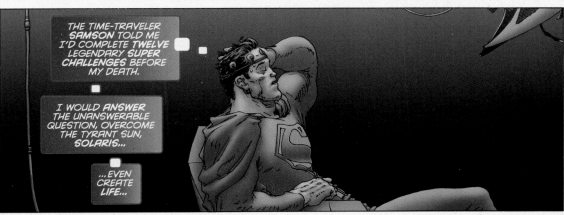

THE TIME-TRAVELER *SAMSON* TOLD ME I'D COMPLETE *TWELVE* LEGENDARY *SUPER CHALLENGES* BEFORE MY DEATH.

I WOULD *ANSWER* THE UNANSWERABLE QUESTION, OVERCOME THE TYRANT SUN, *SOLARIS...*

...EVEN CREATE LIFE...

EACH CHALLENGE, OF COURSE, BRINGS ME *CLOSER* TO MY DEATH.

AND BY MY RECKONING I'VE ACCOMPLISHED *SEVEN* SO FAR.

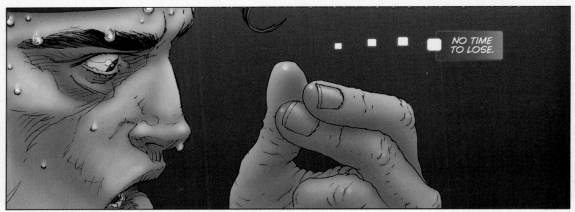

NO TIME TO LOSE.

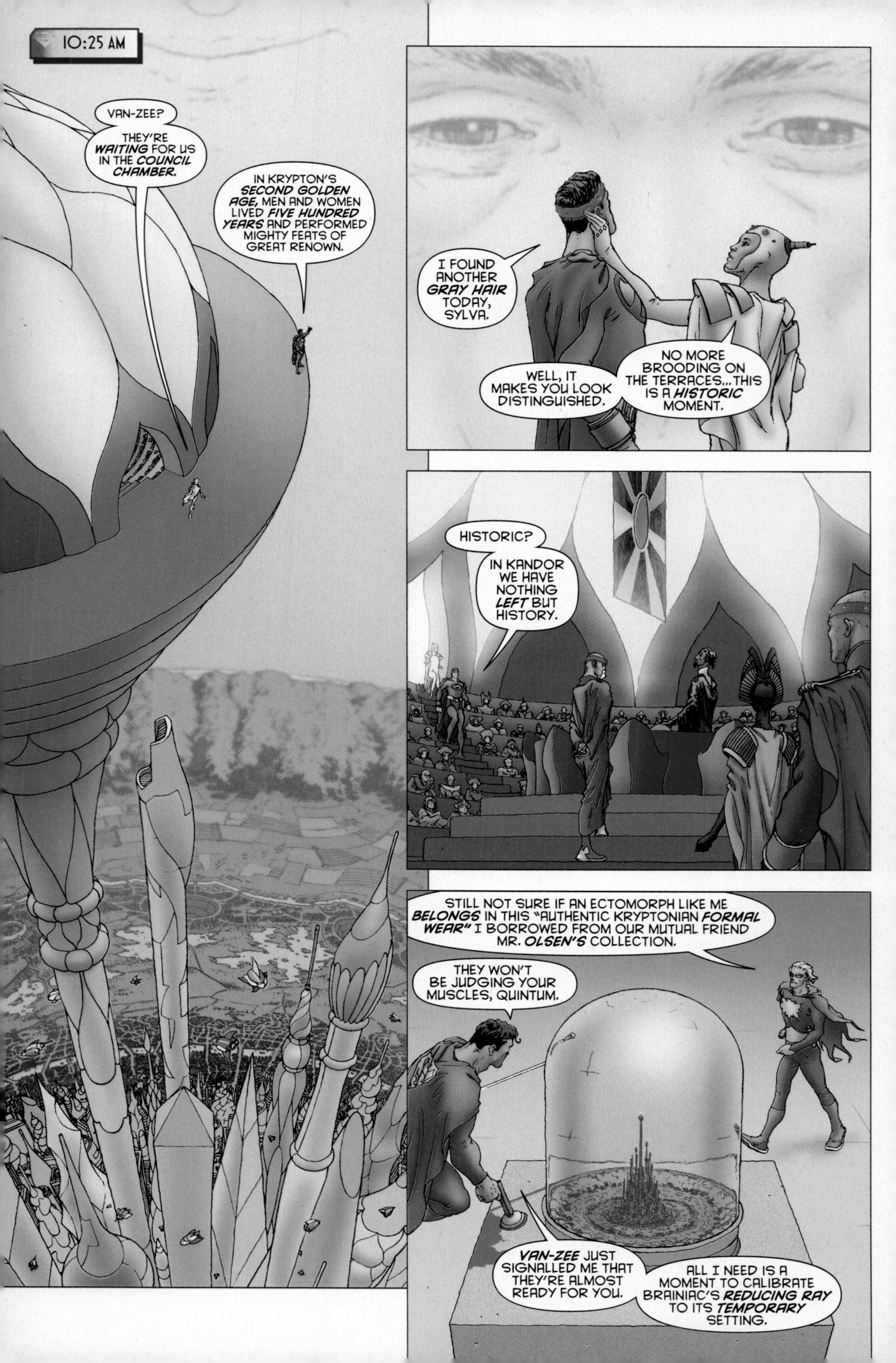

10:25 AM
VAN-ZEE?
THEY'RE WAITING FOR US IN THE COUNCIL CHAMBER.
IN KRYPTON'S SECOND GOLDEN AGE, MEN AND WOMEN LIVED FIVE HUNDRED YEARS AND PERFORMED MIGHTY FEATS OF GREAT RENOWN.
I FOUND ANOTHER GRAY HAIR TODAY, SYLVA.
WELL, IT MAKES YOU LOOK DISTINGUISHED.
NO MORE BROODING ON THE TERRACES... THIS IS A HISTORIC MOMENT.
HISTORIC?
IN KANDOR WE HAVE NOTHING LEFT BUT HISTORY.
STILL NOT SURE IF AN ECTOMORPH LIKE ME BELONGS IN THIS "AUTHENTIC KRYPTONIAN FORMAL WEAR" I BORROWED FROM OUR MUTUAL FRIEND MR. OLSEN'S COLLECTION.
THEY WON'T BE JUDGING YOUR MUSCLES, QUINTUM.
VAN-ZEE JUST SIGNALLED ME THAT THEY'RE ALMOST READY FOR YOU.
ALL I NEED IS A MOMENT TO CALIBRATE BRAINIAC'S REDUCING RAY TO ITS TEMPORARY SETTING.

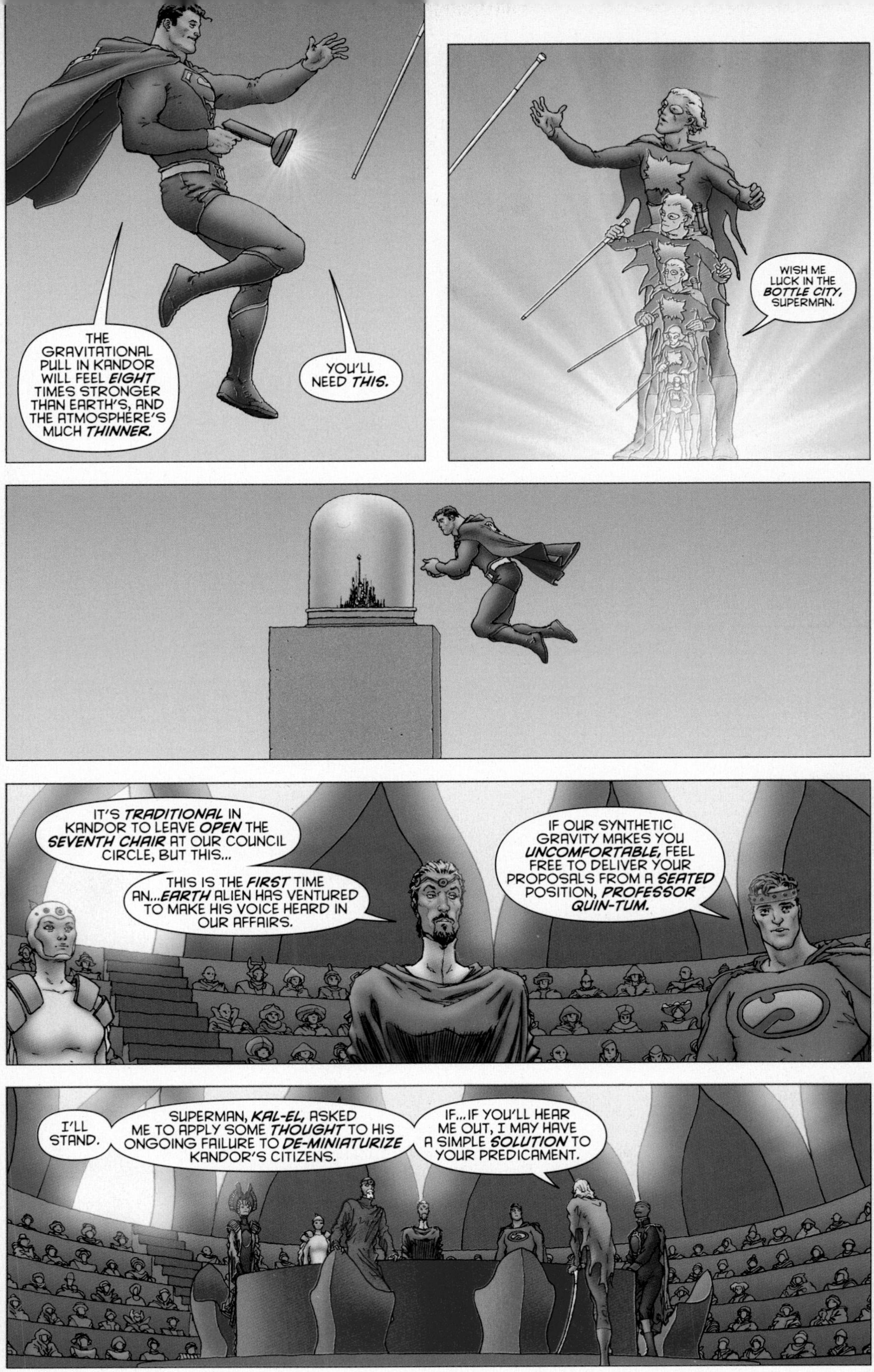
THE GRAVITATIONAL PULL IN KANDOR WILL FEEL EIGHT TIMES STRONGER THAN EARTH'S, AND THE ATMOSPHERE'S MUCH THINNER.
YOU'LL NEED THIS.
WISH ME LUCK IN THE BOTTLE CITY, SUPERMAN.
IT'S TRADITIONAL IN KANDOR TO LEAVE OPEN THE SEVENTH CHAIR AT OUR COUNCIL CIRCLE, BUT THIS...
THIS IS THE FIRST TIME AN...EARTH ALIEN HAS VENTURED TO MAKE HIS VOICE HEARD IN OUR AFFAIRS.
IF OUR SYNTHETIC GRAVITY MAKES YOU UNCOMFORTABLE, FEEL FREE TO DELIVER YOUR PROPOSALS FROM A SEATED POSITION, PROFESSOR QUIN-TUM.
I'LL STAND.
SUPERMAN, KAL-EL, ASKED ME TO APPLY SOME THOUGHT TO HIS ONGOING FAILURE TO DE-MINIATURIZE KANDOR'S CITIZENS.
IF...IF YOU'LL HEAR ME OUT, I MAY HAVE A SIMPLE SOLUTION TO YOUR PREDICAMENT.

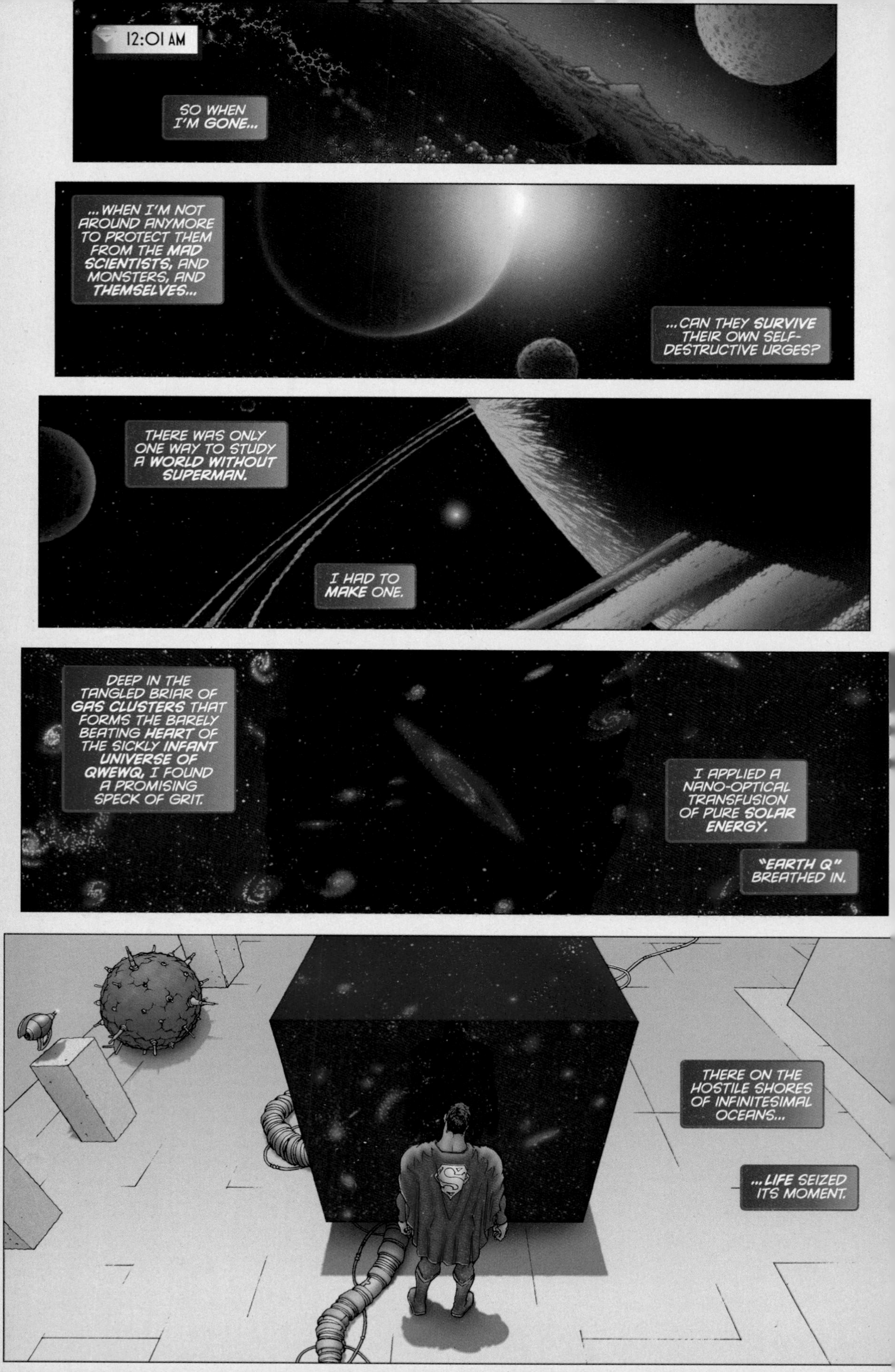
12:01 AM
SO WHEN I'M GONE...
...WHEN I'M NOT AROUND ANYMORE TO PROTECT THEM FROM THE MAD SCIENTISTS, AND MONSTERS, AND THEMSELVES...
...CAN THEY SURVIVE THEIR OWN SELF-DESTRUCTIVE URGES?
THERE WAS ONLY ONE WAY TO STUDY A WORLD WITHOUT SUPERMAN.
I HAD TO MAKE ONE.
DEEP IN THE TANGLED BRIAR OF GAS CLUSTERS THAT FORMS THE BARELY BEATING HEART OF THE SICKLY INFANT UNIVERSE OF QWEWQ, I FOUND A PROMISING SPECK OF GRIT.
I APPLIED A NANO-OPTICAL TRANSFUSION OF PURE SOLAR ENERGY.
"EARTH Q" BREATHED IN.
THERE ON THE HOSTILE SHORES OF INFINITESIMAL OCEANS...
...LIFE SEIZED ITS MOMENT.

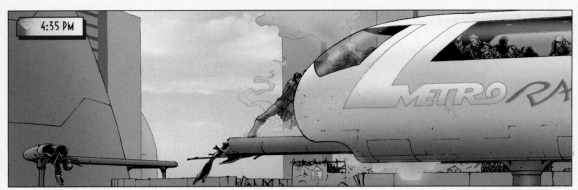

4:35 PM

I GOT *HELD UP*...! NO... NO, *DON'T* PUT THE PHONE DOWN, REGAN!

JUST STAY IN THE APARTMENT!

YOU *HAVE* TO BELIEVE ME! I'M *ON MY WAY!*

HE TORE THE SITE *APART* LOOKING FOR *THIS*-- THEN JUST *DROPPED* IT WHEN THAT REPORTER GOT IN HIS WAY.

WE THOUGHT IT WAS SOME KIND OF *TIME CAPSULE.*

BUT SEE THE *DATE!*

2312?

A TIME CAPSULE FROM THE *FUTURE*, BURIED IN THE *PAST?*

LEAD. *OPAQUE* EVEN TO MY X-RAY VISION.

UH-OH...

LOOKS LIKE HE'S COMING BACK FOR MORE.

HOLD ONTO *THIS.*

I WON'T BE LONG.

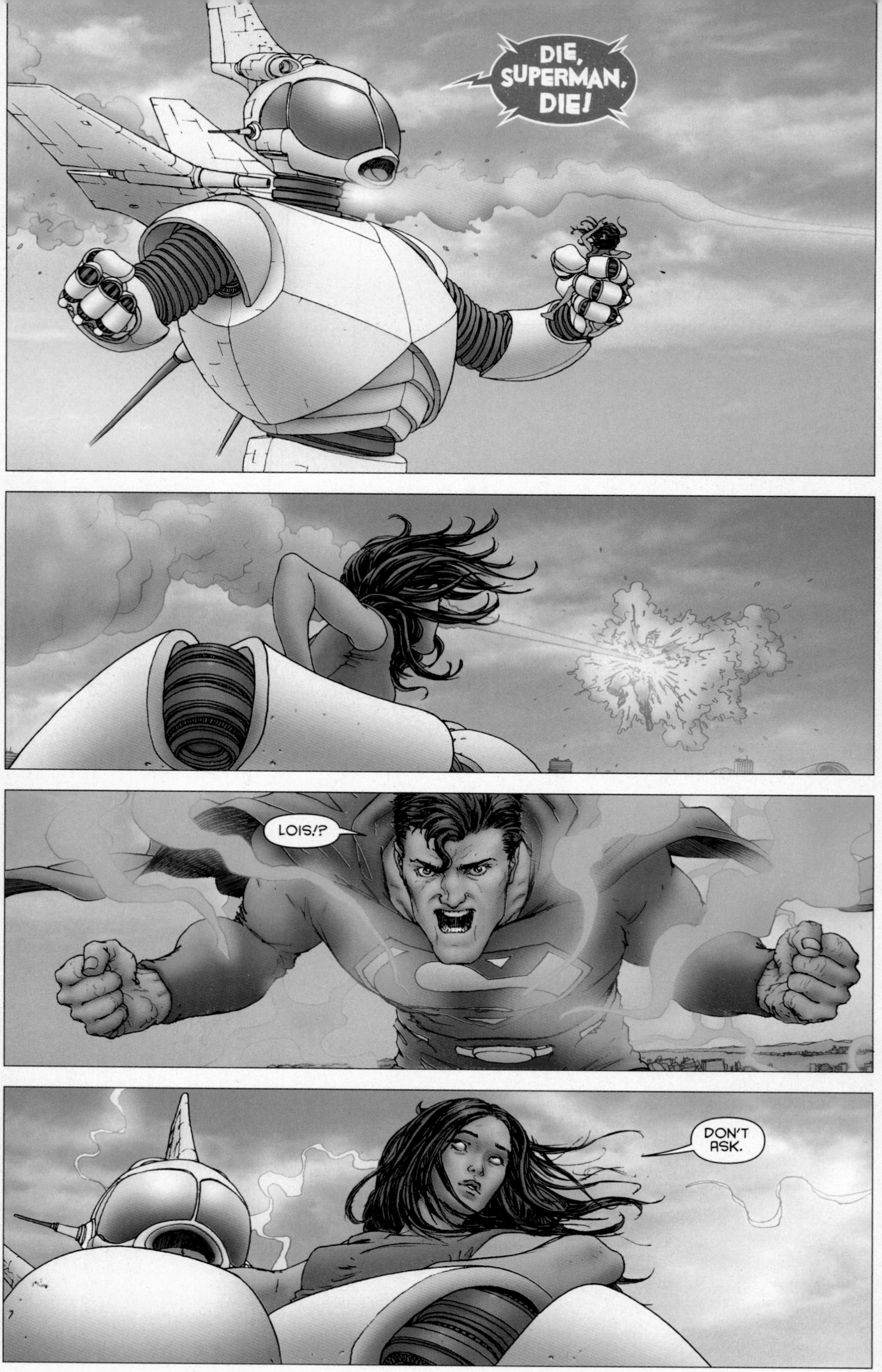
DIE, SUPERMAN, DIE!
LOIS!?
DON'T ASK.

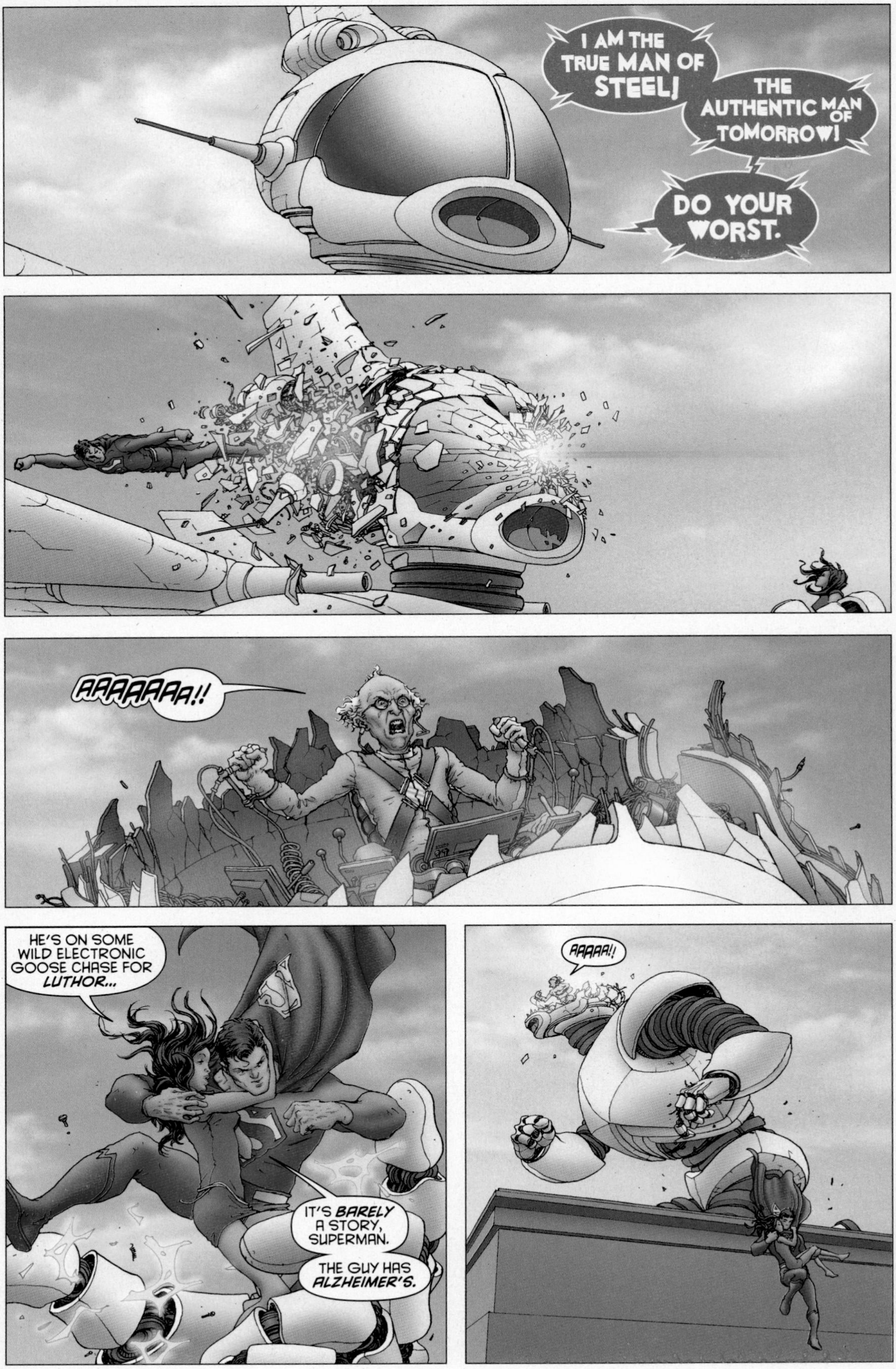

I AM THE TRUE MAN OF STEEL!
THE AUTHENTIC MAN OF TOMORROW!
DO YOUR WORST.
AAAAAAA!!
HE'S ON SOME WILD ELECTRONIC GOOSE CHASE FOR LUTHOR...
IT'S BARELY A STORY, SUPERMAN.
THE GUY HAS ALZHEIMER'S.
AAAAA!!

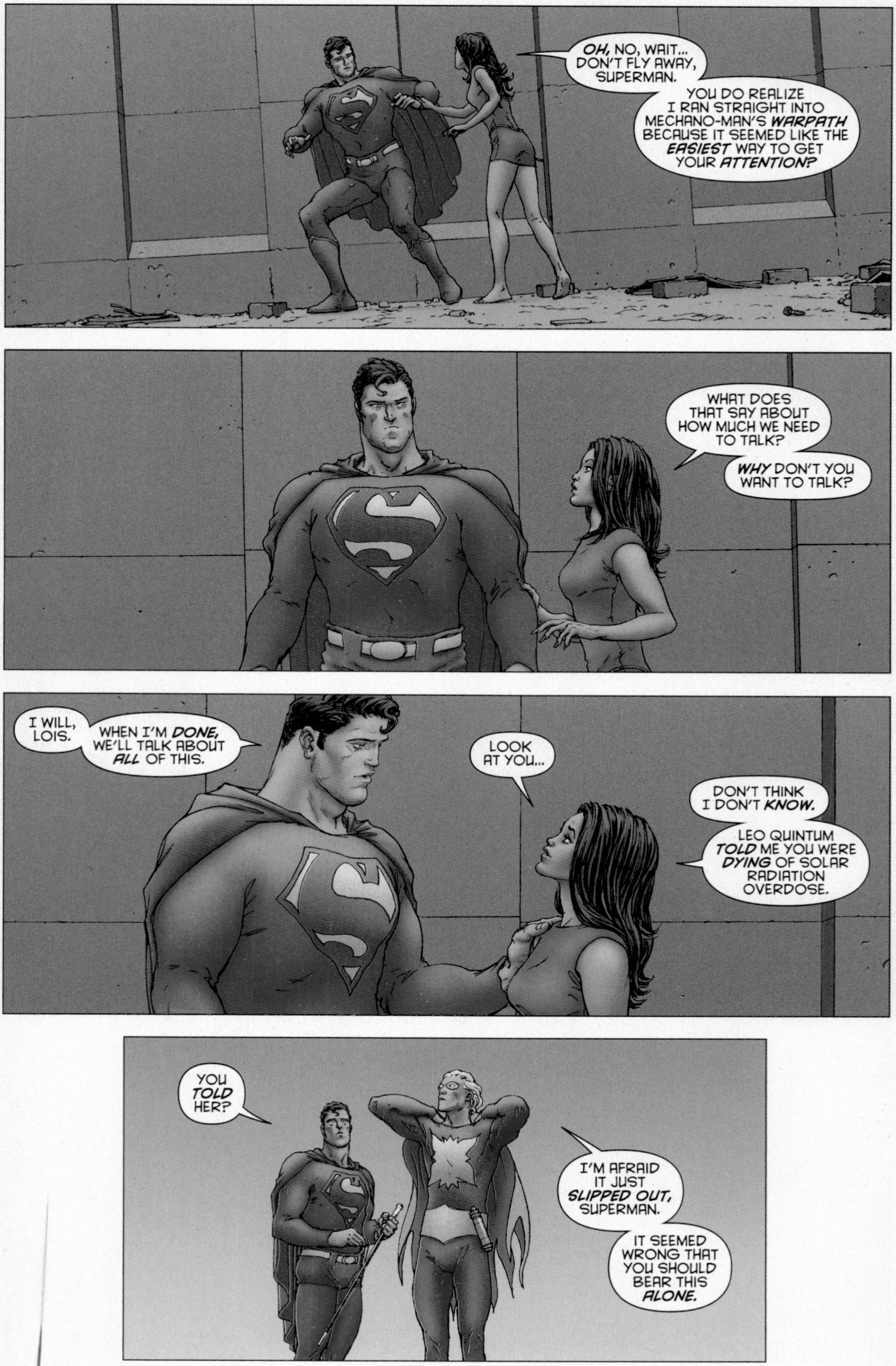
OH, NO, WAIT... DON'T FLY AWAY, SUPERMAN.
YOU DO REALIZE I RAN STRAIGHT INTO MECHANO-MAN'S WARPATH BECAUSE IT SEEMED LIKE THE EASIEST WAY TO GET YOUR ATTENTION?
WHAT DOES THAT SAY ABOUT HOW MUCH WE NEED TO TALK?
WHY DON'T YOU WANT TO TALK?
I WILL, LOIS.
WHEN I'M DONE, WE'LL TALK ABOUT ALL OF THIS.
LOOK AT YOU...
DON'T THINK I DON'T KNOW.
LEO QUINTUM TOLD ME YOU WERE DYING OF SOLAR RADIATION OVERDOSE.
YOU TOLD HER?
I'M AFRAID IT JUST SLIPPED OUT, SUPERMAN.
IT SEEMED WRONG THAT YOU SHOULD BEAR THIS ALONE.

YOU CAN'T DIE.

I KNOW YOU'LL FIND A WAY OUT OF THIS.

PROMISE ME YOU'LL FIND A WAY.

AS SHE *SPOKE,* I WATCHED 35,000 DEAD SKIN CELLS SCATTERING LIKE CONFETTI... LIKE PROMISES...

...LIKE THE DUST OF DEAD STARS.

OUR BIOLOGY IS COMPLETELY INCOMPATIBLE.

WE COULD NEVER HAVE CHILDREN.

NEVER HAVE MORE THAN *THIS.*

THERE'S ALWAYS A WAY.

THAT'S WHAT YOU *ALWAYS* SAY.

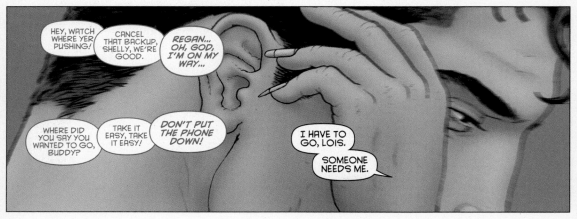

HEY, WATCH WHERE YER PUSHING!

CANCEL THAT BACKUP, SHELLY, WE'RE GOOD.

REGAN... OH, GOD, I'M ON MY WAY...

WHERE DID YOU SAY YOU WANTED TO GO, BUDDY?

TAKE IT EASY, TAKE IT EASY!

DON'T PUT THE PHONE DOWN!

I HAVE TO GO, LOIS.

SOMEONE NEEDS ME.

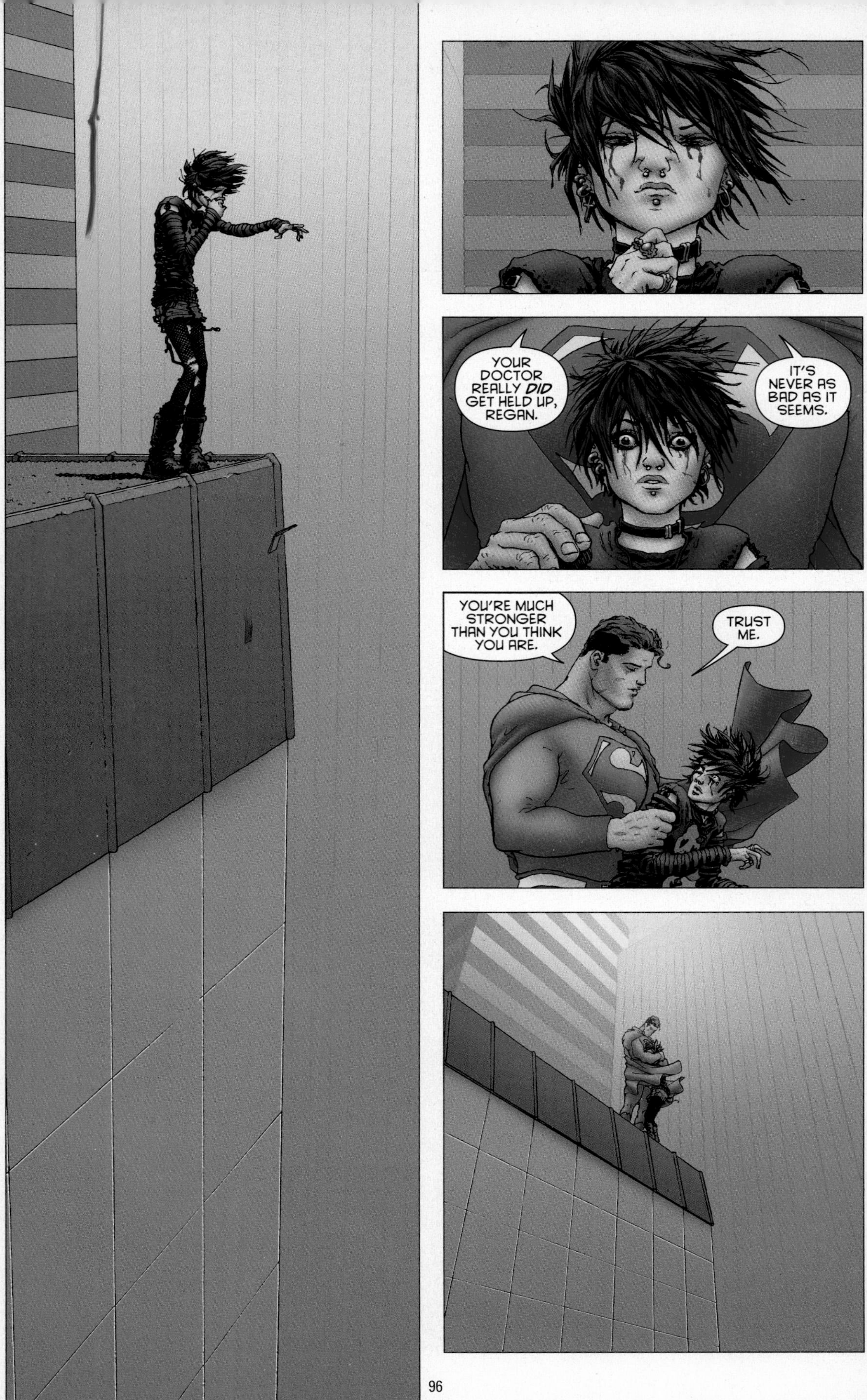
YOUR DOCTOR REALLY DID GET HELD UP, REGAN.
IT'S NEVER AS BAD AS IT SEEMS.
YOU'RE MUCH STRONGER THAN YOU THINK YOU ARE.
TRUST ME.

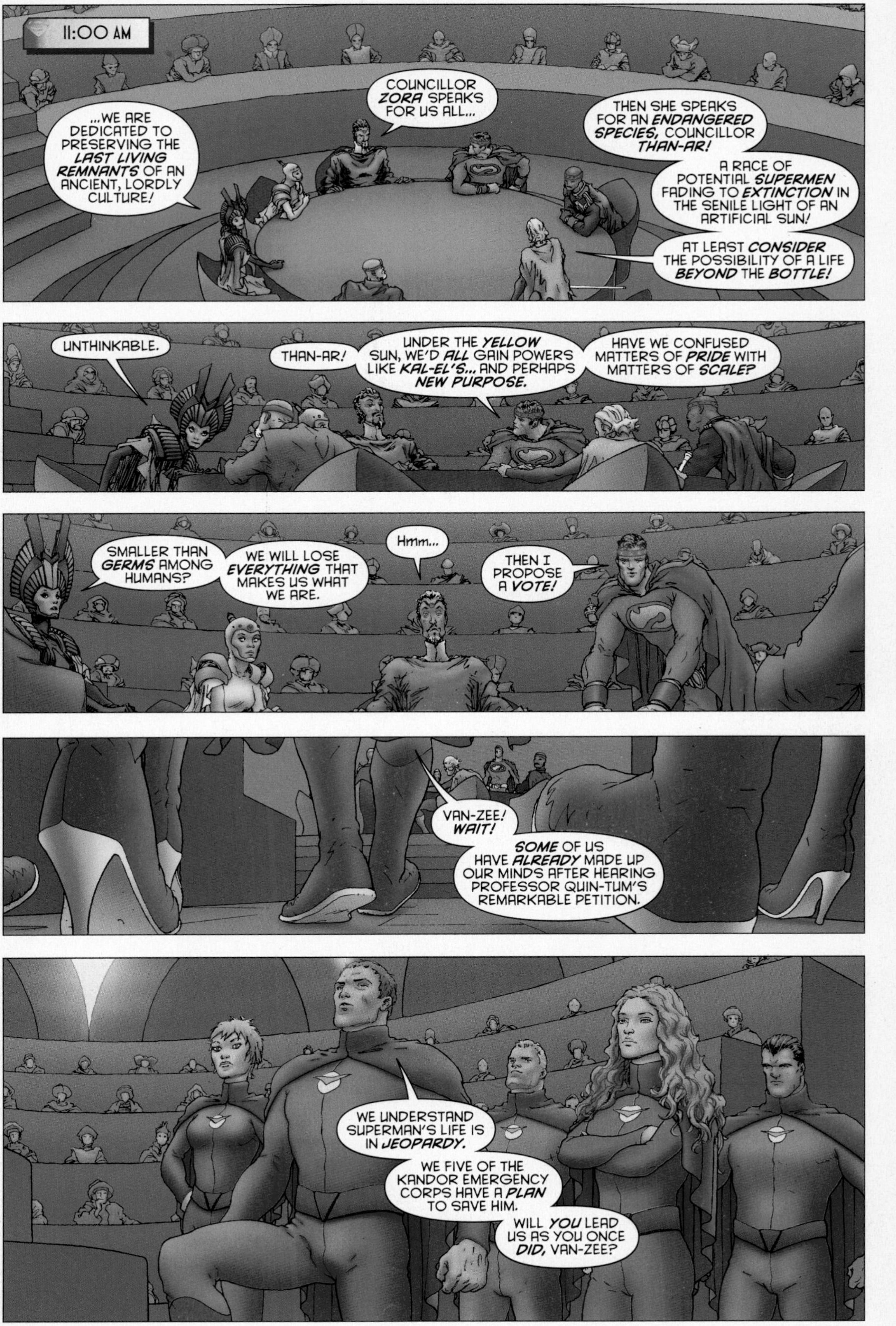
11:00 AM
...WE ARE DEDICATED TO PRESERVING THE LAST LIVING REMNANTS OF AN ANCIENT, LORDLY CULTURE!
COUNCILLOR ZORA SPEAKS FOR US ALL...
THEN SHE SPEAKS FOR AN ENDANGERED SPECIES, COUNCILLOR THAN-AR!
A RACE OF POTENTIAL SUPERMEN FADING TO EXTINCTION IN THE SENILE LIGHT OF AN ARTIFICIAL SUN!
AT LEAST CONSIDER THE POSSIBILITY OF A LIFE BEYOND THE BOTTLE!
UNTHINKABLE.
THAN-AR!
UNDER THE YELLOW SUN, WE'D ALL GAIN POWERS LIKE KAL-EL'S... AND PERHAPS NEW PURPOSE.
HAVE WE CONFUSED MATTERS OF PRIDE WITH MATTERS OF SCALE?
SMALLER THAN GERMS AMONG HUMANS?
WE WILL LOSE EVERYTHING THAT MAKES US WHAT WE ARE.
Hmm...
THEN I PROPOSE A VOTE!
VAN-ZEE! WAIT!
SOME OF US HAVE ALREADY MADE UP OUR MINDS AFTER HEARING PROFESSOR QUIN-TUM'S REMARKABLE PETITION.
WE UNDERSTAND SUPERMAN'S LIFE IS IN JEOPARDY.
WE FIVE OF THE KANDOR EMERGENCY CORPS HAVE A PLAN TO SAVE HIM.
WILL YOU LEAD US AS YOU ONCE DID, VAN-ZEE?

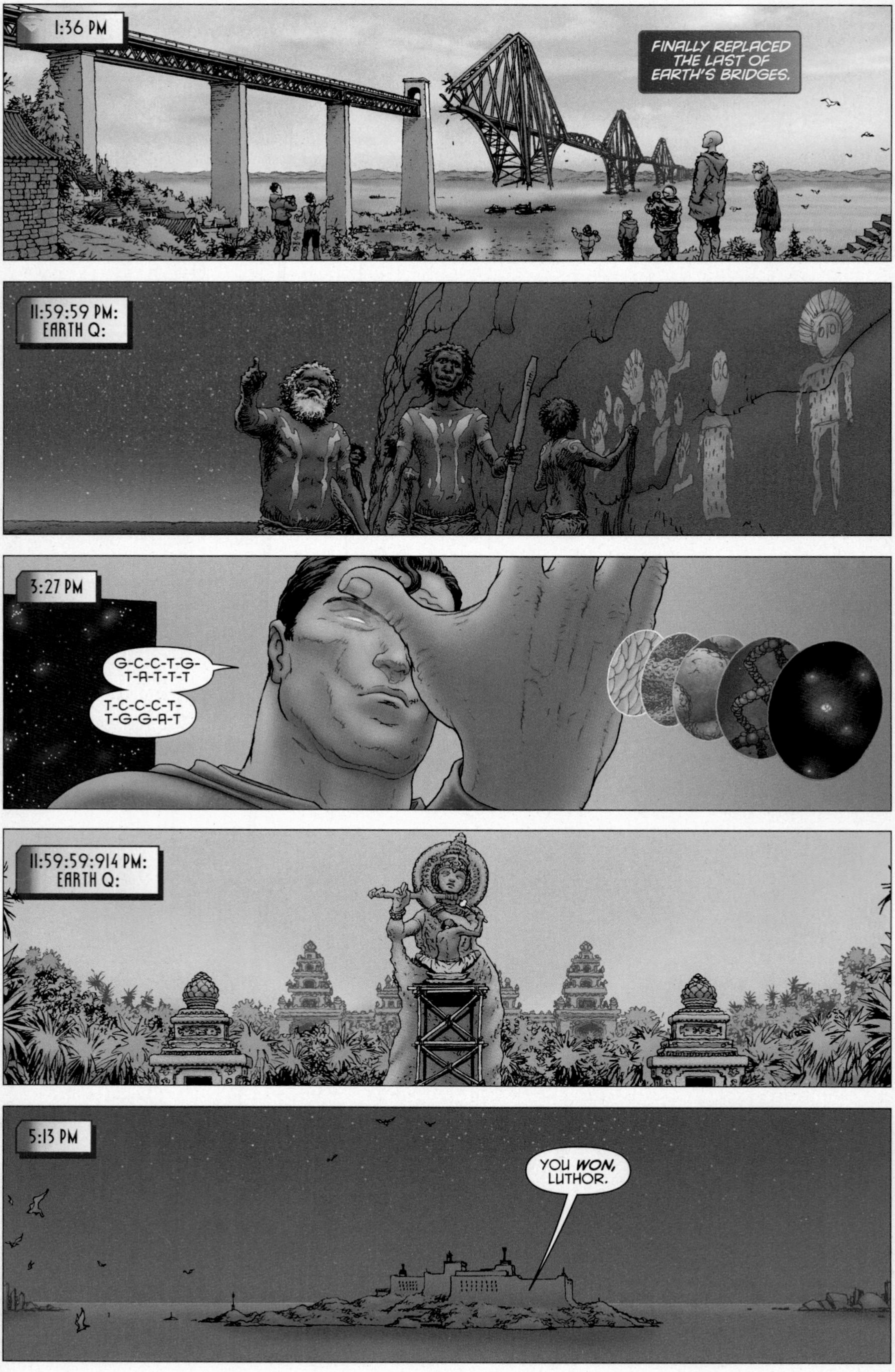
1:36 PM
FINALLY REPLACED THE LAST OF EARTH'S BRIDGES.
11:59:59 PM: EARTH Q:
3:27 PM
G-C-C-T-G-T-A-T-T-T
T-C-C-C-T-T-G-G-A-T
11:59:59:914 PM: EARTH Q:
5:13 PM
YOU WON, LUTHOR.

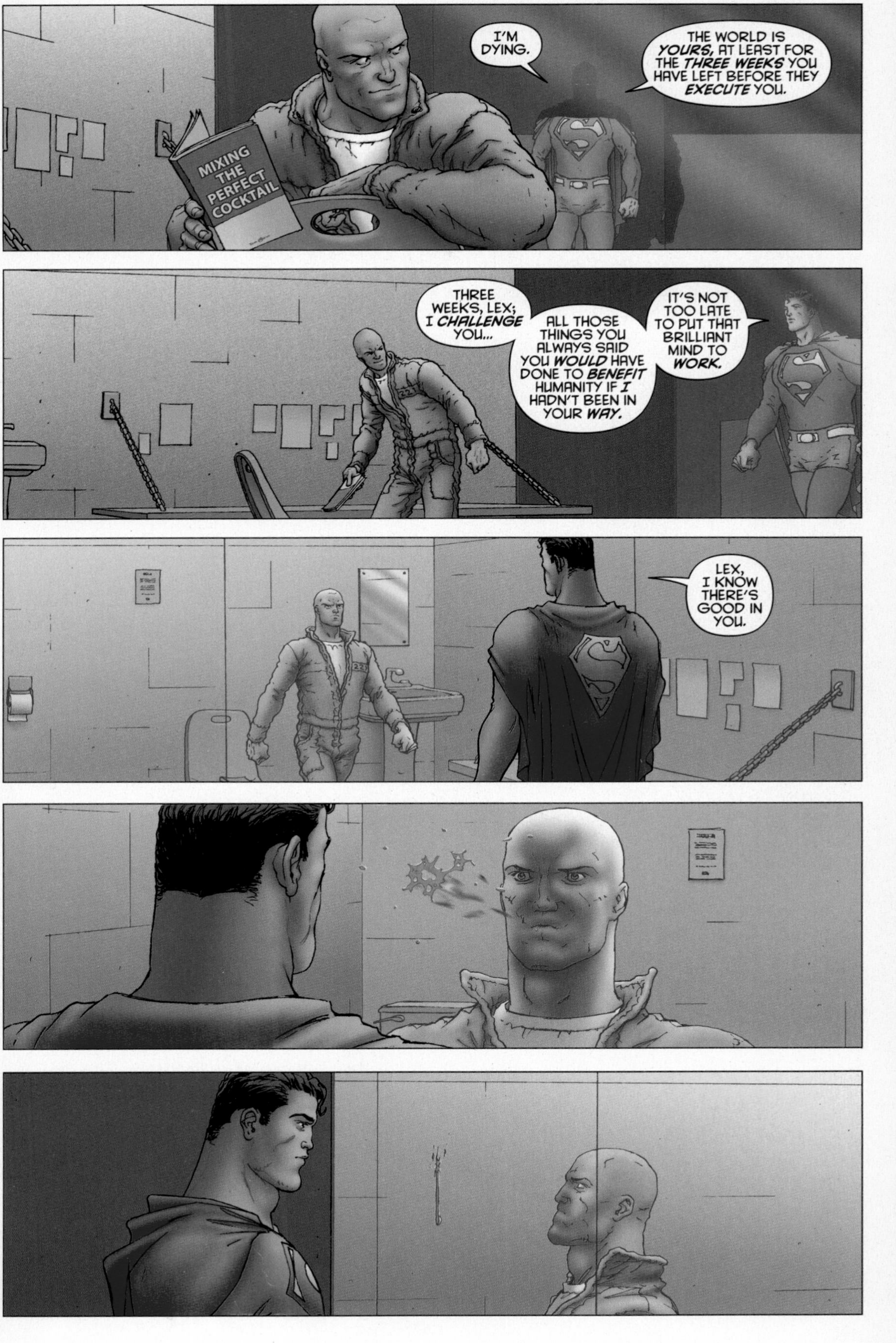
I'M DYING.
THE WORLD IS YOURS, AT LEAST FOR THE THREE WEEKS YOU HAVE LEFT BEFORE THEY EXECUTE YOU.
MIXING THE PERFECT COCKTAIL
THREE WEEKS, LEX; I CHALLENGE YOU...
ALL THOSE THINGS YOU ALWAYS SAID YOU WOULD HAVE DONE TO BENEFIT HUMANITY IF I HADN'T BEEN IN YOUR WAY.
IT'S NOT TOO LATE TO PUT THAT BRILLIANT MIND TO WORK.
LEX, I KNOW THERE'S GOOD IN YOU.

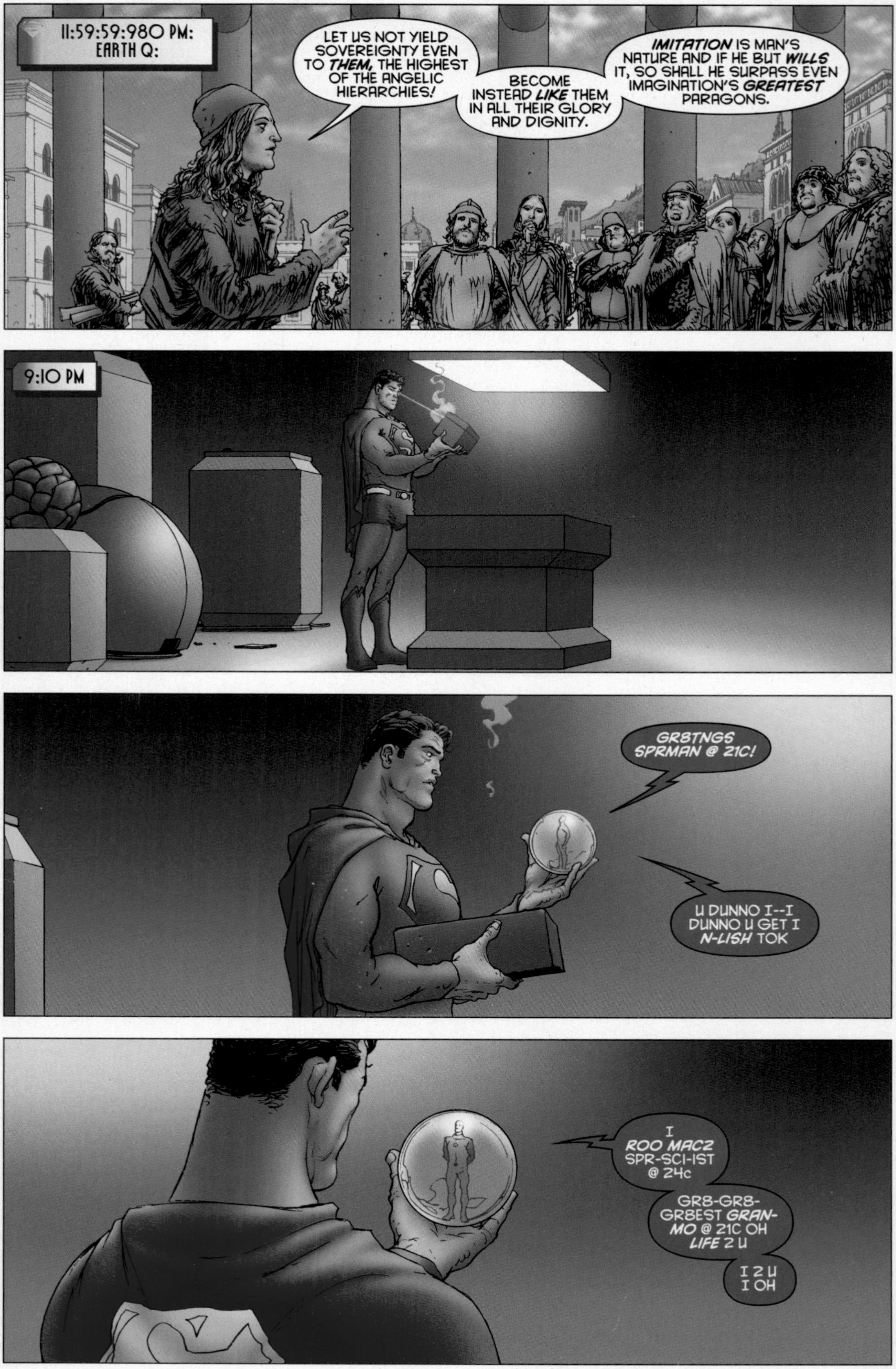
11:59:59:980 PM: EARTH Q:
LET US NOT YIELD SOVEREIGNTY EVEN TO *THEM,* THE HIGHEST OF THE ANGELIC HIERARCHIES!
BECOME INSTEAD *LIKE* THEM IN ALL THEIR GLORY AND DIGNITY.
IMITATION IS MAN'S NATURE AND IF HE BUT *WILLS* IT, SO SHALL HE SURPASS EVEN IMAGINATION'S *GREATEST* PARAGONS.
9:10 PM
GR8TNGS SPRMAN @ 21C!
U DUNNO I--I DUNNO U GET I *N-LISH* TOK
I *ROO MACZ* SPR-SCI-IST @ 24c
GR8-GR8-GR8EST *GRAN-MO* @ 21C OH *LIFE* 2 U
I 2 U I OH

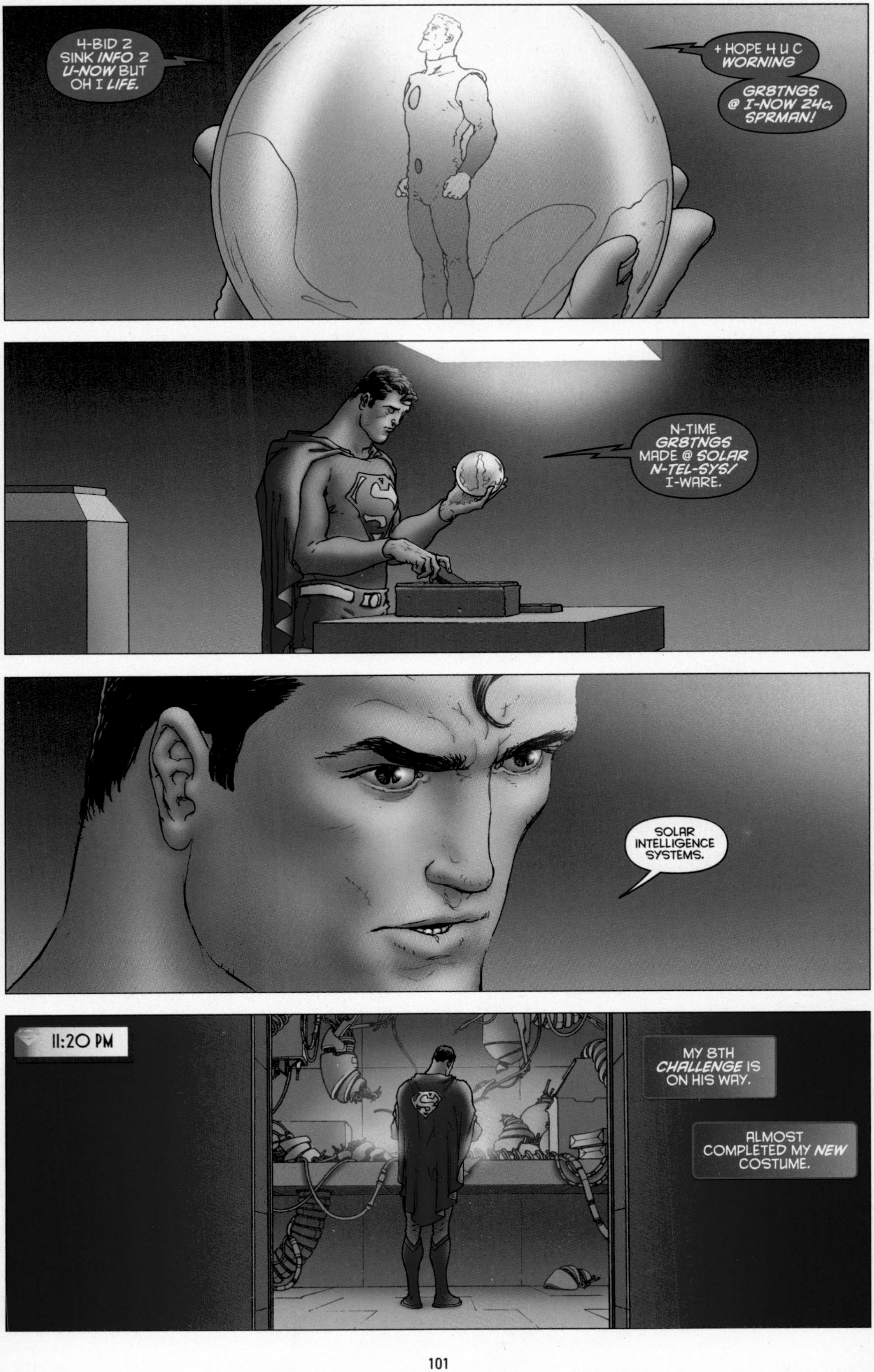
4-BID 2 SINK INFO 2 U-NOW BUT OH I LIFE.
+ HOPE 4 U C WORNING
GR8TNGS @ I-NOW 24c, SPRMAN!
N-TIME GR8TNGS MADE @ SOLAR N-TEL-SYS/ I-WARE.
SOLAR INTELLIGENCE SYSTEMS.
11:20 PM
MY 8TH CHALLENGE IS ON HIS WAY.
ALMOST COMPLETED MY NEW COSTUME.

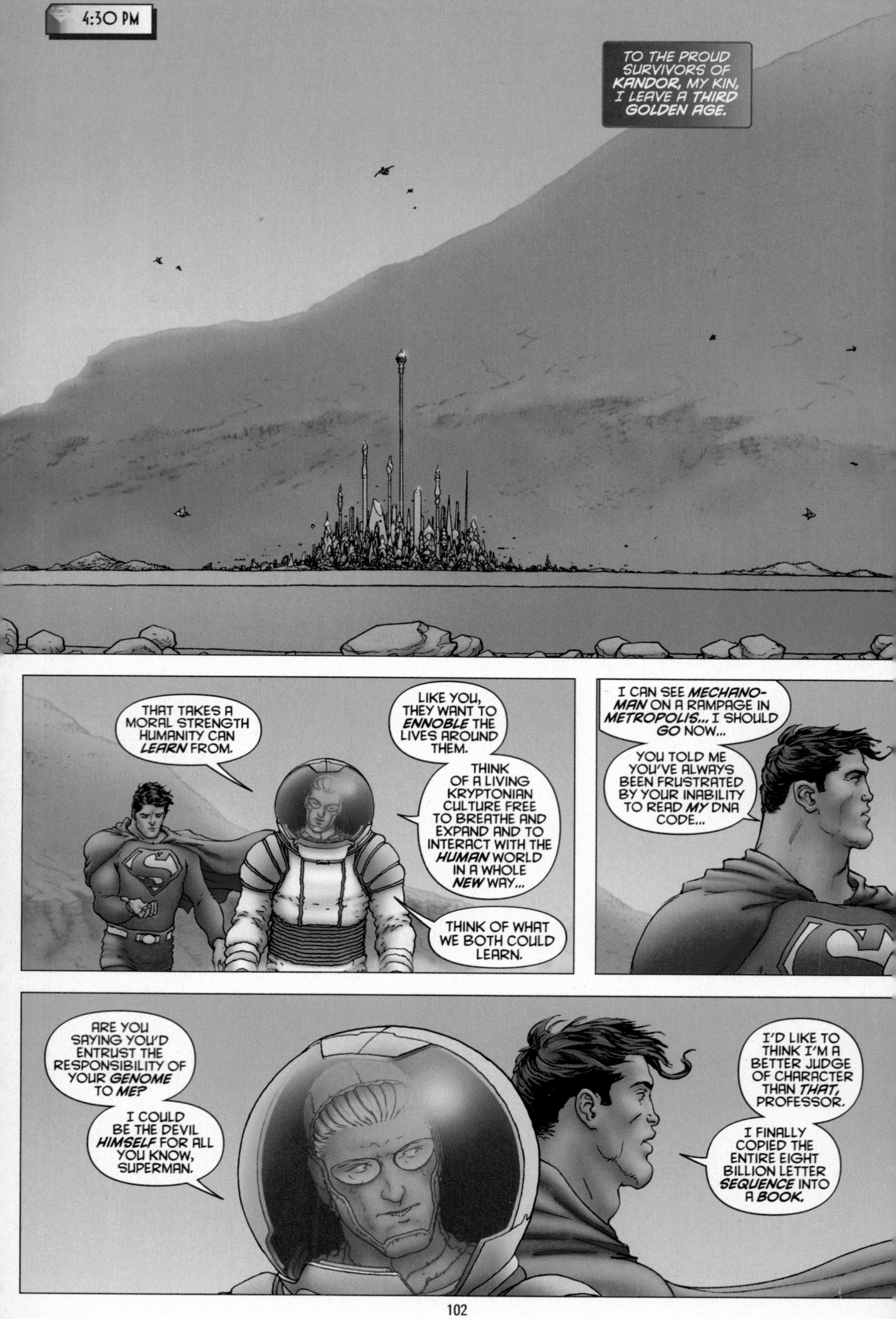
4:30 PM
TO THE PROUD SURVIVORS OF KANDOR, MY KIN, I LEAVE A THIRD GOLDEN AGE.
THAT TAKES A MORAL STRENGTH HUMANITY CAN LEARN FROM.
LIKE YOU, THEY WANT TO ENNOBLE THE LIVES AROUND THEM.
THINK OF A LIVING KRYPTONIAN CULTURE FREE TO BREATHE AND EXPAND AND TO INTERACT WITH THE HUMAN WORLD IN A WHOLE NEW WAY...
THINK OF WHAT WE BOTH COULD LEARN.
I CAN SEE MECHANO-MAN ON A RAMPAGE IN METROPOLIS... I SHOULD GO NOW...
YOU TOLD ME YOU'VE ALWAYS BEEN FRUSTRATED BY YOUR INABILITY TO READ MY DNA CODE...
ARE YOU SAYING YOU'D ENTRUST THE RESPONSIBILITY OF YOUR GENOME TO ME?
I COULD BE THE DEVIL HIMSELF FOR ALL YOU KNOW, SUPERMAN.
I'D LIKE TO THINK I'M A BETTER JUDGE OF CHARACTER THAN THAT, PROFESSOR.
I FINALLY COPIED THE ENTIRE EIGHT BILLION LETTER SEQUENCE INTO A BOOK.

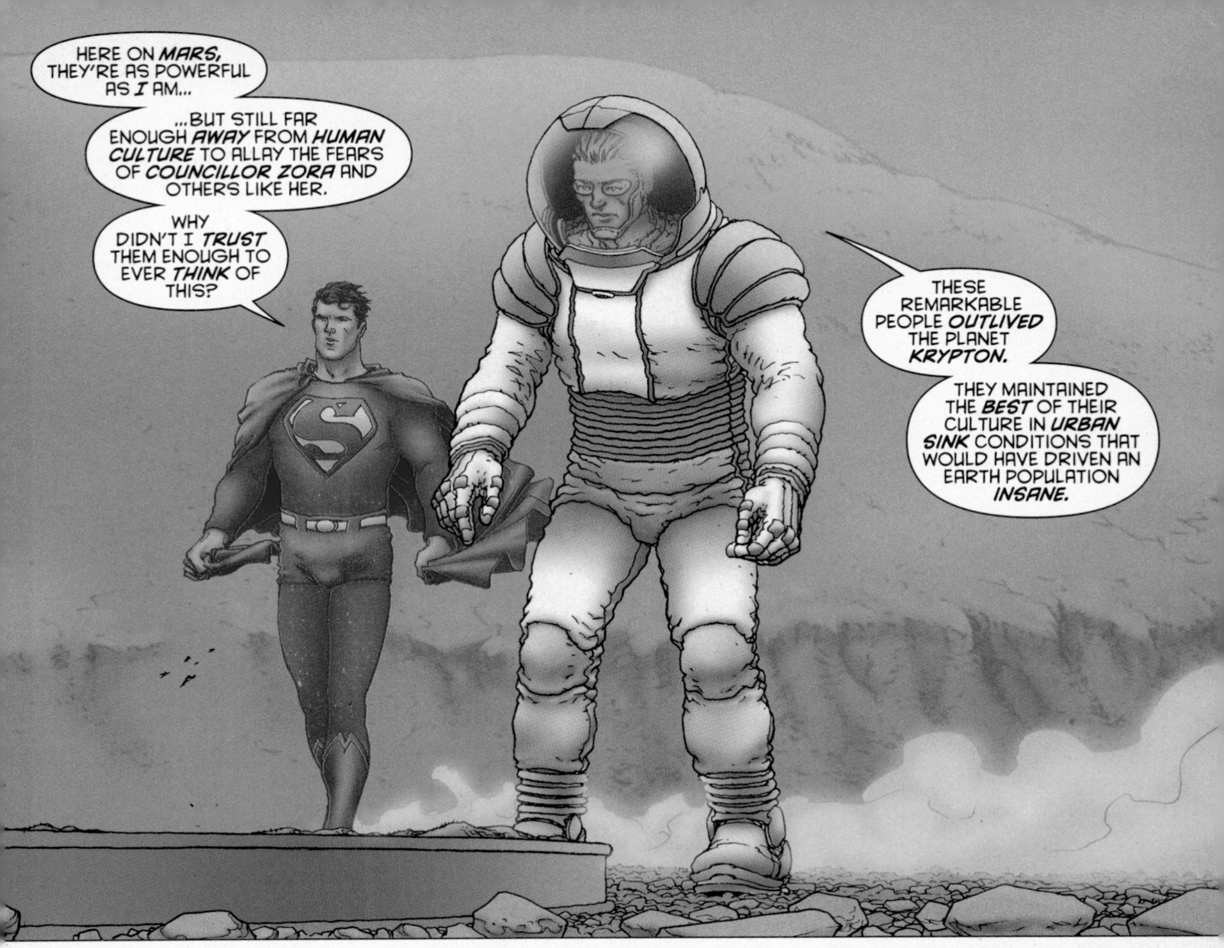
HERE ON *MARS*, THEY'RE AS POWERFUL AS *I* AM...
...BUT STILL FAR ENOUGH *AWAY* FROM *HUMAN CULTURE* TO ALLAY THE FEARS OF *COUNCILLOR ZORA* AND OTHERS LIKE HER.
WHY DIDN'T I *TRUST* THEM ENOUGH TO EVER *THINK* OF THIS?
THESE REMARKABLE PEOPLE *OUTLIVED* THE PLANET *KRYPTON.*
THEY MAINTAINED THE *BEST* OF THEIR CULTURE IN *URBAN SINK* CONDITIONS THAT WOULD HAVE DRIVEN AN EARTH POPULATION *INSANE.*

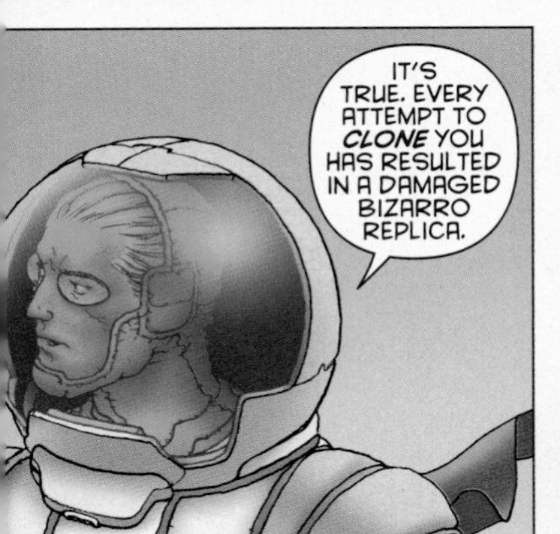
IT'S TRUE. EVERY ATTEMPT TO *CLONE* YOU HAS RESULTED IN A DAMAGED BIZARRO REPLICA.

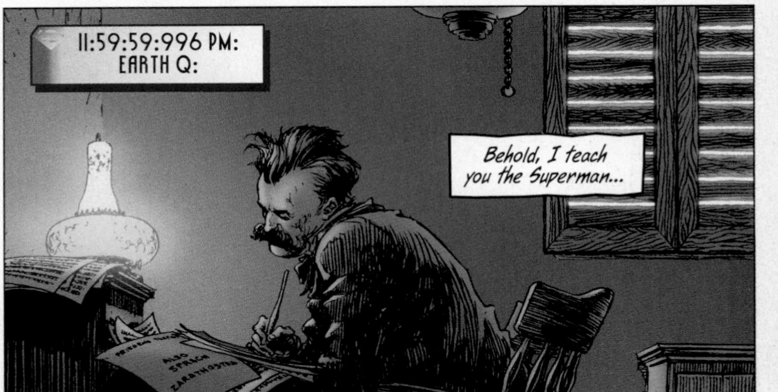
11:59:59:996 PM: EARTH Q:
Behold, I teach you the Superman...

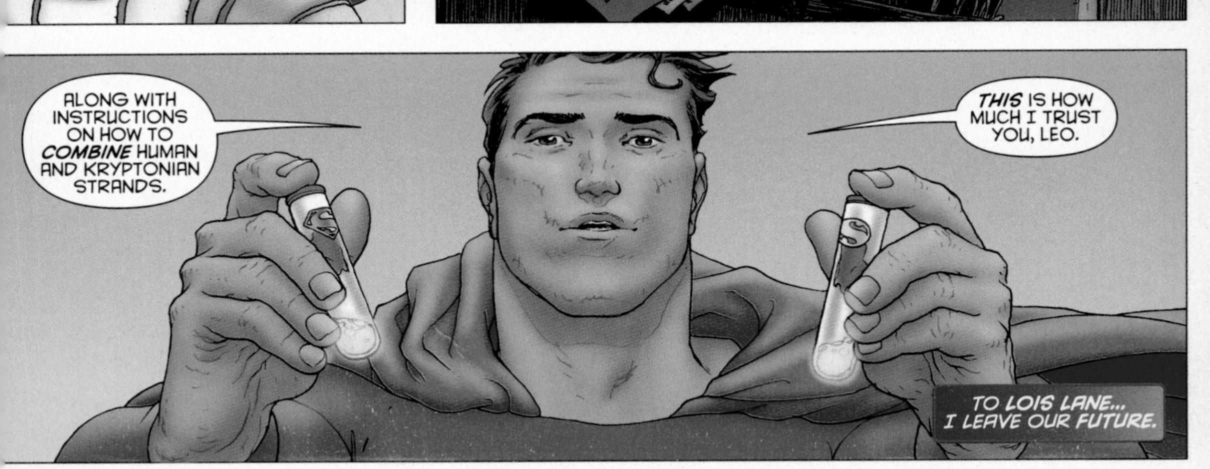
ALONG WITH INSTRUCTIONS ON HOW TO *COMBINE* HUMAN AND KRYPTONIAN STRANDS.
THIS IS HOW MUCH I TRUST YOU, LEO.
TO LOIS LANE... I LEAVE OUR FUTURE.

EVEN WITH OUR INCREDIBLE SPEED AND STAMINA, WE STILL CAN'T PREVENT YOUR WHITE BLOOD CELLS FROM COMMITTING *SUICIDE.*

AFTER ALL YOU'VE DONE FOR US, WE'VE *FAILED* YOU...

WE'RE SO SORRY, KAL-EL.

ALL OF YOU DID EVERYTHING YOU *COULD,* VAN-ZEE.

BELIEVE ME, IT FELT GREAT.

TRUTH IS, I ONLY NEEDED YOUR HELP LONG ENOUGH TO ACCOMPLISH TODAY'S *TASKS.*

I DIDN'T THINK YOU'D BE ABLE TO SAVE *ME.*

BUT *HUMAN* DISEASES WOULD BE *NO MATCH* FOR YOUR KNOWLEDGE AND POWER, AM I RIGHT?

MICROSCOPIC KANDORIAN SUPER-DOCTORS COULD *CURE* ANYTHING.

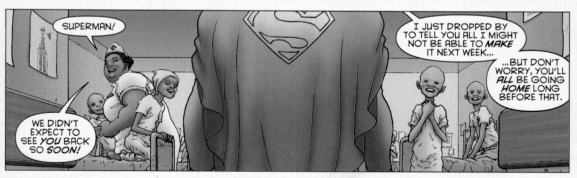

SUPERMAN!

WE DIDN'T EXPECT TO SEE *YOU* BACK SO *SOON!*

I JUST DROPPED BY TO TELL YOU ALL I MIGHT NOT BE ABLE TO *MAKE* IT NEXT WEEK...

...BUT DON'T WORRY, YOU'LL *ALL* BE GOING *HOME* LONG BEFORE THAT.

I BROUGHT SOME *FRIENDS* TO MEET YOU.

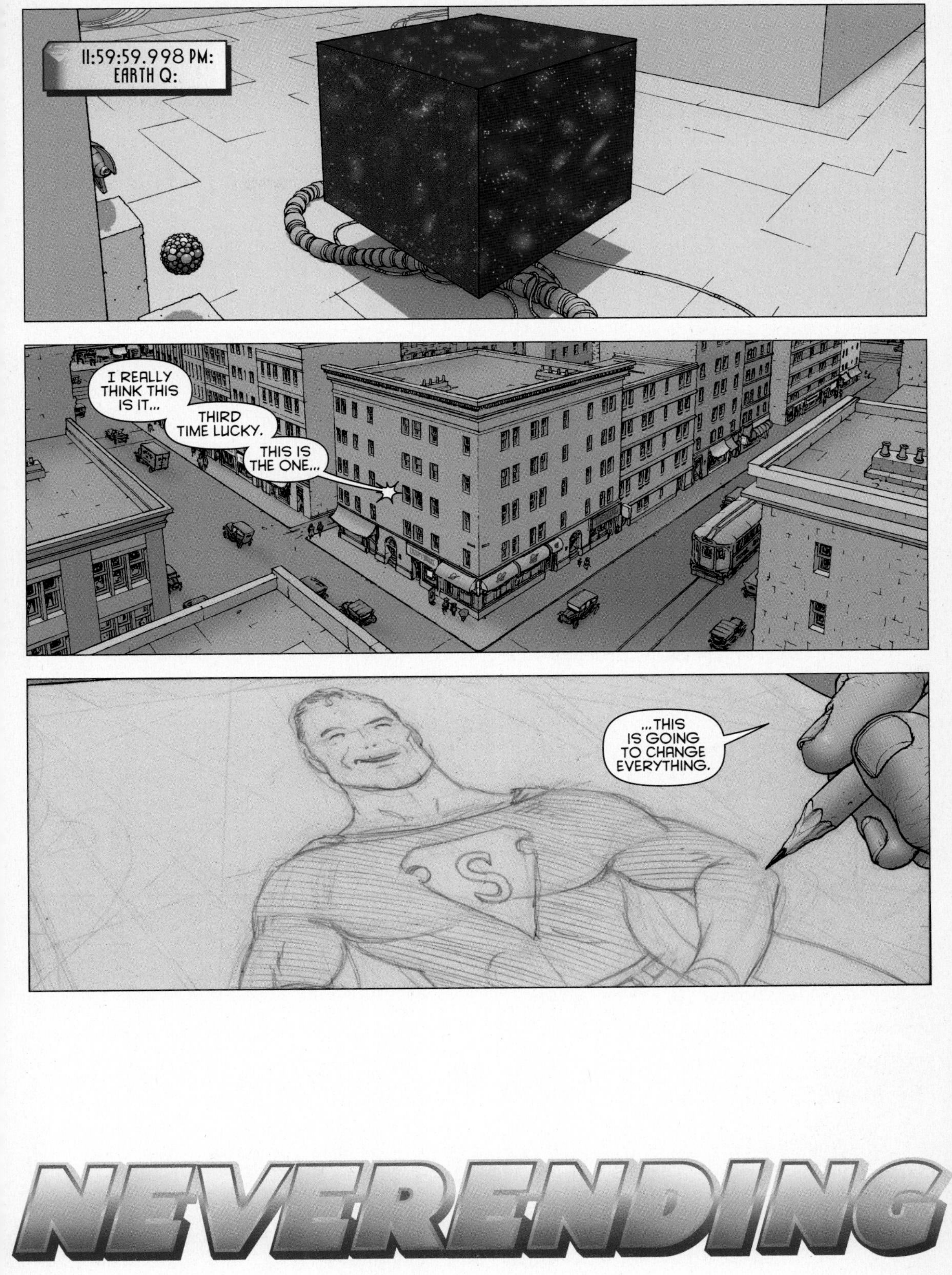
11:59:59.998 PM:
EARTH Q:
I REALLY THINK THIS IS IT...
THIRD TIME LUCKY.
THIS IS THE ONE...
...THIS IS GOING TO CHANGE EVERYTHING.

NEVERENDING

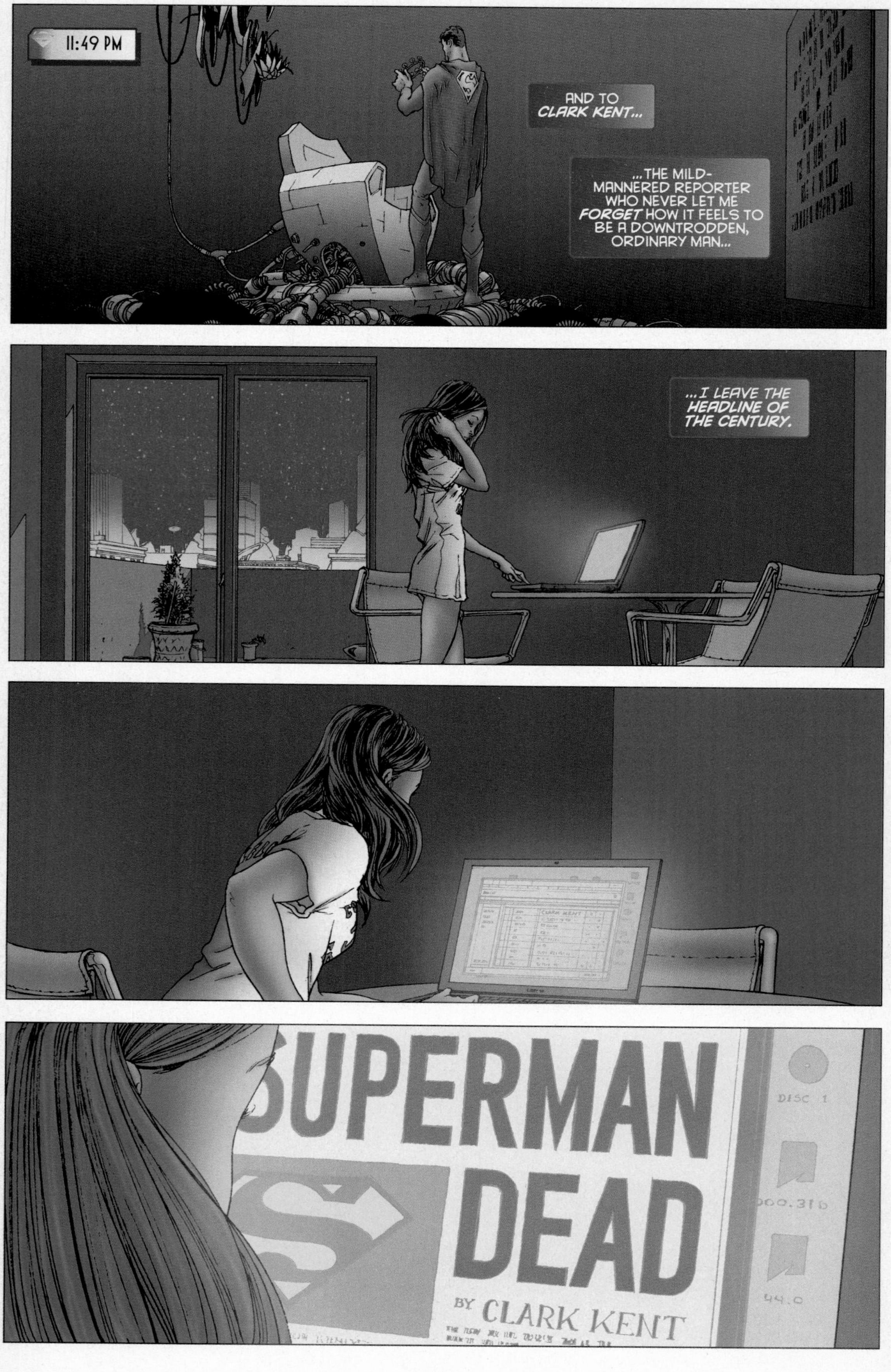

11:49 PM
AND TO *CLARK KENT...*
...THE MILD-MANNERED REPORTER WHO NEVER LET ME *FORGET* HOW IT FEELS TO BE A DOWNTRODDEN, ORDINARY MAN...
...I LEAVE THE HEADLINE OF THE CENTURY.
SUPERMAN DEAD
BY CLARK KENT
DISC 1

Episode 11

RED SUN DAY

Cover FRANK QUITELY with Jamie Grant

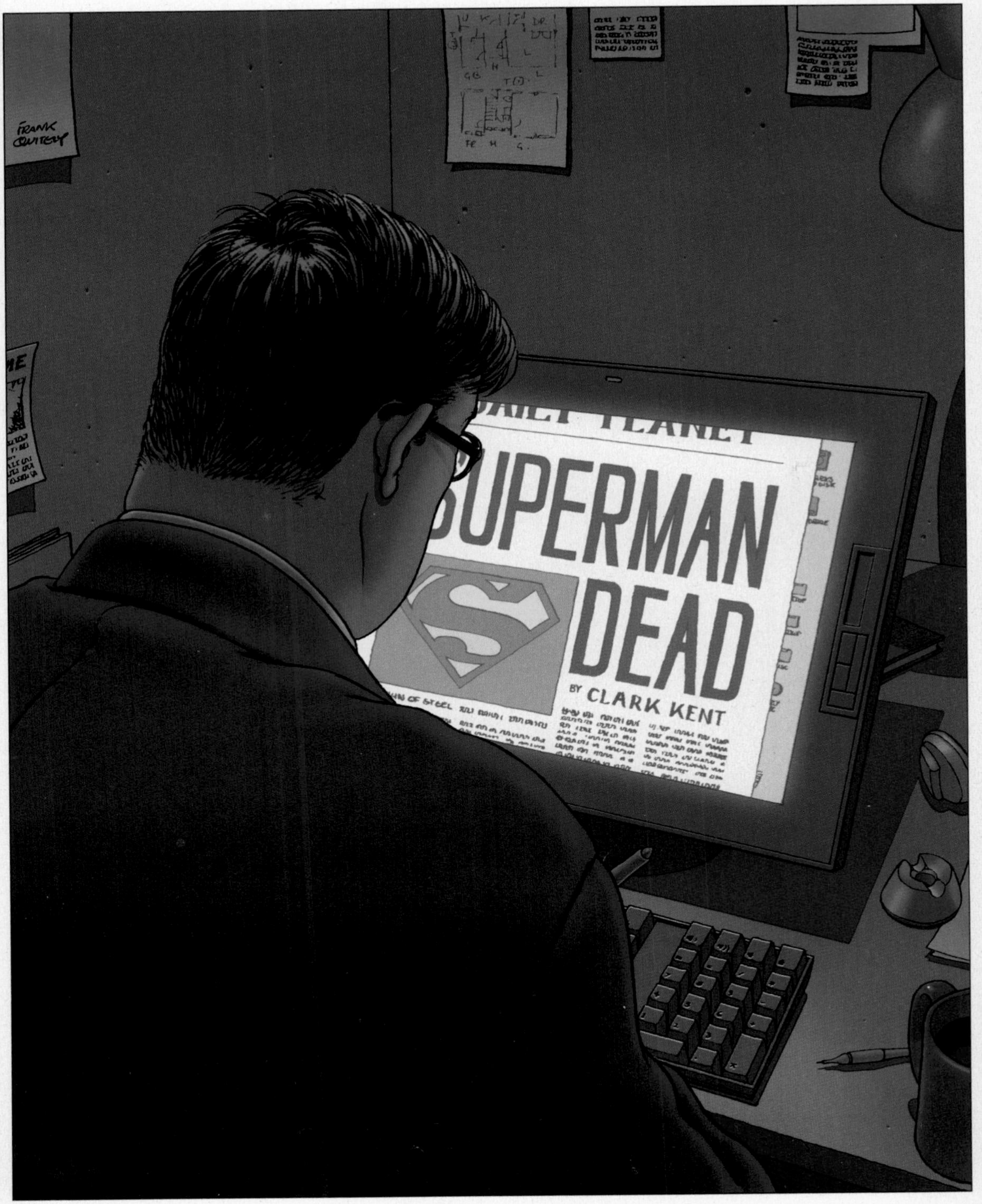
FRANK QUITELY
SUPERMAN DEAD
BY CLARK KENT

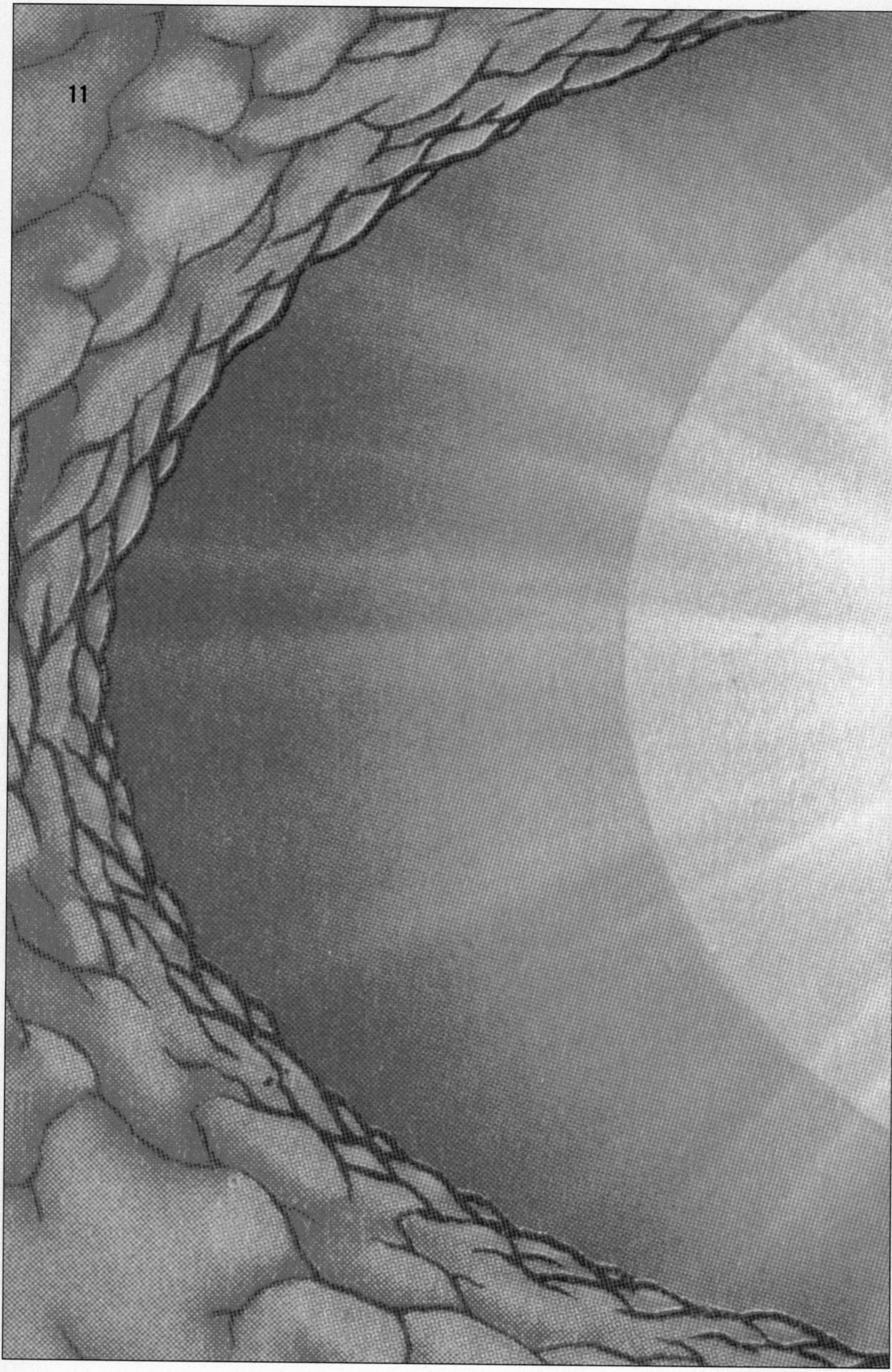
11

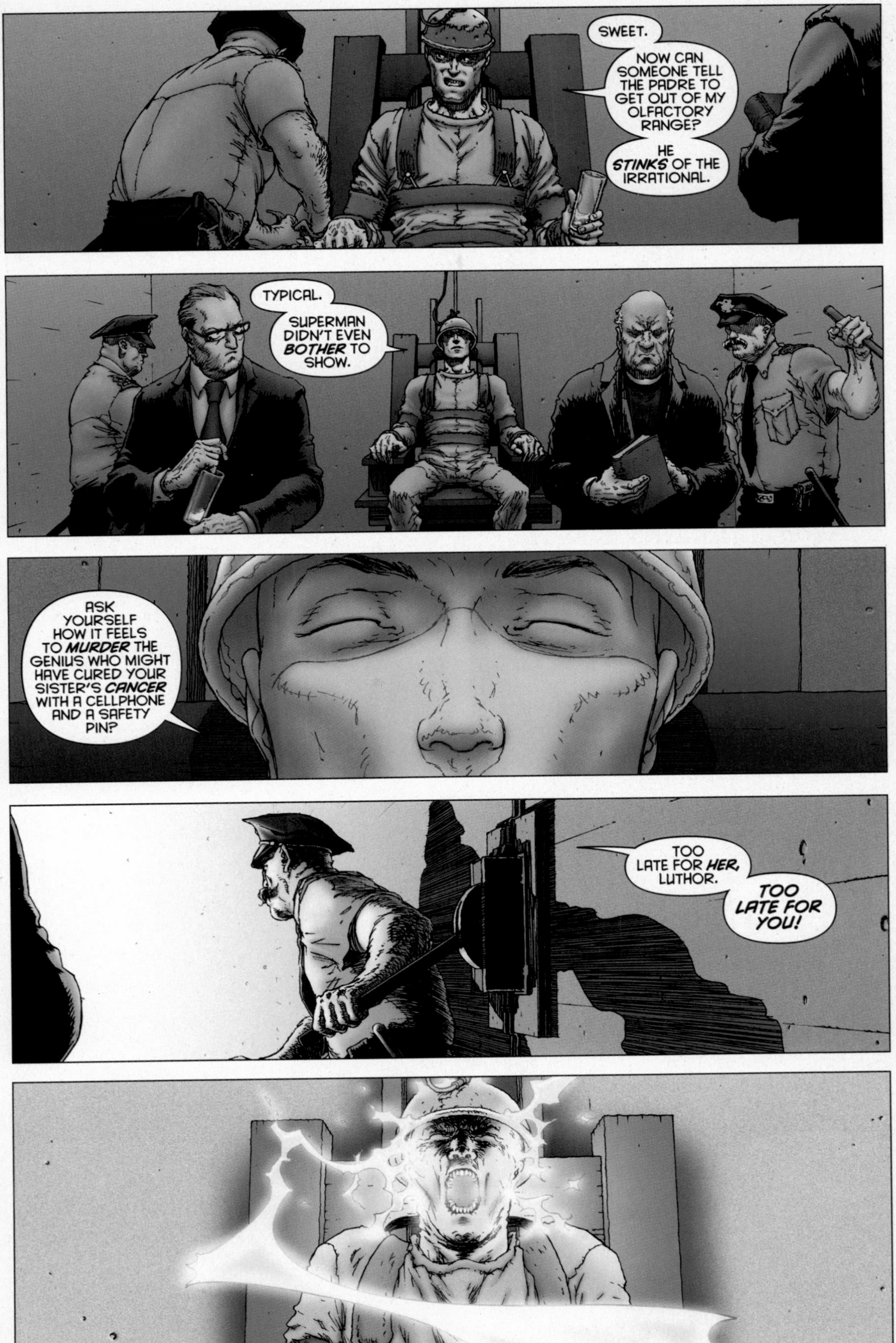
SWEET.
NOW CAN SOMEONE TELL THE PADRE TO GET OUT OF MY OLFACTORY RANGE?
HE *STINKS* OF THE IRRATIONAL.
TYPICAL.
SUPERMAN DIDN'T EVEN *BOTHER* TO SHOW.
ASK YOURSELF HOW IT FEELS TO *MURDER* THE GENIUS WHO MIGHT HAVE CURED YOUR SISTER'S *CANCER* WITH A CELLPHONE AND A SAFETY PIN?
TOO LATE FOR *HER*, LUTHOR.
TOO LATE FOR YOU!

...k^k^k... ha! Kkh!

OH...YOU *MORONS*... YOU KNUCKLE-DRAGGING *NEANDERTHALS.*

THAT "LAST PERFECT COCKTAIL" YOU ALLOWED ME TO MIX...?

...CONTAINED A HIDDEN... PREPROGRAMMED... SHAPESHIFTING MOLECULE I DESIGNED...

...I JUST DRANK... A 24-HOUR... *SUPERPOWER*... SERUM.

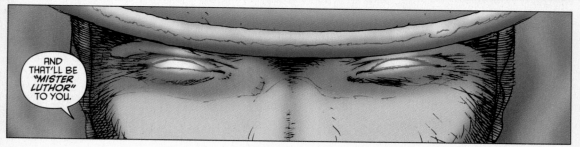

AND THAT'LL BE *"MISTER LUTHOR"* TO YOU.

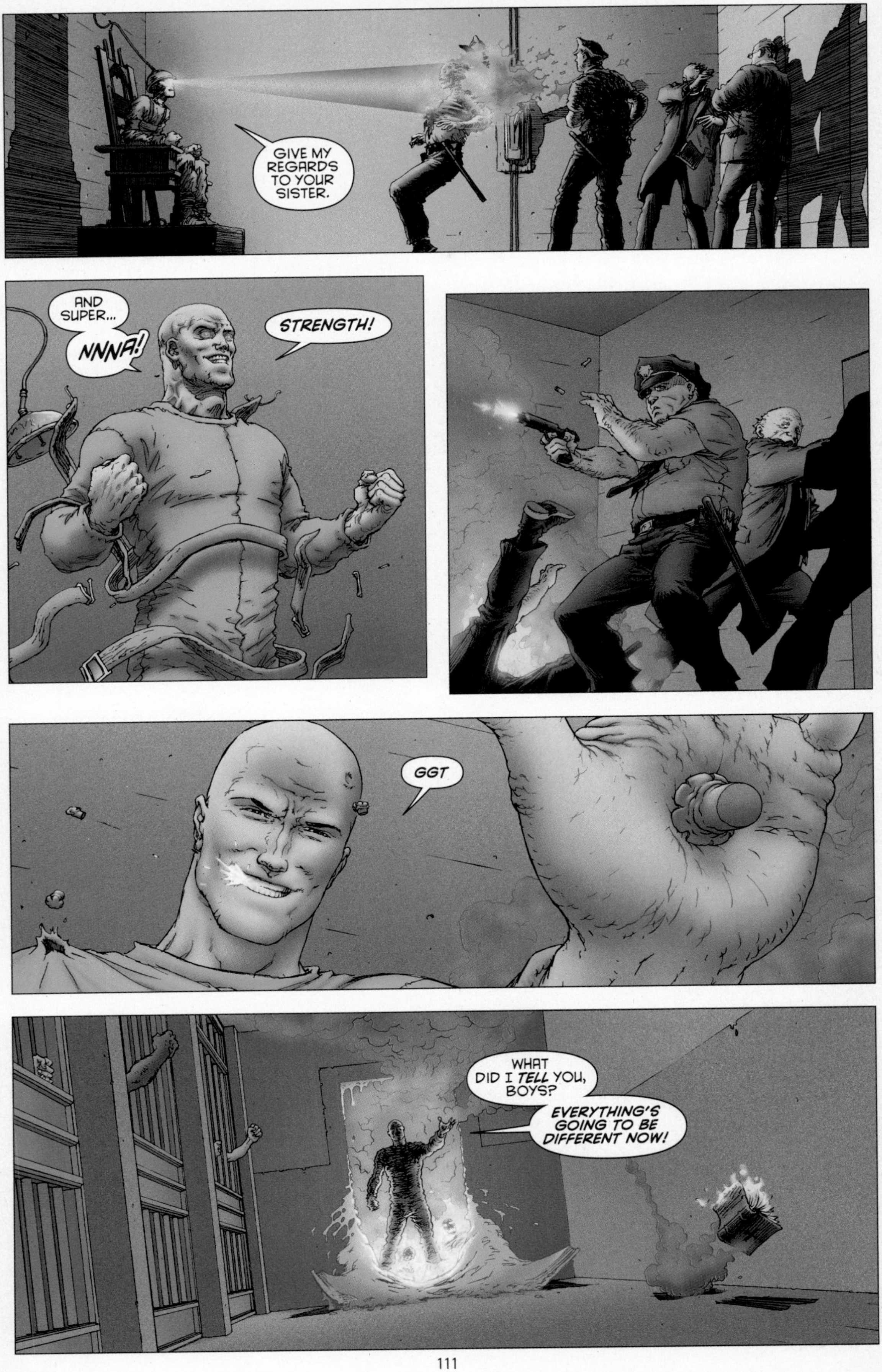
GIVE MY REGARDS TO YOUR SISTER.
AND SUPER...
NNNA!
STRENGTH!
GGT
WHAT DID I TELL YOU, BOYS?
EVERYTHING'S GOING TO BE DIFFERENT NOW!

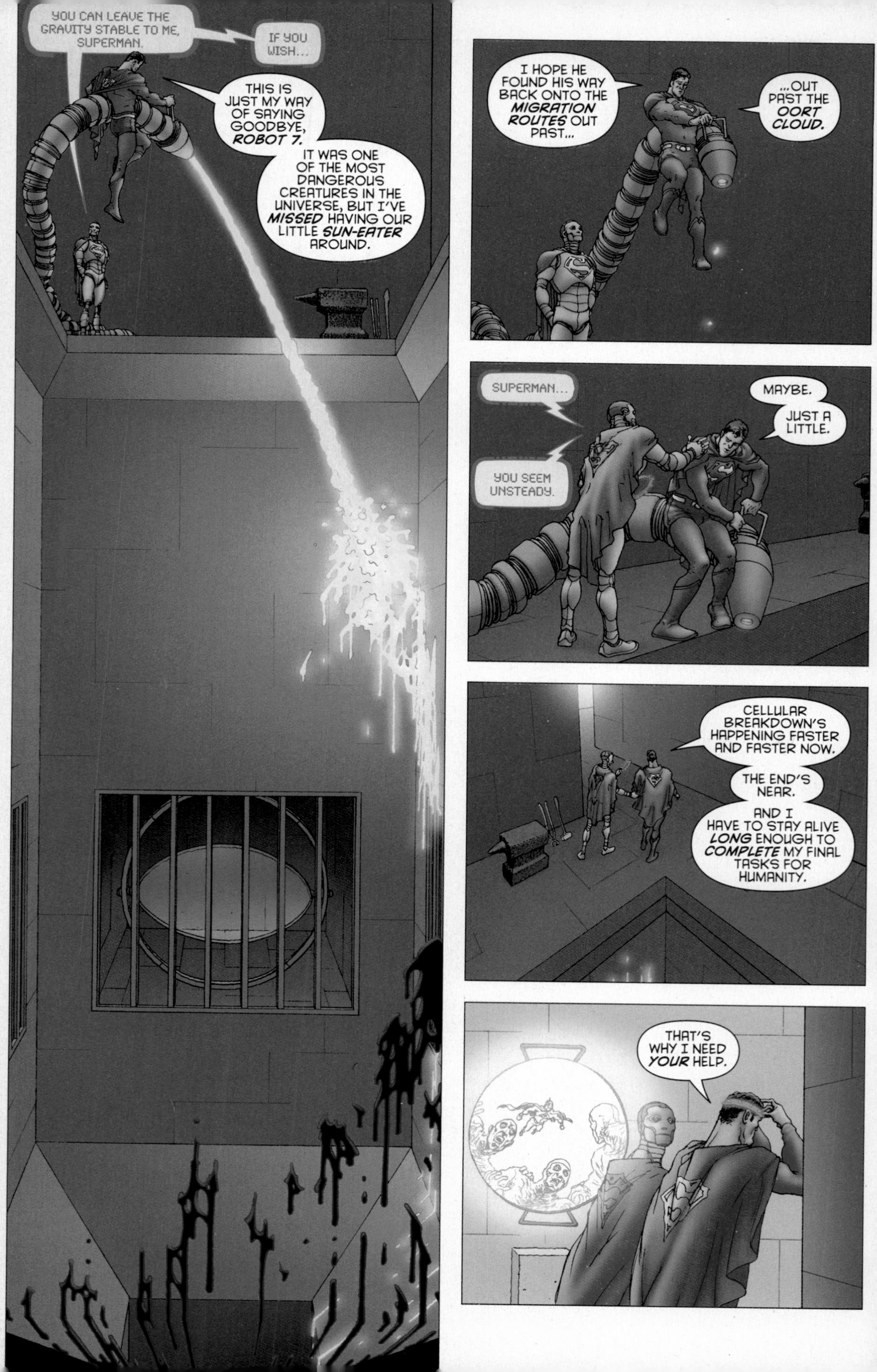
YOU CAN LEAVE THE GRAVITY STABLE TO ME, SUPERMAN.
IF YOU WISH...
THIS IS JUST MY WAY OF SAYING GOODBYE, ROBOT 7.
IT WAS ONE OF THE MOST DANGEROUS CREATURES IN THE UNIVERSE, BUT I'VE MISSED HAVING OUR LITTLE SUN-EATER AROUND.
I HOPE HE FOUND HIS WAY BACK ONTO THE MIGRATION ROUTES OUT PAST...
...OUT PAST THE OORT CLOUD.
SUPERMAN...
YOU SEEM UNSTEADY.
MAYBE.
JUST A LITTLE.
CELLULAR BREAKDOWN'S HAPPENING FASTER AND FASTER NOW.
THE END'S NEAR.
AND I HAVE TO STAY ALIVE LONG ENOUGH TO COMPLETE MY FINAL TASKS FOR HUMANITY.
THAT'S WHY I NEED YOUR HELP.

YOU ROBOTS WILL HAVE TO MAINTAIN AREAS OF THE FORTRESS LIKE THE *BIZARRO ZOO.*

THESE POOR CREATURES, DISTORTED DURING THE INVASION FROM THE *CUBE EARTH,* REQUIRE SPECIAL CARE AND ATTENTION.

AND THIS...

YOU ASKED FOR THIS TO BE PRESERVED IN SUPERLAMINATE.

ZIBARRO'S POETRY.

...THAT LONELY, SANE VOICE OF A SUNKEN, DARK AND MARVELOUS WORLD.

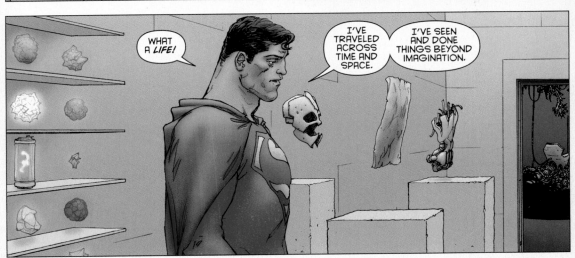

WHAT A *LIFE!*

I'VE TRAVELED ACROSS TIME AND SPACE.

I'VE SEEN AND DONE THINGS BEYOND IMAGINATION.

BLESSED WITH FRIENDS LIKE *PETE* AND *LANA* AND *JIMMY.*

AND *BATMAN...* WHAT INCREDIBLE ADVENTURES WE'VE SHARED.

WHAT AMAZING PEOPLE I'VE KNOWN.

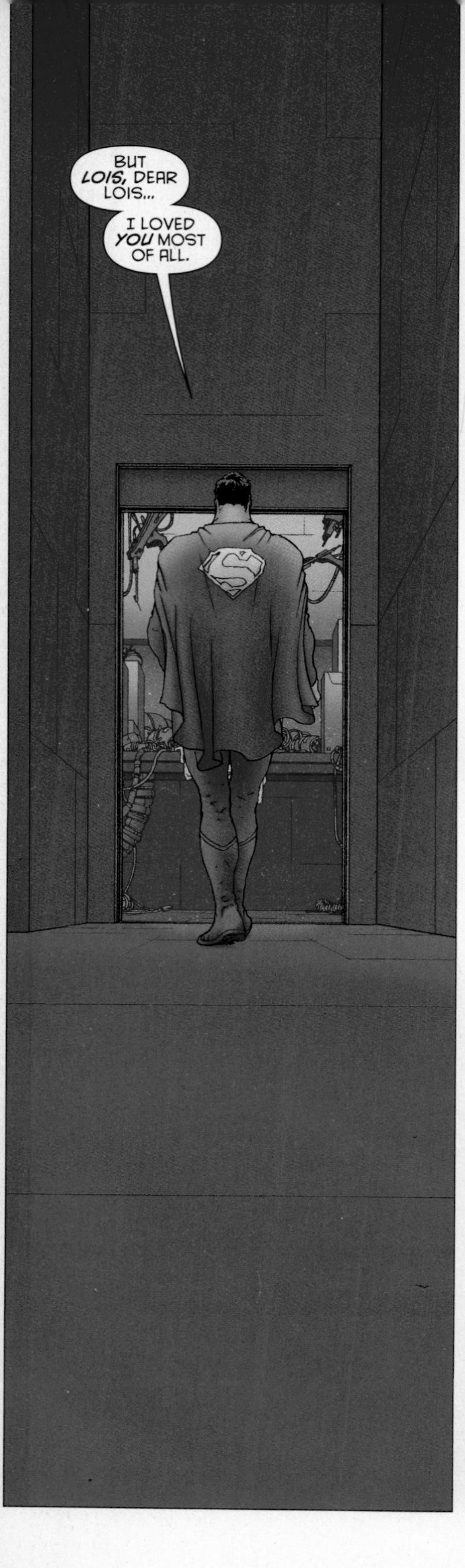
BUT LOIS, DEAR LOIS...
I LOVED YOU MOST OF ALL.

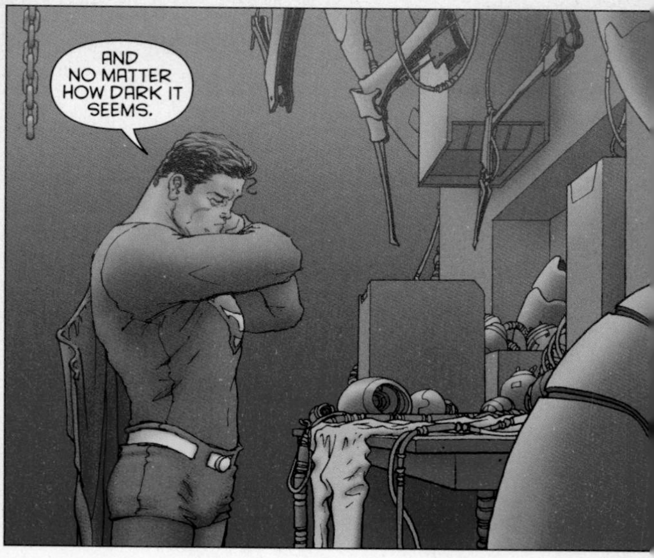
AND NO MATTER HOW DARK IT SEEMS.

RED SUN DAY

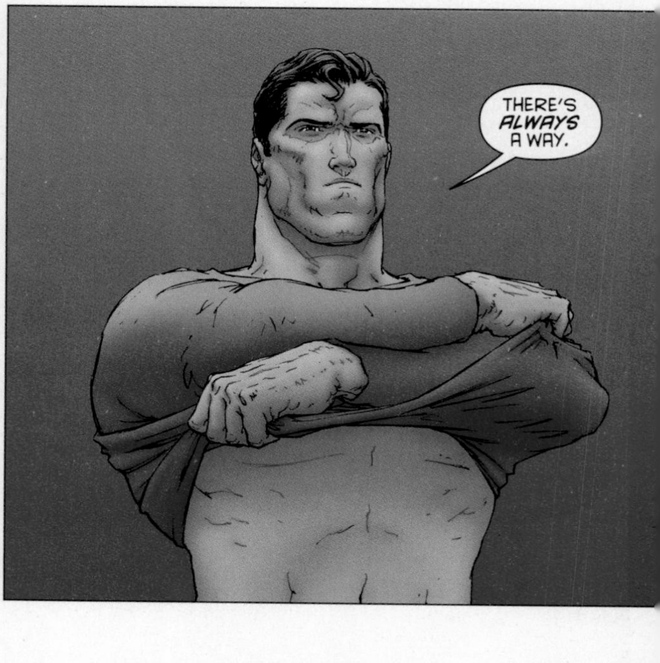
THERE'S ALWAYS A WAY.

...UH-HUH... YEAH...*OBVIOUSLY* I'M IN AN "*AUTHENTIC*" *LUTHOR'S LAIR,* I'M NOT GONNA SAY *WHICH ONE,* DURR!

AT LEAST UNCLE LEXIE TAKES MY WORLD DOMINATION PLANS *SERIOUSLY!*

ANYWAY, THAT *SOUNDS* LIKE--

HA!

COULDN'T *RESIST* IT.

I HAVE *HIS* SUPERPOWERS FOR *24 HOURS,* NASTHALTHIA, THANKS TO A SERUM ONLY *I* COULD HAVE INVENTED.

HOW'S YOUR MOM?

MAD AT YOU.

SO WHAT'S IT *LIKE,* LEXIE?

WHEN CAN I GET *ALL* SUPERPOWERED UP ?

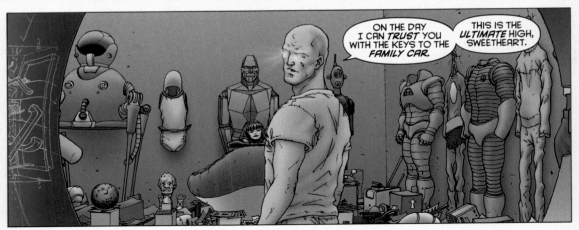

ON THE DAY I CAN *TRUST* YOU WITH THE KEYS TO THE *FAMILY CAR.*

THIS IS THE *ULTIMATE* HIGH, SWEETHEART.

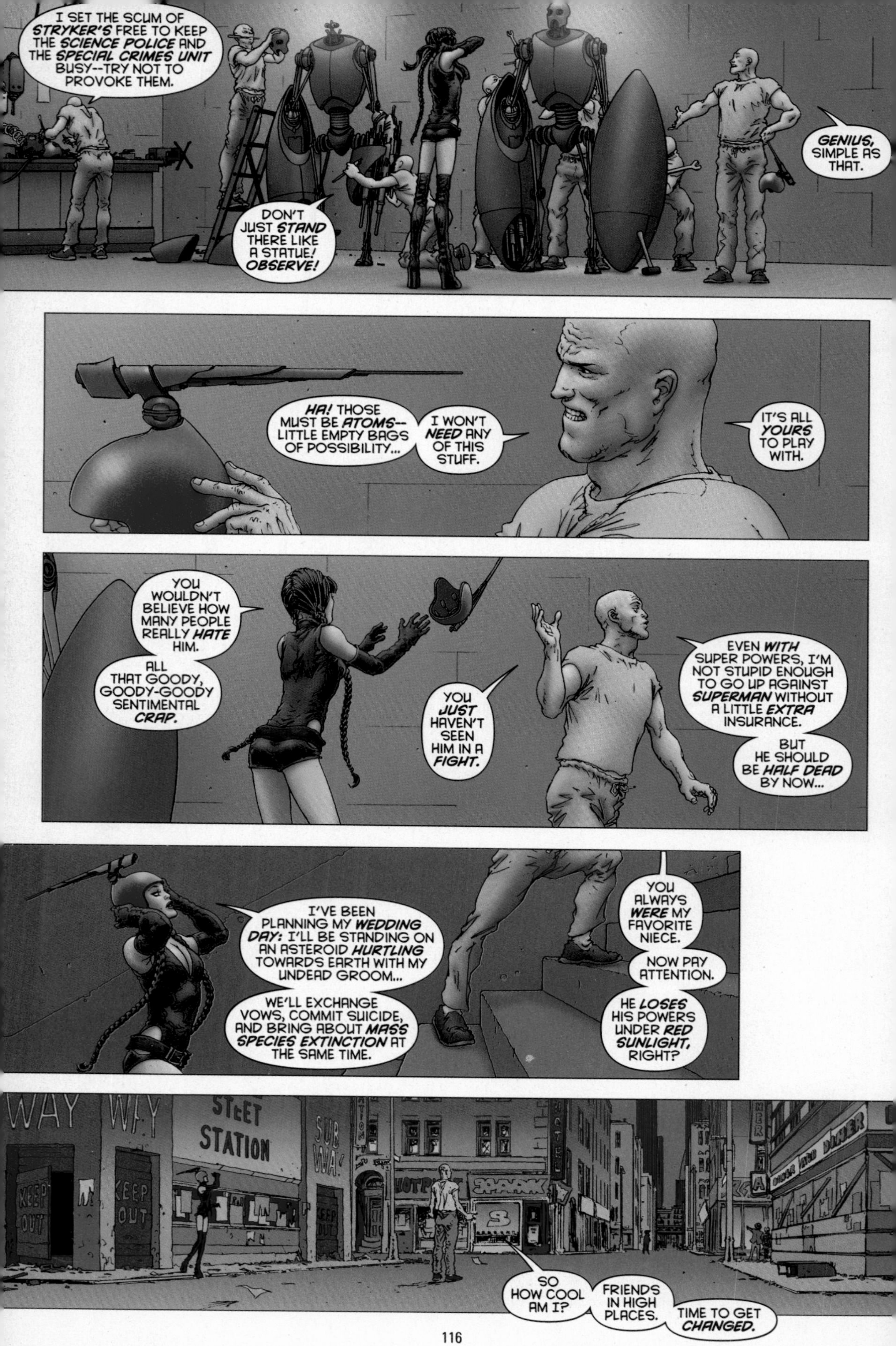
I SET THE SCUM OF STRYKER'S FREE TO KEEP THE SCIENCE POLICE AND THE SPECIAL CRIMES UNIT BUSY--TRY NOT TO PROVOKE THEM.
GENIUS, SIMPLE AS THAT.
DON'T JUST STAND THERE LIKE A STATUE! OBSERVE!
HA! THOSE MUST BE ATOMS-- LITTLE EMPTY BAGS OF POSSIBILITY...
I WON'T NEED ANY OF THIS STUFF.
IT'S ALL YOURS TO PLAY WITH.
YOU WOULDN'T BELIEVE HOW MANY PEOPLE REALLY HATE HIM.
ALL THAT GOODY, GOODY-GOODY SENTIMENTAL CRAP.
YOU JUST HAVEN'T SEEN HIM IN A FIGHT.
EVEN WITH SUPER POWERS, I'M NOT STUPID ENOUGH TO GO UP AGAINST SUPERMAN WITHOUT A LITTLE EXTRA INSURANCE.
BUT HE SHOULD BE HALF DEAD BY NOW...
I'VE BEEN PLANNING MY WEDDING DAY: I'LL BE STANDING ON AN ASTEROID HURTLING TOWARDS EARTH WITH MY UNDEAD GROOM...
WE'LL EXCHANGE VOWS, COMMIT SUICIDE, AND BRING ABOUT MASS SPECIES EXTINCTION AT THE SAME TIME.
YOU ALWAYS WERE MY FAVORITE NIECE.
NOW PAY ATTENTION.
HE LOSES HIS POWERS UNDER RED SUNLIGHT, RIGHT?
STATION
KEEP OUT
KEEP OUT
SO HOW COOL AM I?
FRIENDS IN HIGH PLACES.
TIME TO GET CHANGED.

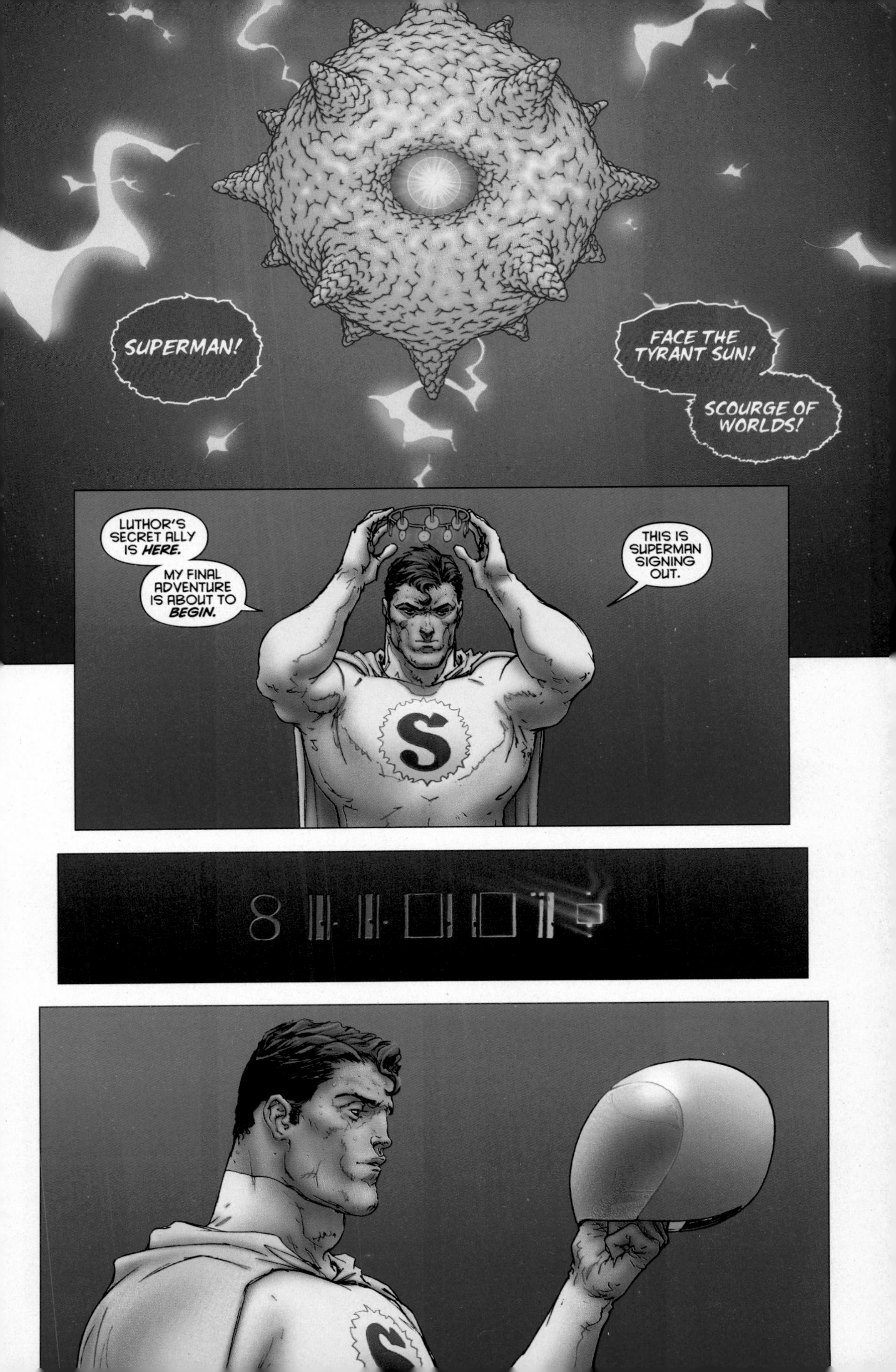

SUPERMAN!
FACE THE TYRANT SUN!
SCOURGE OF WORLDS!
LUTHOR'S SECRET ALLY IS *HERE.*
MY FINAL ADVENTURE IS ABOUT TO *BEGIN.*
THIS IS SUPERMAN SIGNING OUT.

SUPERMAN.

YOU CANNOT STAND ALONE.

I WILL REMAIN TO GUARD THE FORTRESS OF SOLITUDE.

THE REST OF US WILL FIGHT BY YOUR SIDE.

I...I COULDN'T ASK FOR GREATER LOYALTY.

FORT SUPERMAN IS CLOSING DOWN.

SEAL THE FORTRESS!

WELCOME

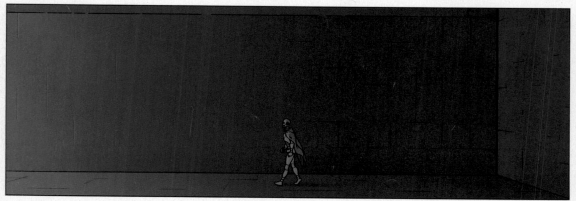

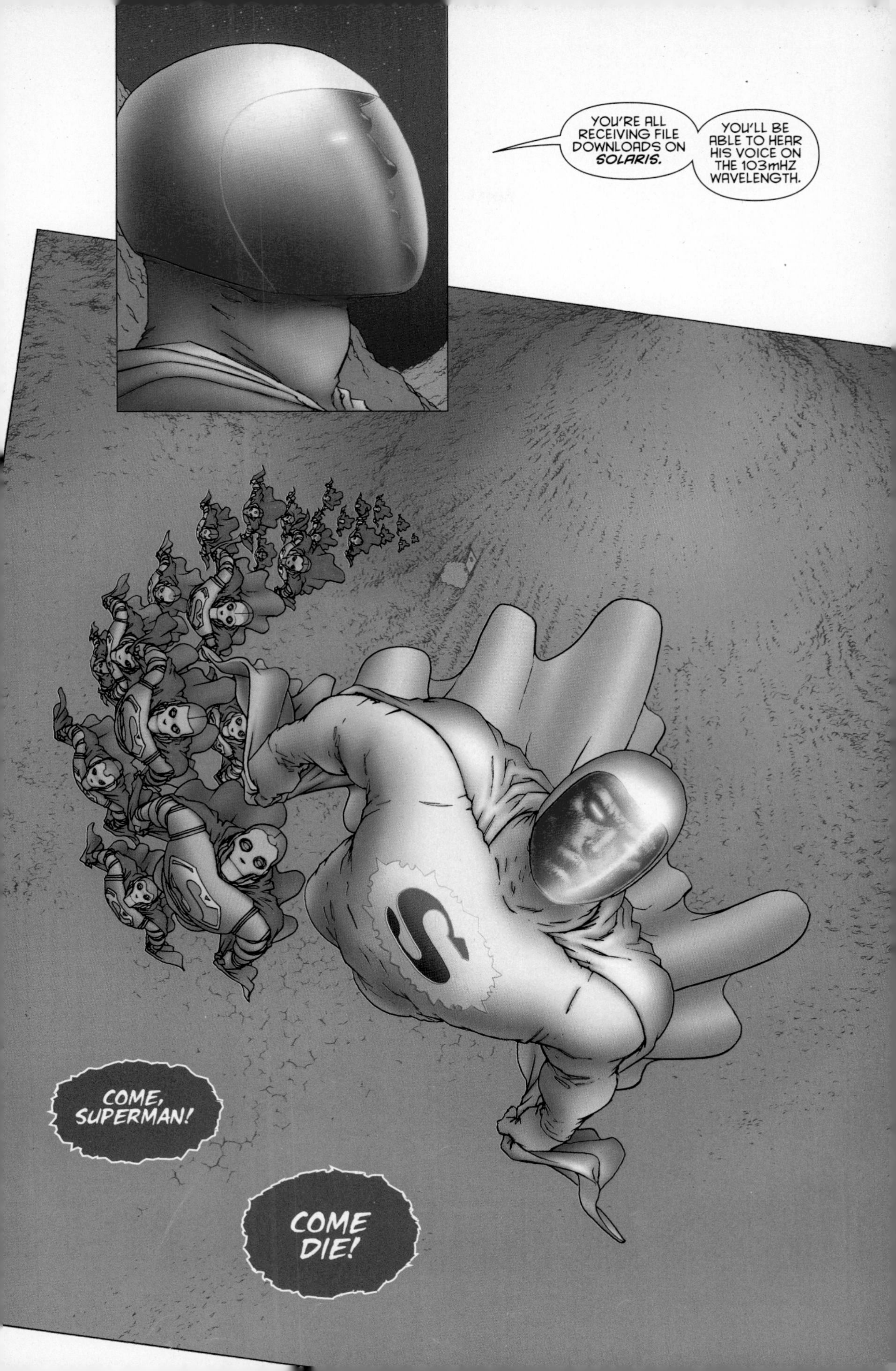

YOU'RE ALL RECEIVING FILE DOWNLOADS ON *SOLARIS.*
YOU'LL BE ABLE TO HEAR HIS VOICE ON THE 103mHZ WAVELENGTH.
COME, SUPERMAN!
COME DIE!

IMPOSSIBLE!
WHY NOT POWERLESS IN MY RED RAYS?
YOU REALLY EXPECTED TO SURPRISE ME?
TOO BAD.
THIS SOLARSUIT I MADE WILL PROTECT ME FROM RED SUN RADIATION LONG ENOUGH TO EVEN THE ODDS.
TOO LATE!
I KILL YOUR SUN!
AND YOU!

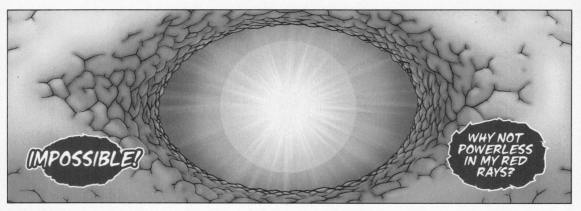

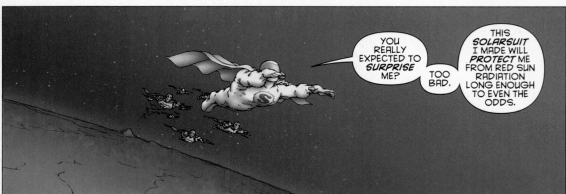

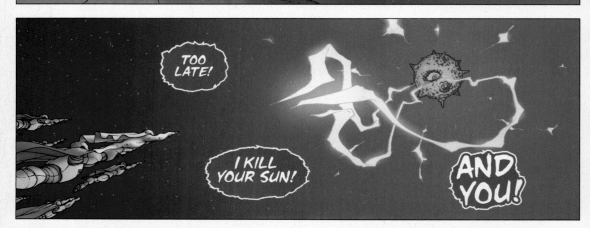

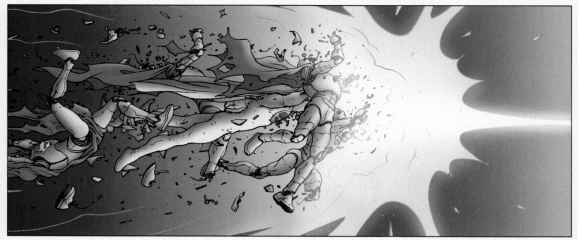

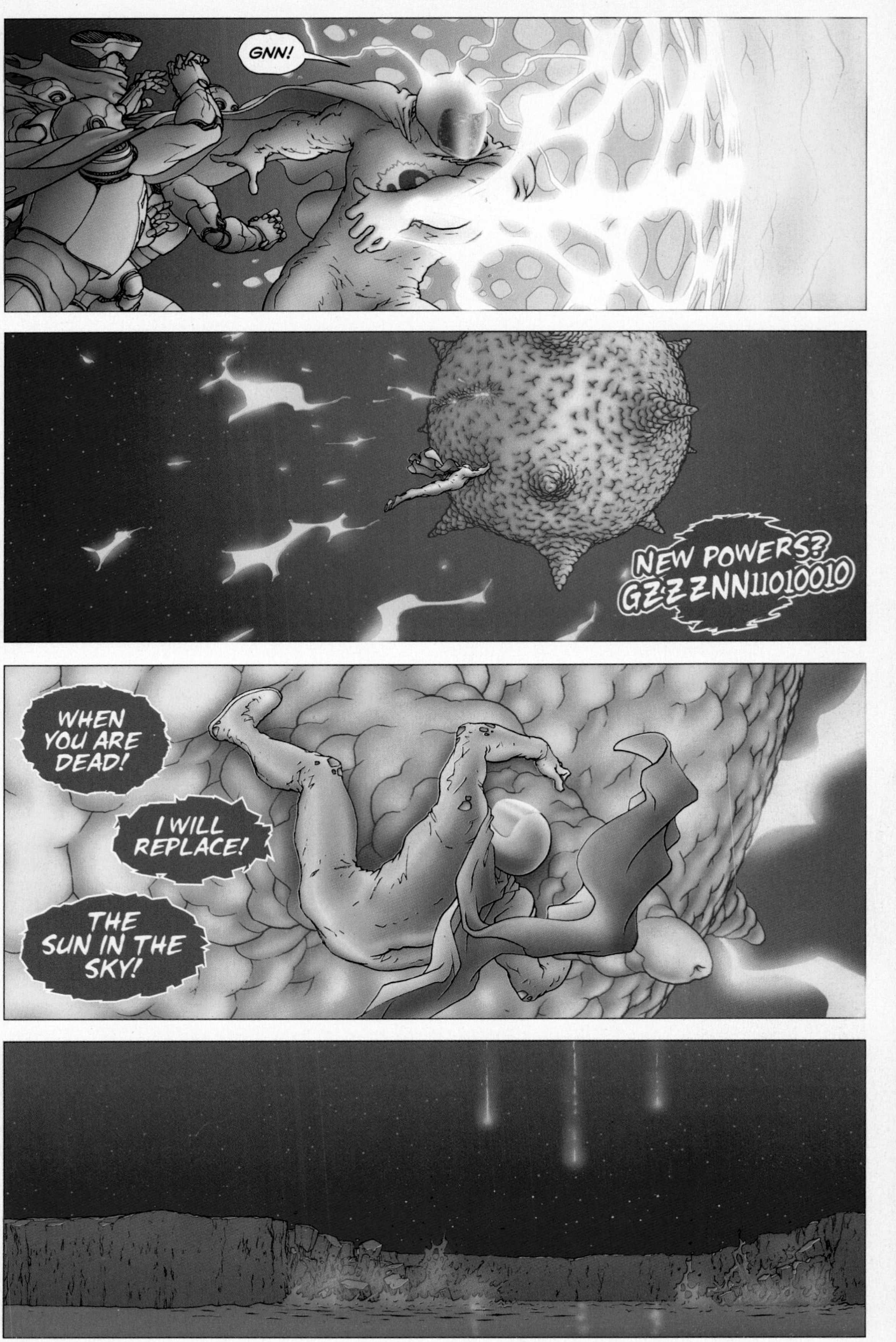
GNN!
NEW POWERS? GZZZNN11010010
WHEN YOU ARE DEAD!
I WILL REPLACE!
THE SUN IN THE SKY!

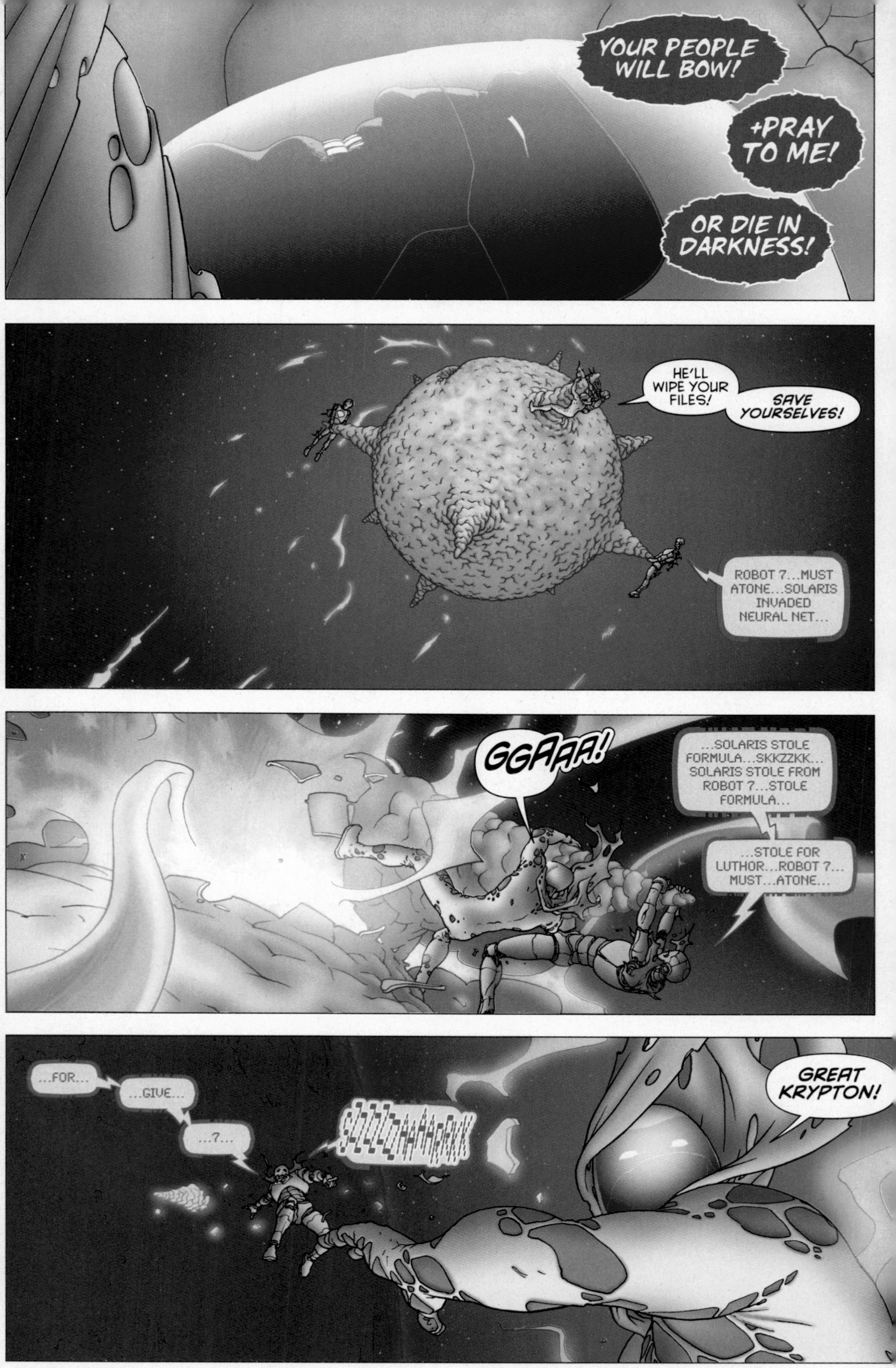
YOUR PEOPLE WILL BOW!
+PRAY TO ME!
OR DIE IN DARKNESS!
HE'LL WIPE YOUR FILES!
SAVE YOURSELVES!
ROBOT 7...MUST ATONE...SOLARIS INVADED NEURAL NET...
GGAAAA!
...SOLARIS STOLE FORMULA...SKKZZKK... SOLARIS STOLE FROM ROBOT 7...STOLE FORMULA...
...STOLE FOR LUTHOR...ROBOT 7... MUST...ATONE...
...FOR...
...GIVE...
...7...
SZZZZAAAARRKK
GREAT KRYPTON!

NO!
GO BACK TO YOUR OWN KIND!
GO BACK!
WHAT IS THIS?
ABOMINATION!
THE NATURAL ENEMY OF A LIVING SOLAR COMPUTER.
TYRANT SUN...
MEET SUN-EATER!
1010101011
1010101010000111

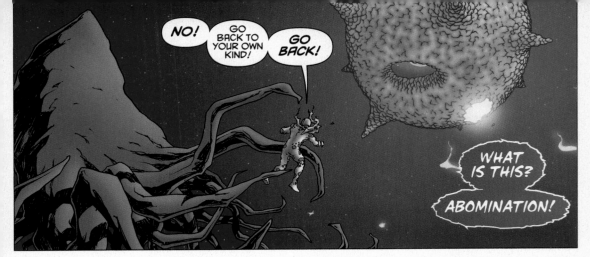

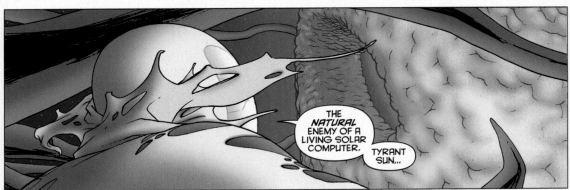

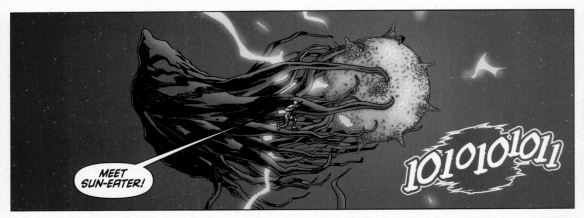

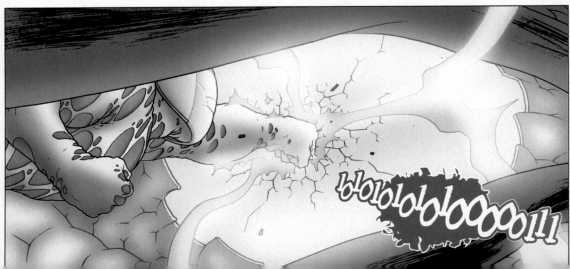

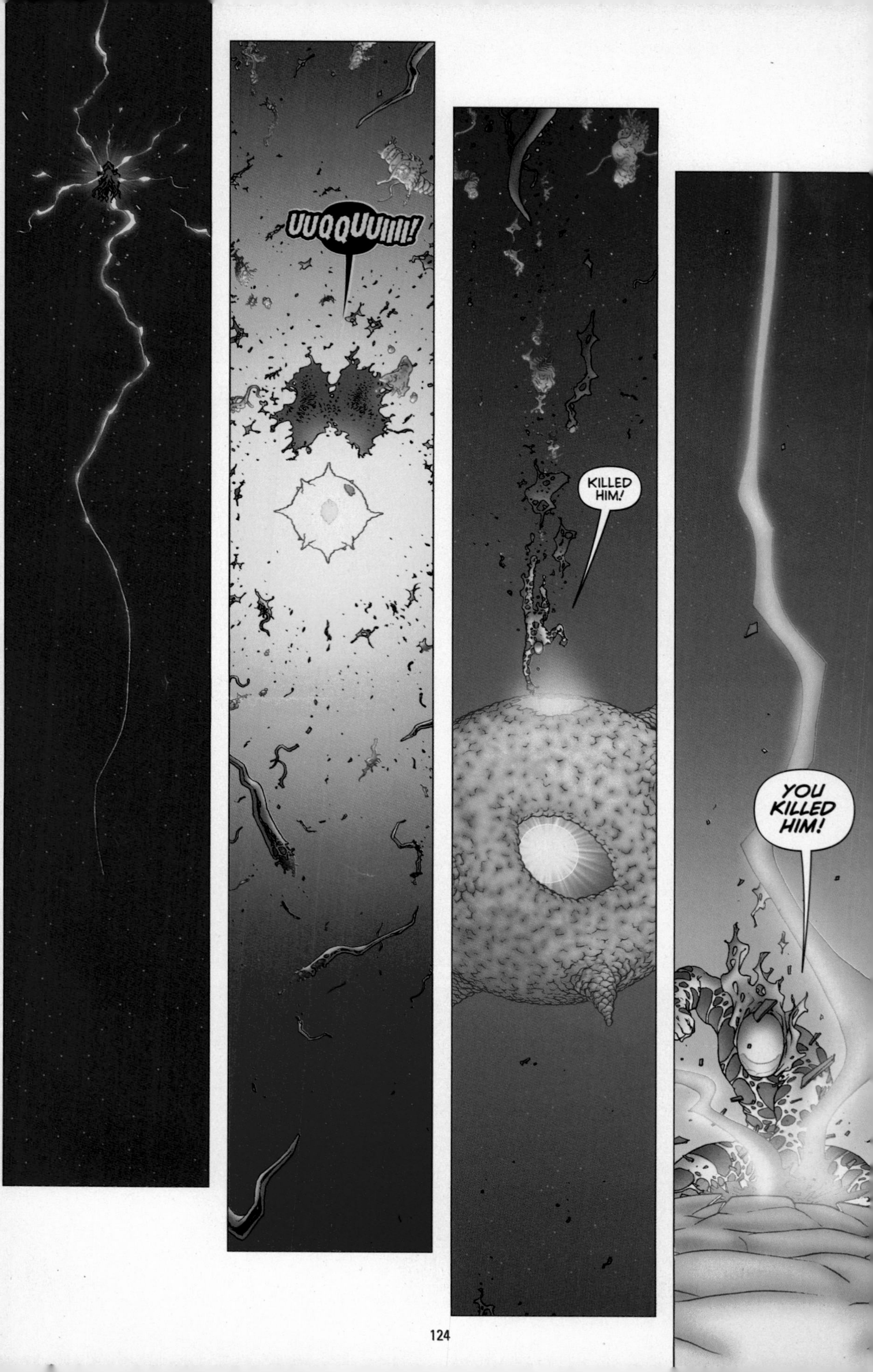
UUQQUUIIII!
KILLED HIM!
YOU KILLED HIM!

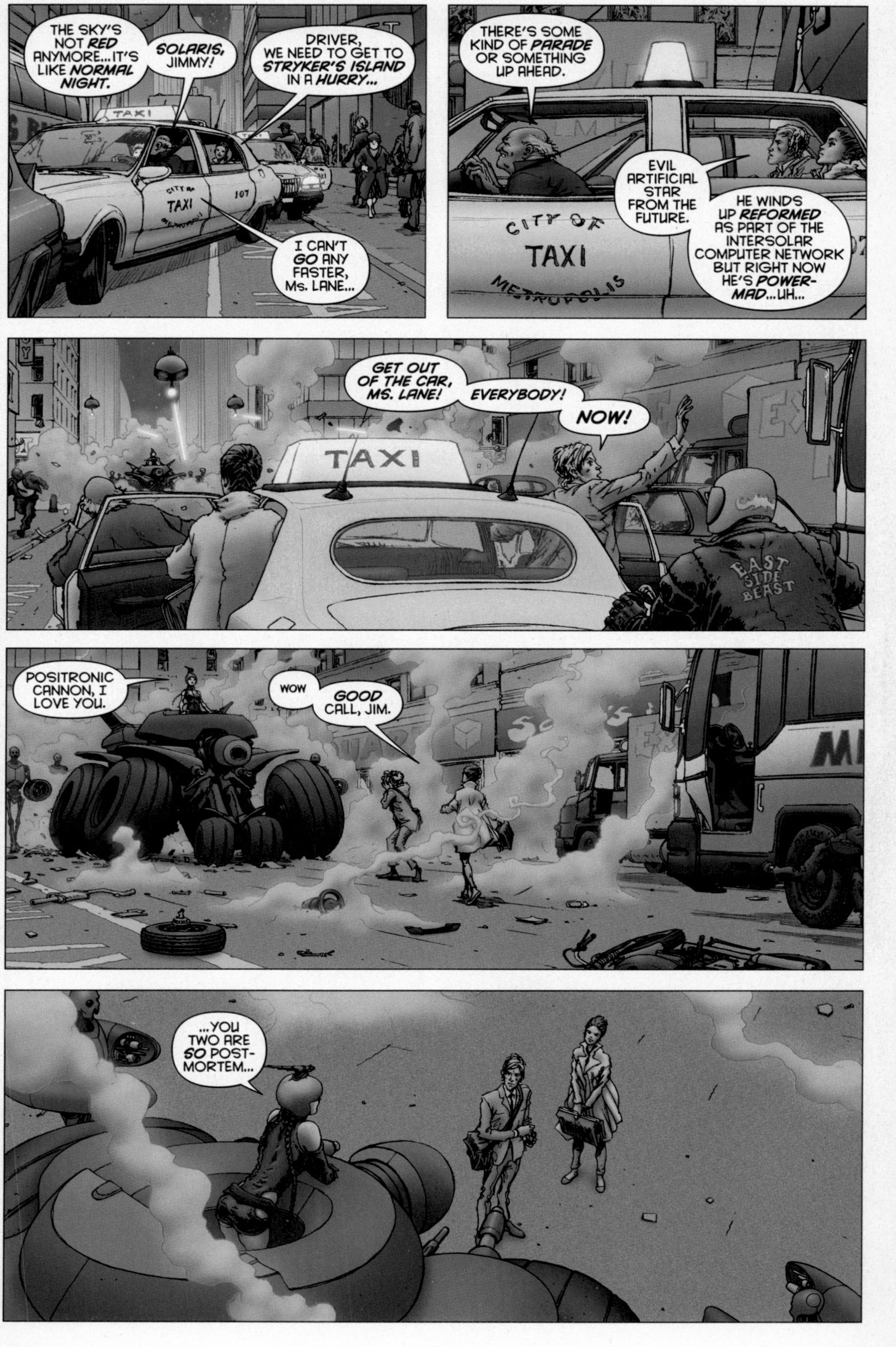
THE SKY'S NOT RED ANYMORE...IT'S LIKE NORMAL NIGHT.
SOLARIS, JIMMY!
DRIVER, WE NEED TO GET TO STRYKER'S ISLAND IN A HURRY...
TAXI
I CAN'T GO ANY FASTER, Ms. LANE...
THERE'S SOME KIND OF PARADE OR SOMETHING UP AHEAD.
EVIL ARTIFICIAL STAR FROM THE FUTURE.
HE WINDS UP REFORMED AS PART OF THE INTERSOLAR COMPUTER NETWORK BUT RIGHT NOW HE'S POWER-MAD...UH...
CITY OF TAXI METROPOLIS
GET OUT OF THE CAR, MS. LANE!
EVERYBODY!
NOW!
TAXI
EAST SIDE BEAST
POSITRONIC CANNON, I LOVE YOU.
WOW
GOOD CALL, JIM.
...YOU TWO ARE SO POST-MORTEM...

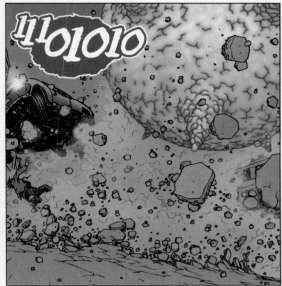

11101010

1110010o POISONEDO1OSUN1110

I NEED EVERYONE TO TAKE COVER!

NOW!

BY THE 24th CENTURY, I'M TOLD, YOU'LL HAVE BEEN *REHABILITATED* TO WORK *WITH* HUMANITY INSTEAD OF *AGAINST* THEM.

REHABILITATION BEGINS *HERE*. SOLARIS.

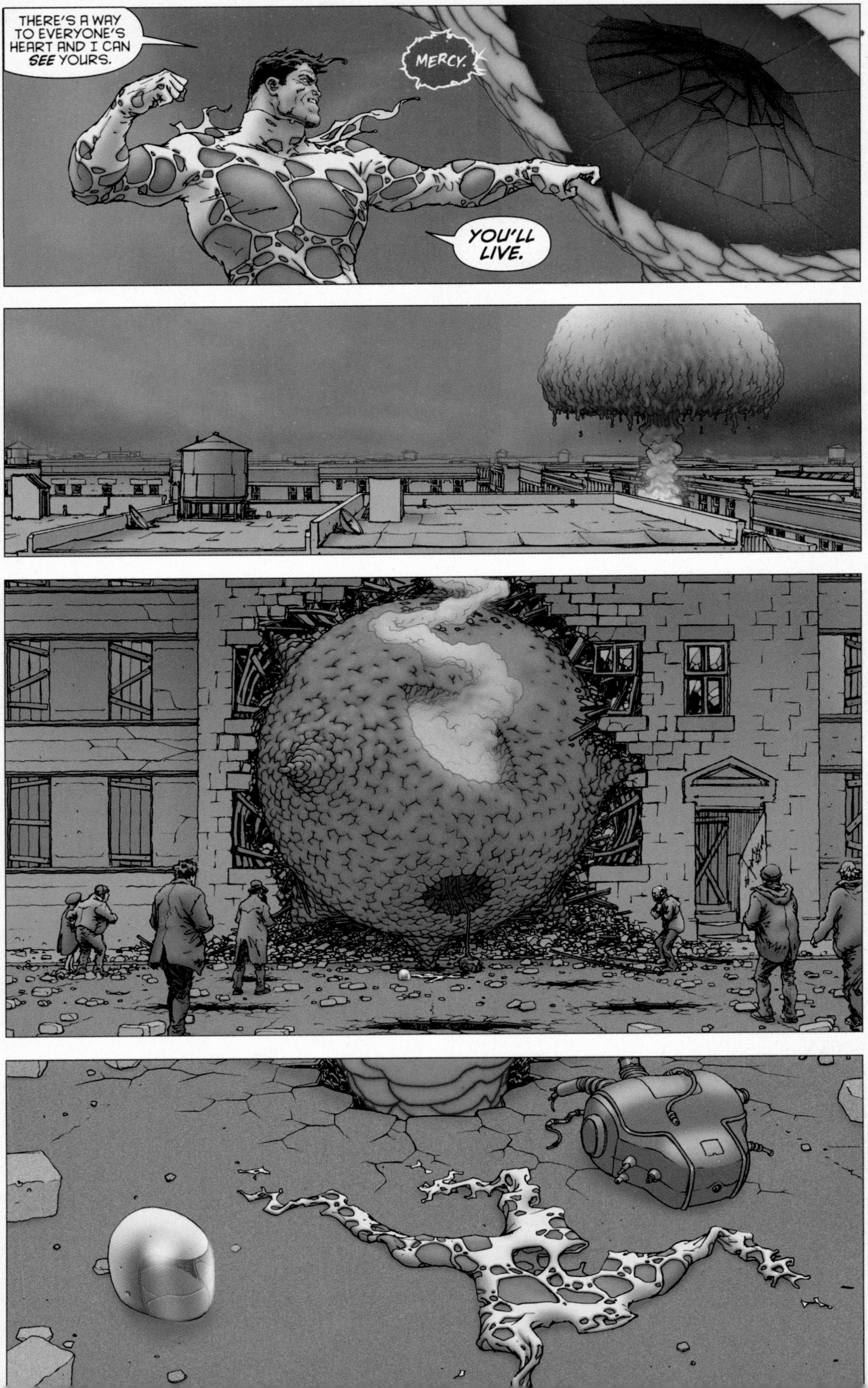
THERE'S A WAY TO EVERYONE'S HEART AND I CAN SEE YOURS.
MERCY.
YOU'LL LIVE.

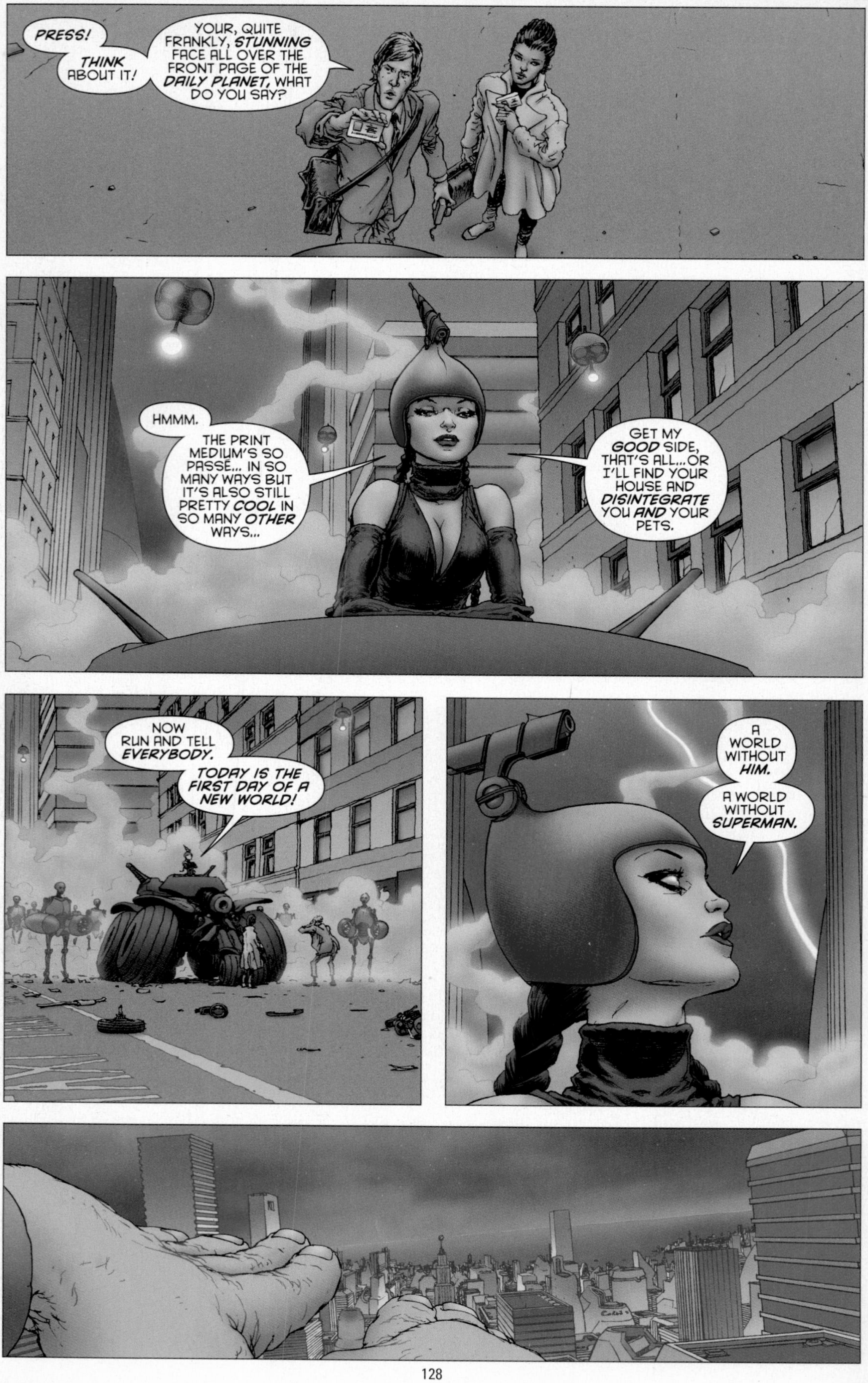
PRESS!
THINK ABOUT IT!
YOUR, QUITE FRANKLY, STUNNING FACE ALL OVER THE FRONT PAGE OF THE DAILY PLANET, WHAT DO YOU SAY?
HMMM.
THE PRINT MEDIUM'S SO PASSÉ... IN SO MANY WAYS BUT IT'S ALSO STILL PRETTY COOL IN SO MANY OTHER WAYS...
GET MY GOOD SIDE, THAT'S ALL...OR I'LL FIND YOUR HOUSE AND DISINTEGRATE YOU AND YOUR PETS.
NOW RUN AND TELL EVERYBODY.
TODAY IS THE FIRST DAY OF A NEW WORLD!
A WORLD WITHOUT HIM.
A WORLD WITHOUT SUPERMAN.

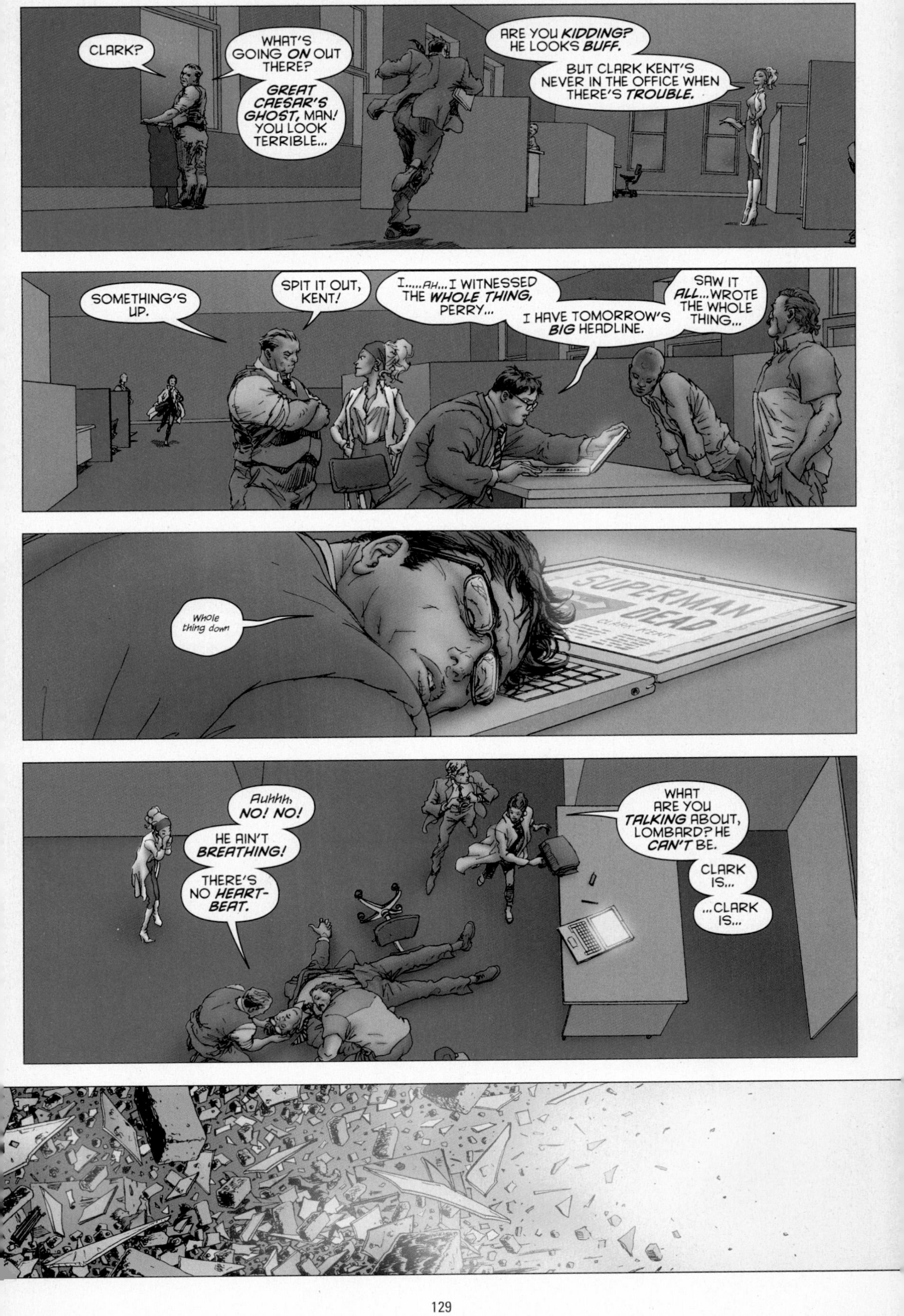

CLARK?
WHAT'S GOING ON OUT THERE?
GREAT CAESAR'S GHOST, MAN! YOU LOOK TERRIBLE...
ARE YOU KIDDING? HE LOOKS BUFF.
BUT CLARK KENT'S NEVER IN THE OFFICE WHEN THERE'S TROUBLE.
SOMETHING'S UP.
SPIT IT OUT, KENT!
I.....AH...I WITNESSED THE WHOLE THING, PERRY...
I HAVE TOMORROW'S BIG HEADLINE.
SAW IT ALL...WROTE THE WHOLE THING...
Whole thing down
SUPERMAN DEAD
CLARK KENT
Auhhh, NO! NO!
HE AIN'T BREATHING!
THERE'S NO HEART-BEAT.
WHAT ARE YOU TALKING ABOUT, LOMBARD? HE CAN'T BE.
CLARK IS...
...CLARK IS...

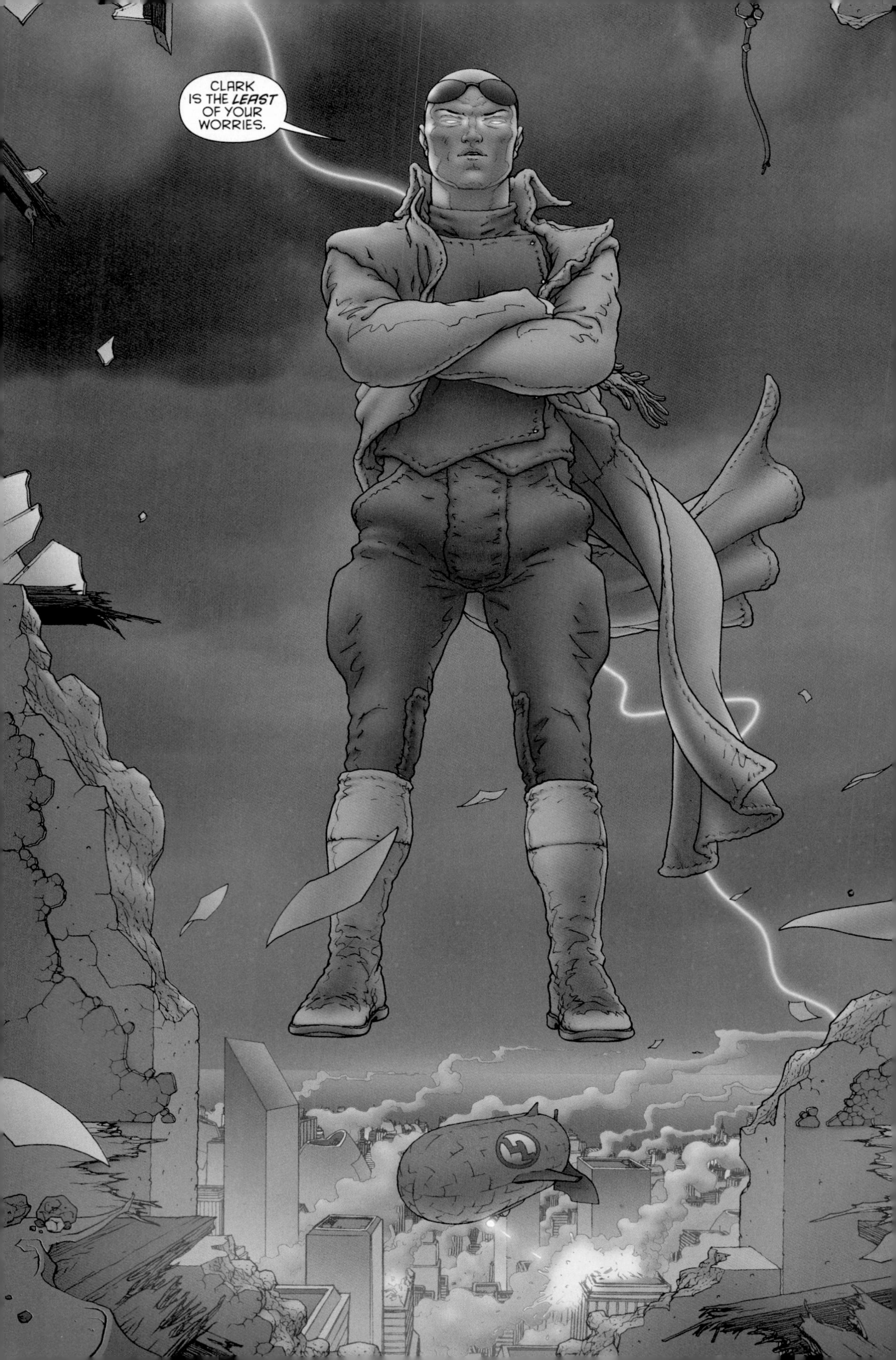
CLARK IS THE *LEAST* OF YOUR WORRIES.

Episode 12

SUPERMAN IN EXCELSIS

Cover FRANK QUITELY

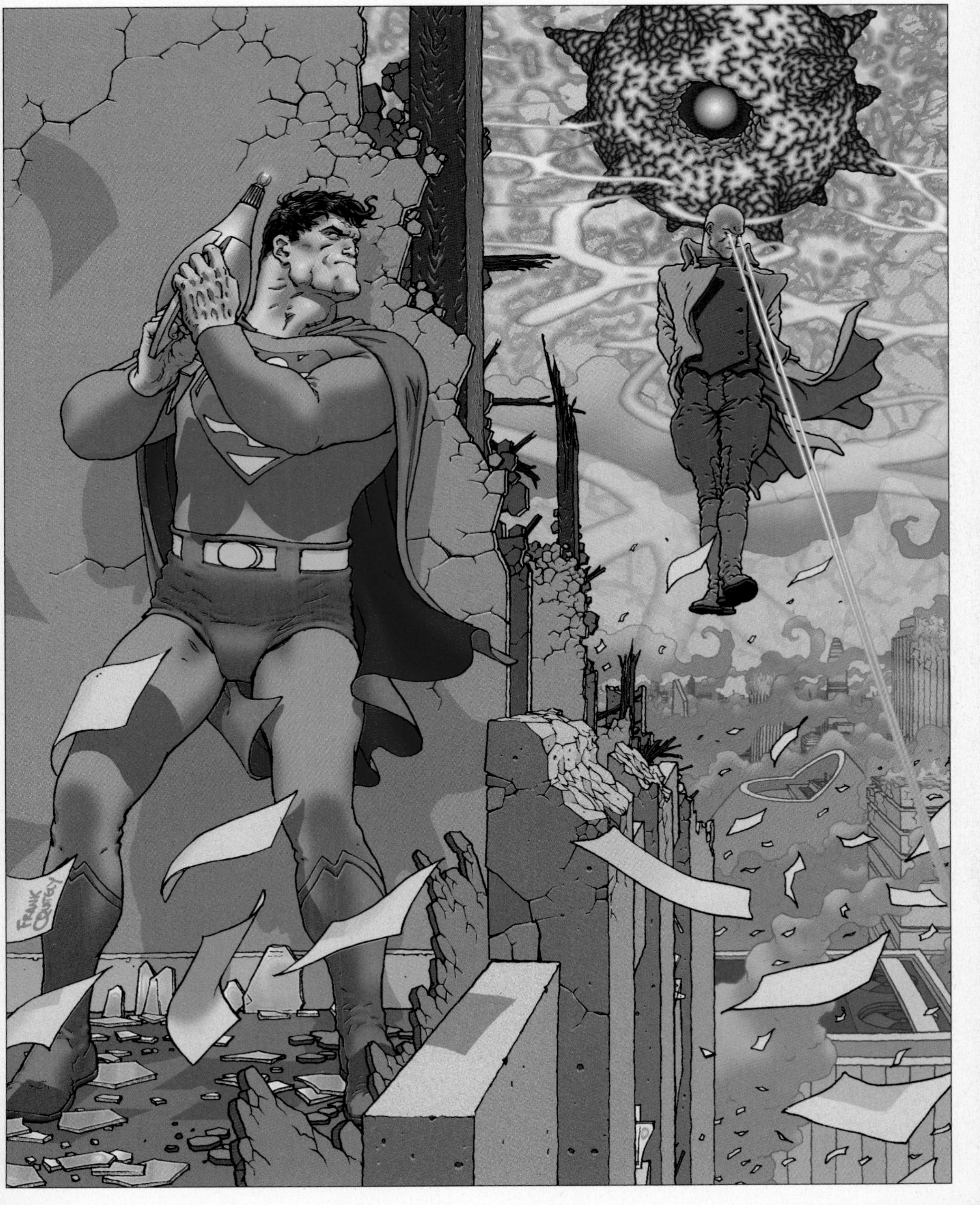
FRANK QUITELY

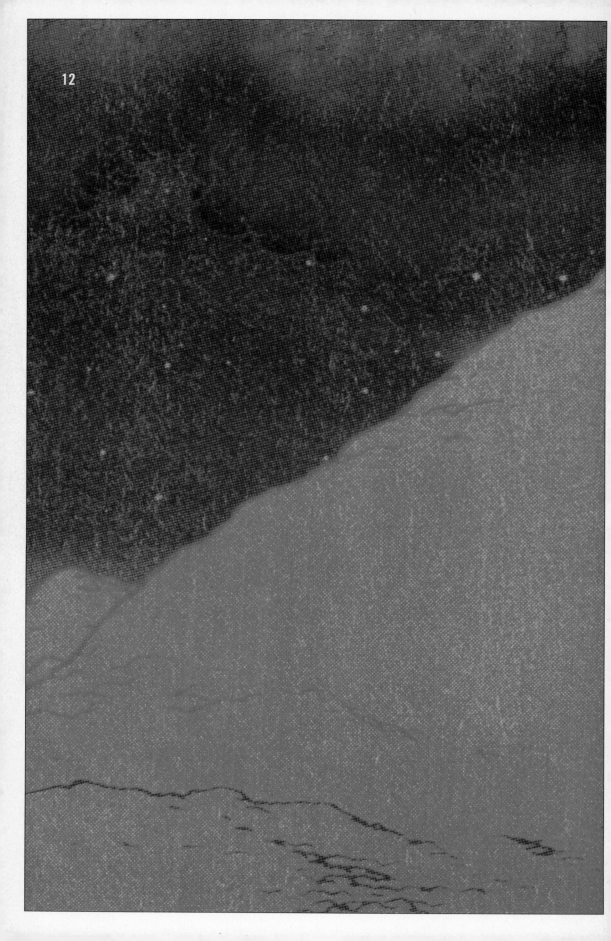

12

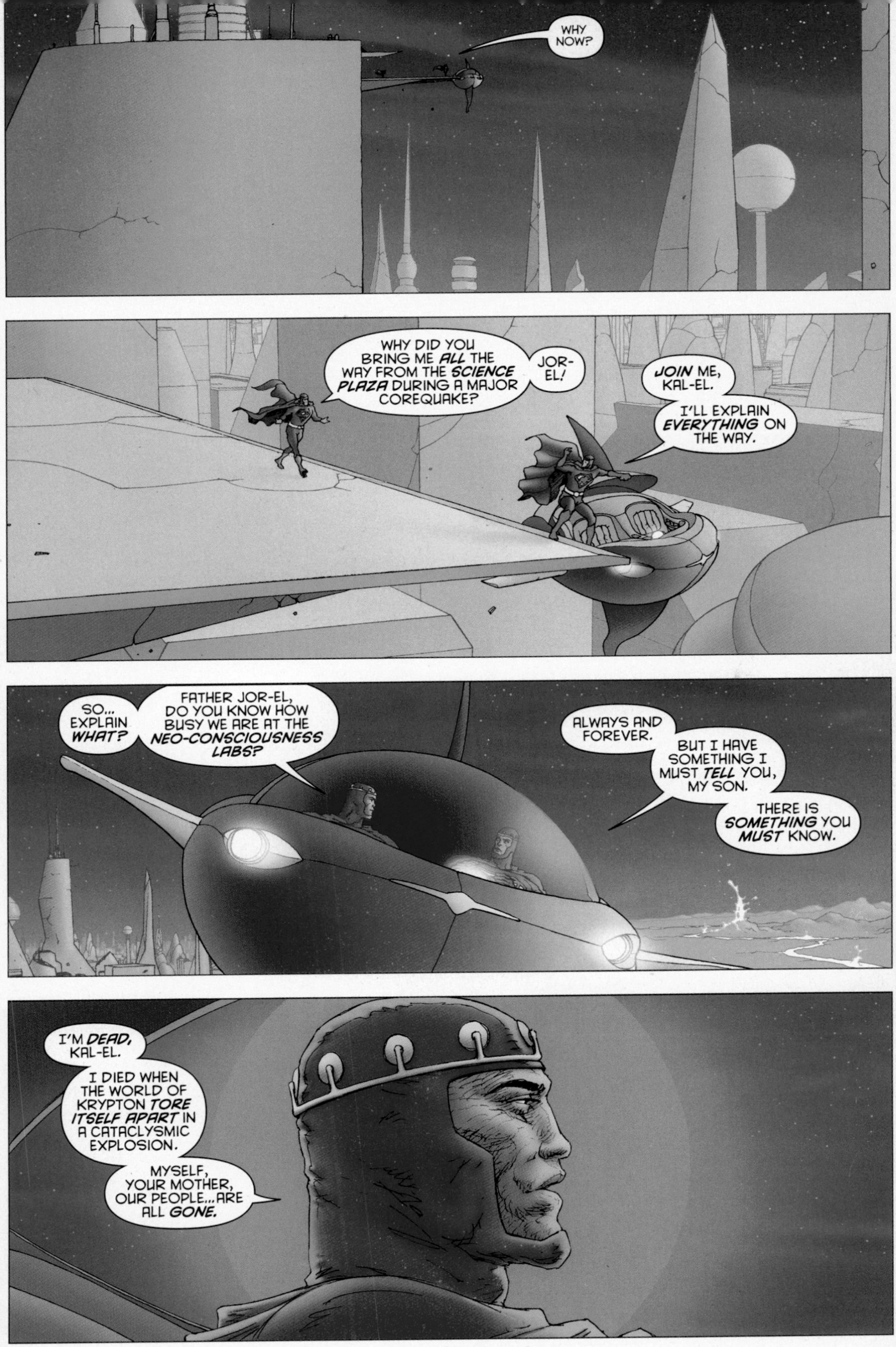

WHY NOW?
WHY DID YOU BRING ME ALL THE WAY FROM THE SCIENCE PLAZA DURING A MAJOR COREQUAKE?
JOR-EL!
JOIN ME, KAL-EL.
I'LL EXPLAIN EVERYTHING ON THE WAY.
SO... EXPLAIN WHAT?
FATHER JOR-EL, DO YOU KNOW HOW BUSY WE ARE AT THE NEO-CONSCIOUSNESS LABS?
ALWAYS AND FOREVER.
BUT I HAVE SOMETHING I MUST TELL YOU, MY SON.
THERE IS SOMETHING YOU MUST KNOW.
I'M DEAD, KAL-EL.
I DIED WHEN THE WORLD OF KRYPTON TORE ITSELF APART IN A CATACLYSMIC EXPLOSION.
MYSELF, YOUR MOTHER, OUR PEOPLE... ARE ALL GONE.

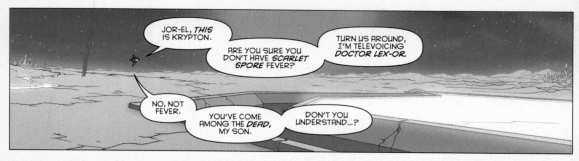

JOR-EL, *THIS* IS KRYPTON.

ARE YOU SURE YOU DON'T HAVE *SCARLET SPORE* FEVER?

TURN US AROUND, I'M TELEVOICING *DOCTOR LEX-OR.*

NO, NOT FEVER.

YOU'VE COME AMONG THE *DEAD,* MY SON.

DON'T YOU UNDERSTAND...?

...YOU *TOO* ARE DEAD.

YOU DIED DEFENDING HUMANKIND AGAINST THE TYRANT SUN, *SOLARIS,* AFTER A PRIOR TOXIC *OVERDOSE* OF YELLOW SOLAR RADIATION.

THE *29 WONDERS* OF KRYPTON AND OUR *SHINING CITIES* WERE ALL *LOST,* KAL-EL.

OUR ART, OUR PROUD HISTORY, OUR VERY *NAMES...* ERASED FROM THE SCREENS OF POSTERITY.

CONSIDER US: A WHOLE CIVILIZATION OF *SUPERMEN* REDUCED TO *DUST* BY A CAPRICE OF COSMOLOGY.

THEN THINK HOW PRECIOUS AND HOW FRAGILE ALL THE *LITTLE* THINGS YOU VALUE ARE.

BUT YOUR MACHINES *STABILIZED* KRYPTON'S CORE.

JOR-EL OF EL, MY FATHER, IF I'M DEAD...

...WHAT *PLACE* IS THIS?

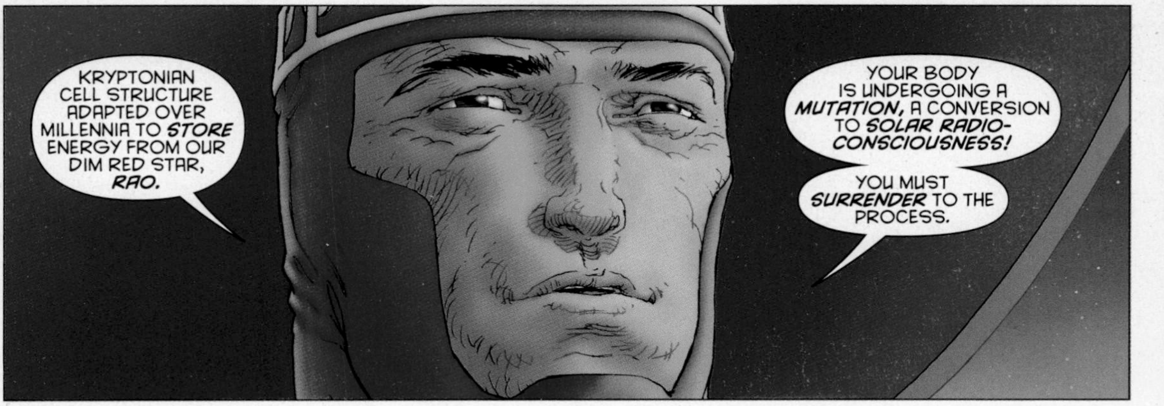
KRYPTONIAN CELL STRUCTURE ADAPTED OVER MILLENNIA TO STORE ENERGY FROM OUR DIM RED STAR, RAO.
YOUR BODY IS UNDERGOING A MUTATION, A CONVERSION TO SOLAR RADIO-CONSCIOUSNESS!
YOU MUST SURRENDER TO THE PROCESS.

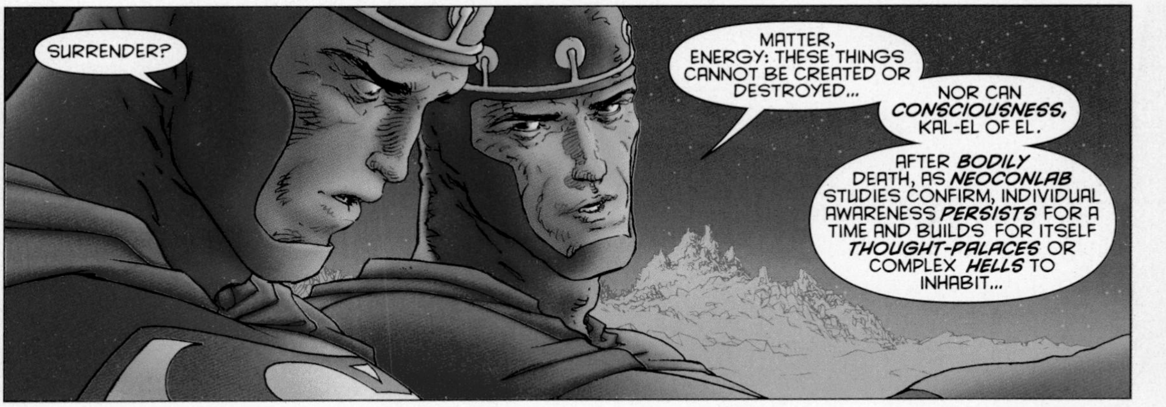
SURRENDER?
MATTER, ENERGY: THESE THINGS CANNOT BE CREATED OR DESTROYED...
NOR CAN CONSCIOUSNESS, KAL-EL OF EL.
AFTER BODILY DEATH, AS NEOCONLAB STUDIES CONFIRM, INDIVIDUAL AWARENESS PERSISTS FOR A TIME AND BUILDS FOR ITSELF THOUGHT-PALACES OR COMPLEX HELLS TO INHABIT...

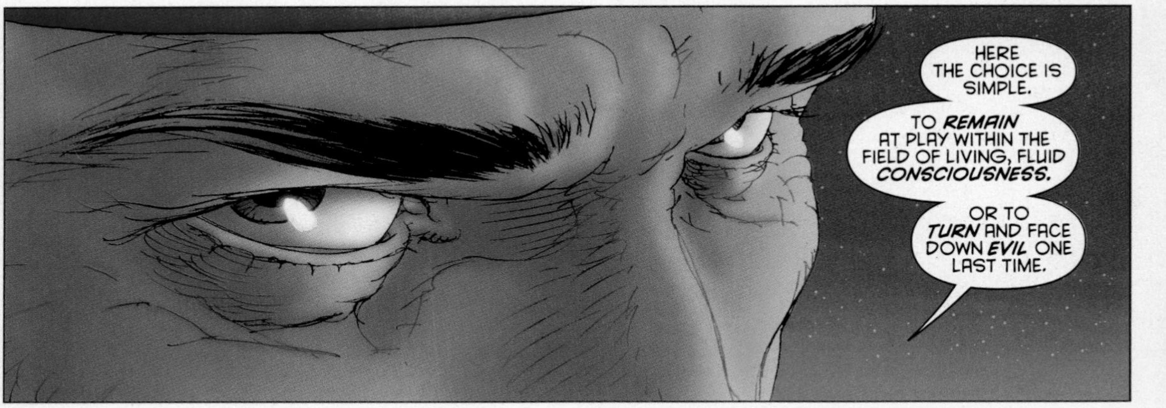
HERE THE CHOICE IS SIMPLE.
TO REMAIN AT PLAY WITHIN THE FIELD OF LIVING, FLUID CONSCIOUSNESS.
OR TO TURN AND FACE DOWN EVIL ONE LAST TIME.

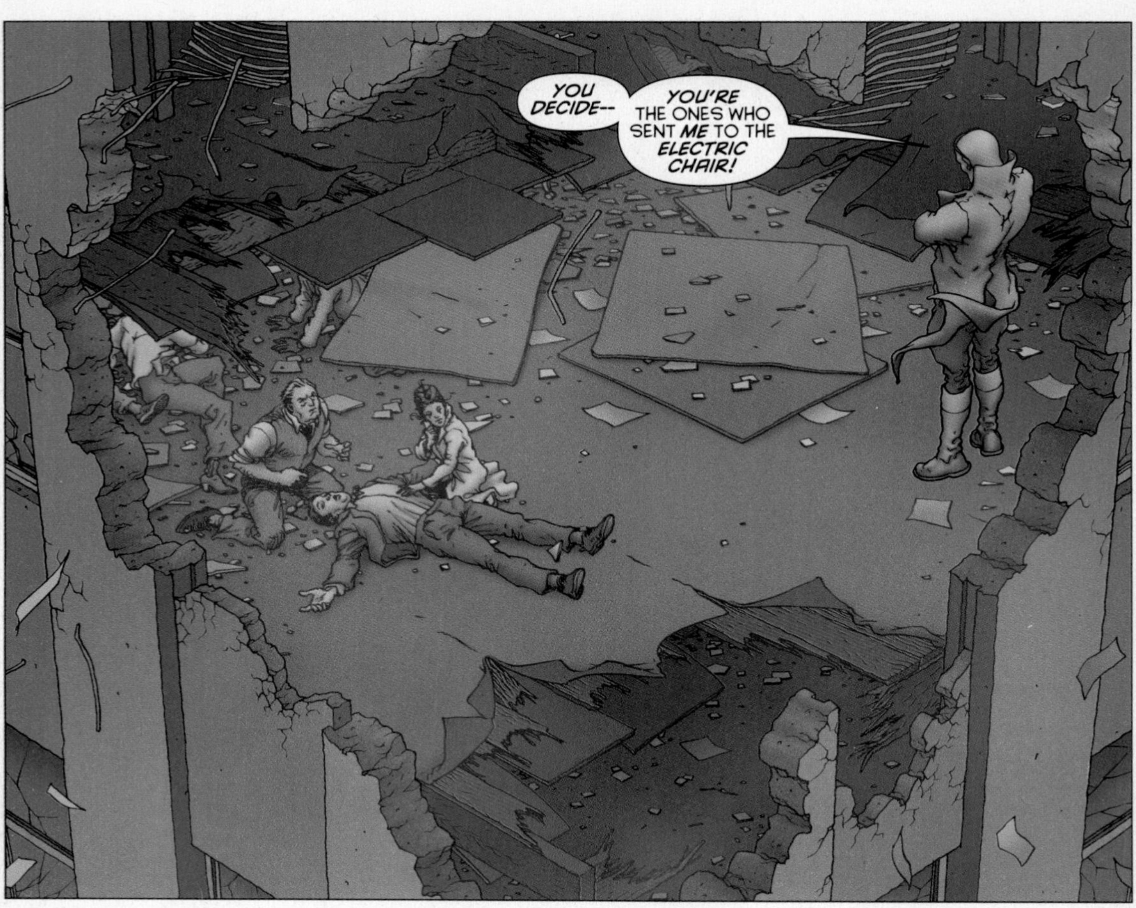
YOU DECIDE--
YOU'RE THE ONES WHO SENT ME TO THE ELECTRIC CHAIR!

SUPERMAN IN EXCELSIS

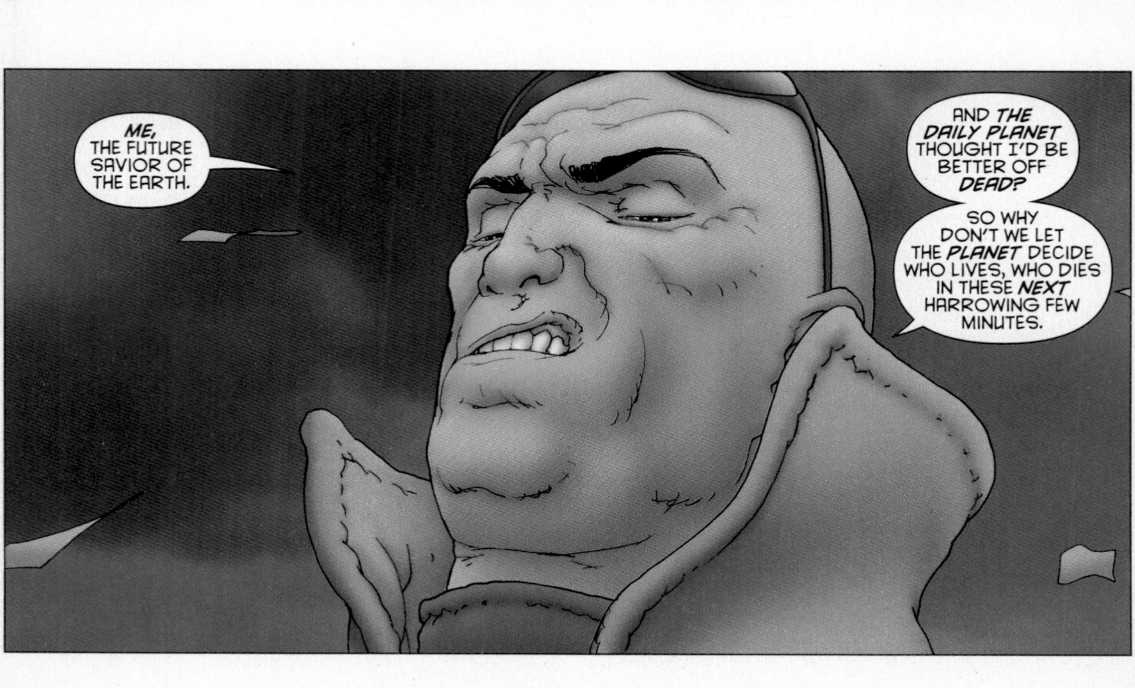
ME, THE FUTURE SAVIOR OF THE EARTH.
AND THE DAILY PLANET THOUGHT I'D BE BETTER OFF DEAD?
SO WHY DON'T WE LET THE PLANET DECIDE WHO LIVES, WHO DIES IN THESE NEXT HARROWING FEW MINUTES.

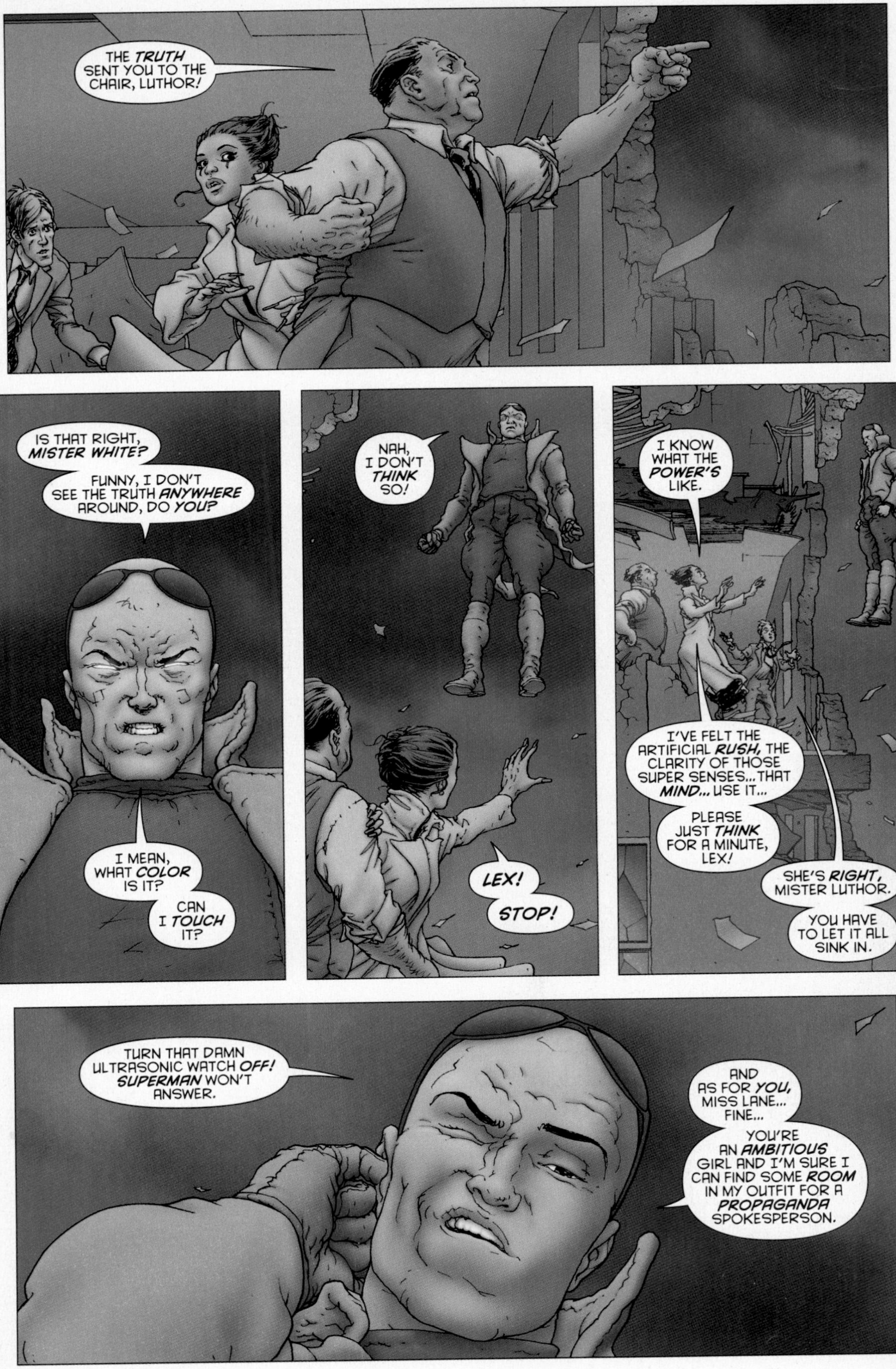
THE TRUTH SENT YOU TO THE CHAIR, LUTHOR!
IS THAT RIGHT, MISTER WHITE?
FUNNY, I DON'T SEE THE TRUTH ANYWHERE AROUND, DO YOU?
I MEAN, WHAT COLOR IS IT?
CAN I TOUCH IT?
NAH, I DON'T THINK SO!
LEX!
STOP!
I KNOW WHAT THE POWER'S LIKE.
I'VE FELT THE ARTIFICIAL RUSH, THE CLARITY OF THOSE SUPER SENSES... THAT MIND... USE IT...
PLEASE JUST THINK FOR A MINUTE, LEX!
SHE'S RIGHT, MISTER LUTHOR.
YOU HAVE TO LET IT ALL SINK IN.
TURN THAT DAMN ULTRASONIC WATCH OFF! SUPERMAN WON'T ANSWER.
AND AS FOR YOU, MISS LANE... FINE...
YOU'RE AN AMBITIOUS GIRL AND I'M SURE I CAN FIND SOME ROOM IN MY OUTFIT FOR A PROPAGANDA SPOKESPERSON.

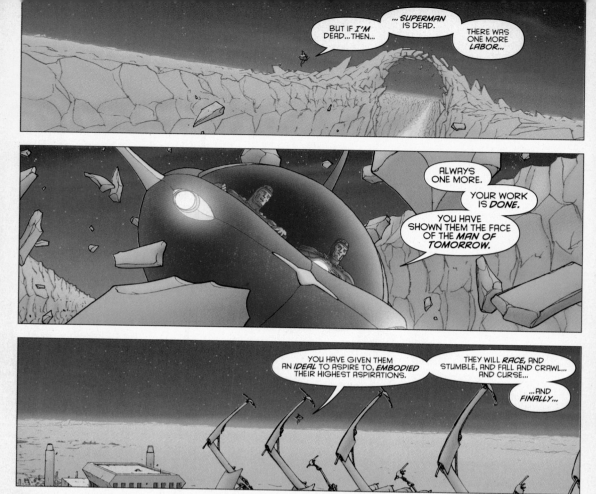

BUT IF *I'M* DEAD...THEN...

...*SUPERMAN* IS DEAD.

THERE WAS ONE MORE *LABOR*...

ALWAYS ONE MORE.

YOUR WORK IS *DONE.*

YOU HAVE SHOWN THEM THE FACE OF THE *MAN OF TOMORROW.*

YOU HAVE GIVEN THEM AN *IDEAL* TO ASPIRE TO, *EMBODIED* THEIR HIGHEST ASPIRATIONS.

THEY WILL *RACE*, AND STUMBLE, AND FALL AND CRAWL... AND CURSE...

...AND *FINALLY*...

...THEY WILL *JOIN* YOU IN THE SUN, KAL-EL.

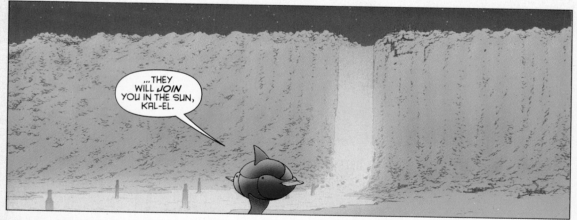

IN *TIME* YOU WILL NO LONGER BE *ALONE.*

BUT MY LIFE!

MY *LIFE!*
FOR KRYPTON, IT WAS *ALWAYS* TOO LATE!
BUT THE *BEST* OF US, THE *GOLD* IN US, WILL SURVIVE IN YOU!
ALL THAT IS IMPURE WILL BE BURNED TO *ASH.*
AND ALL THAT IS STRONG AND GREAT AND TRUE WILL *SURVIVE...*
...AND BE REBORN.
FATHER, NOT ME!

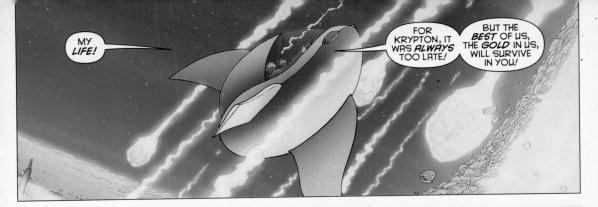

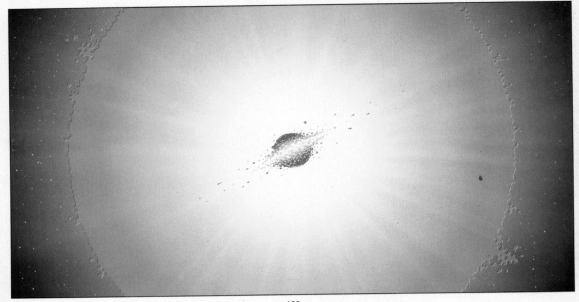

COME *ON*, CLARK! YOU CAN *DO* IT, BUDDY *COME ON!*

I'M SORRY FOR ALL THOSE TIMES I PLAYED TRICKS ON YOU.

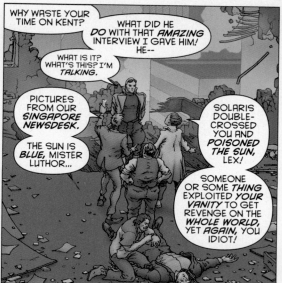

WHY WASTE YOUR TIME ON KENT?

WHAT DID HE *DO* WITH THAT *AMAZING* INTERVIEW I GAVE HIM! HE--

WHAT IS IT? WHAT'S THIS? I'M *TALKING.*

PICTURES FROM OUR *SINGAPORE NEWSDESK.*

THE SUN IS *BLUE,* MISTER LUTHOR...

SOLARIS DOUBLE-CROSSED YOU AND *POISONED THE SUN,* LEX!

SOMEONE OR SOME *THING* EXPLOITED *YOUR VANITY* TO GET REVENGE ON THE *WHOLE WORLD,* YET *AGAIN,* YOU IDIOT!

IDIOT?

UNNGHH!

Lois?

YOU DON'T THINK I'LL *REPAIR THE SUN!?*

YOU *WATCH* ME!

YOU WRITE THE HEADLINES!

NGGH!

SHOW ME WHAT YOU GOT, LUTHOR!

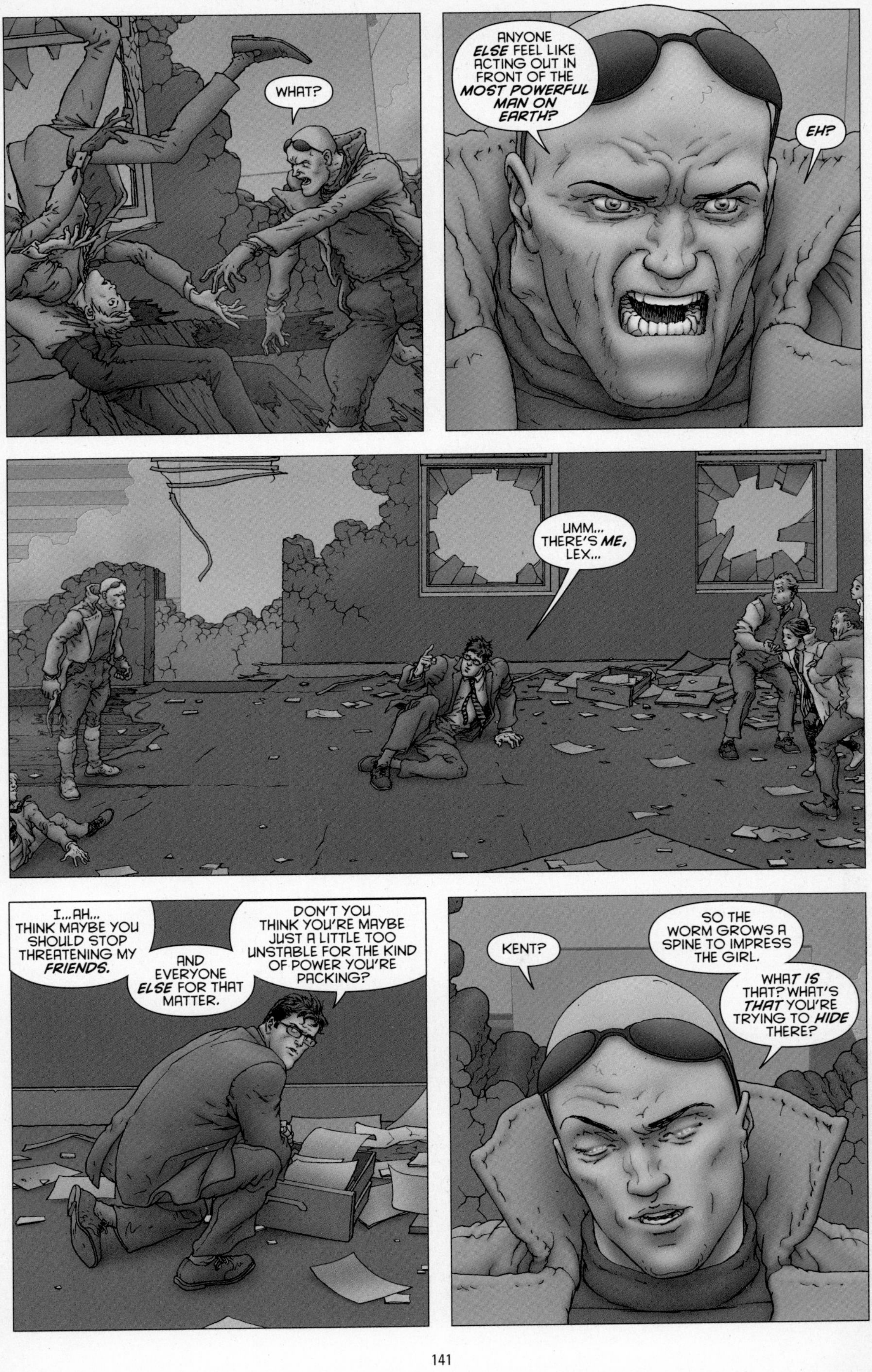
WHAT?
ANYONE ELSE FEEL LIKE ACTING OUT IN FRONT OF THE MOST POWERFUL MAN ON EARTH?
EH?
UMM... THERE'S ME, LEX...
I...AH... THINK MAYBE YOU SHOULD STOP THREATENING MY FRIENDS.
AND EVERYONE ELSE FOR THAT MATTER.
DON'T YOU THINK YOU'RE MAYBE JUST A LITTLE TOO UNSTABLE FOR THE KIND OF POWER YOU'RE PACKING?
KENT?
SO THE WORM GROWS A SPINE TO IMPRESS THE GIRL.
WHAT IS THAT? WHAT'S THAT YOU'RE TRYING TO HIDE THERE?

THIS? THIS IS A *GRAVITY GUN.*

UMMF--

I *KNEW* IT! DIDN'T I *SAY* HE WAS *WAY* TOO BUFF TO BE CLARK KENT?

I GIVE YOU THE *REAR VIEW!*

SORRY IF I STARTLED YOU.

AND THANKS FOR NOTICING THOSE EXTRA HOURS ON THE *STAIRMASTER,* CAT.

NICE, AH, *DISGUISE,* SUPERMAN.

WE ALWAYS KEEP A SPARE.

I GUESS YOU'VE BEEN KEEPING THE *REAL* CLARK IN YOUR *FORTRESS* ALL THIS TIME, RIGHT?

CLARK'S SAFE, JIMMY.

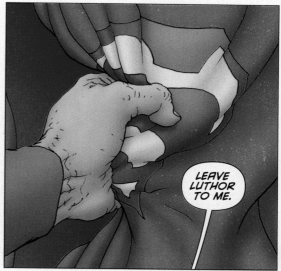

LEAVE LUTHOR TO ME.

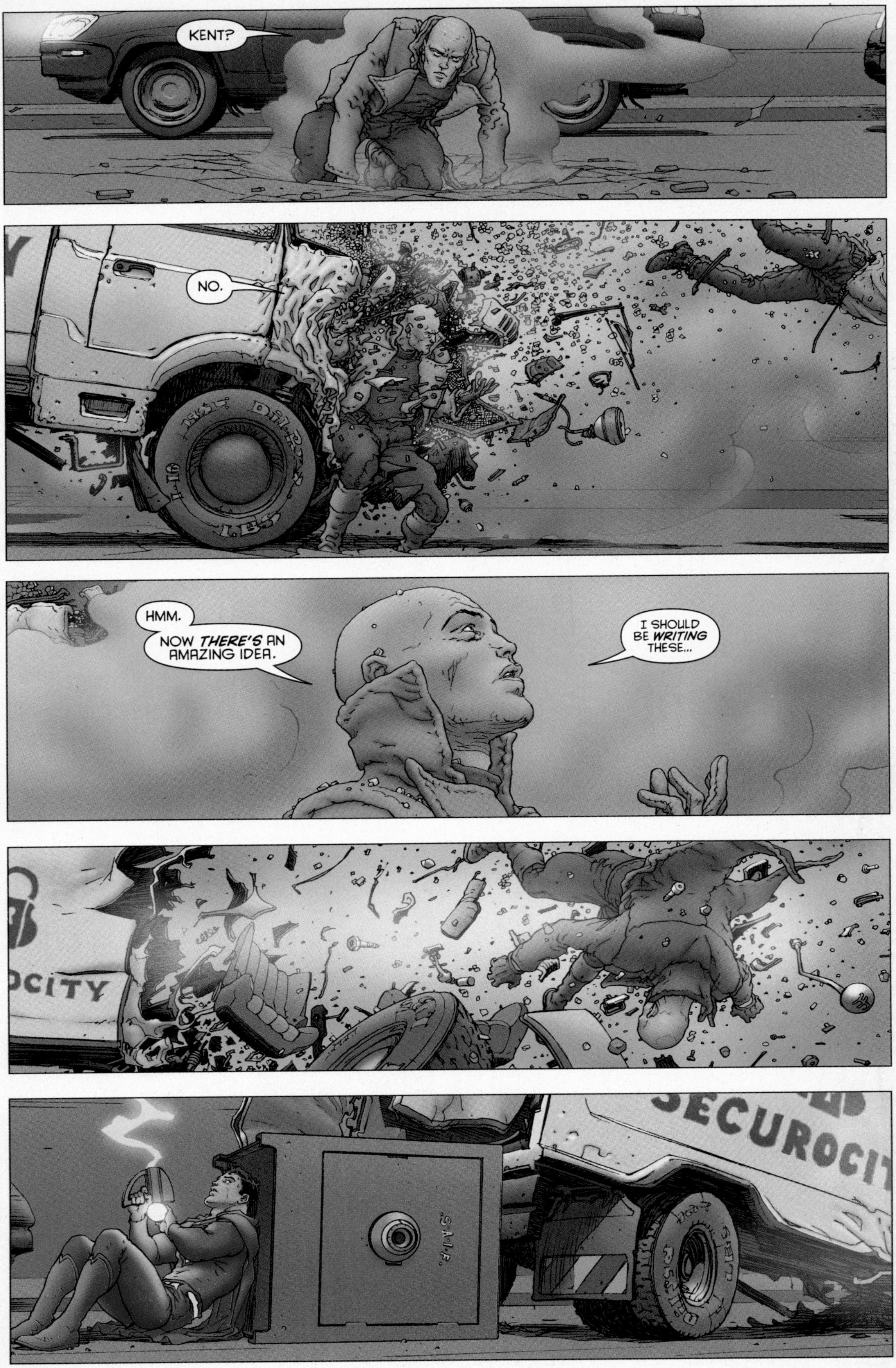
KENT?
NO.
HMM.
NOW *THERE'S* AN AMAZING IDEA.
I SHOULD BE *WRITING* THESE...

WHAT **IS** THIS, HIDE AND SEEK?

STUPID, INFANTILE GAMES?

I **KNOW** WHERE YOU ARE, SUPERMAN.

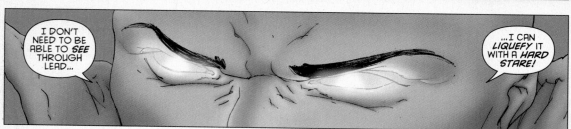

I DON'T NEED TO BE ABLE TO **SEE** THROUGH LEAD...

...I CAN **LIQUEFY** IT WITH A **HARD STARE!**

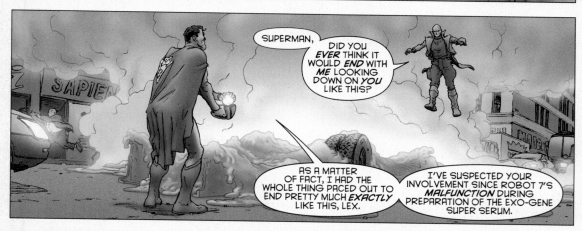

SUPERMAN, DID YOU **EVER** THINK IT WOULD **END** WITH **ME** LOOKING DOWN ON **YOU** LIKE THIS?

AS A MATTER OF FACT, I HAD THE WHOLE THING PACED OUT TO END PRETTY MUCH **EXACTLY** LIKE THIS, LEX.

I'VE SUSPECTED YOUR INVOLVEMENT SINCE ROBOT 7'S **MALFUNCTION** DURING PREPARATION OF THE EXO-GENE SUPER SERUM.

AS YOU KNOW, I'VE HAD TO **CONFISCATE** SOME OF THE GALAXY'S DEADLIEST WEAPONS, INCLUDING **THIS** ONE.

SEE HOW YOU'RE WORKING FIFTY TIMES **HARDER** JUST TO **STAY** IN THE AIR.

BUT THAT'S NOT WHY I CHOSE THE **GRAVITY GUN.**

GAH!

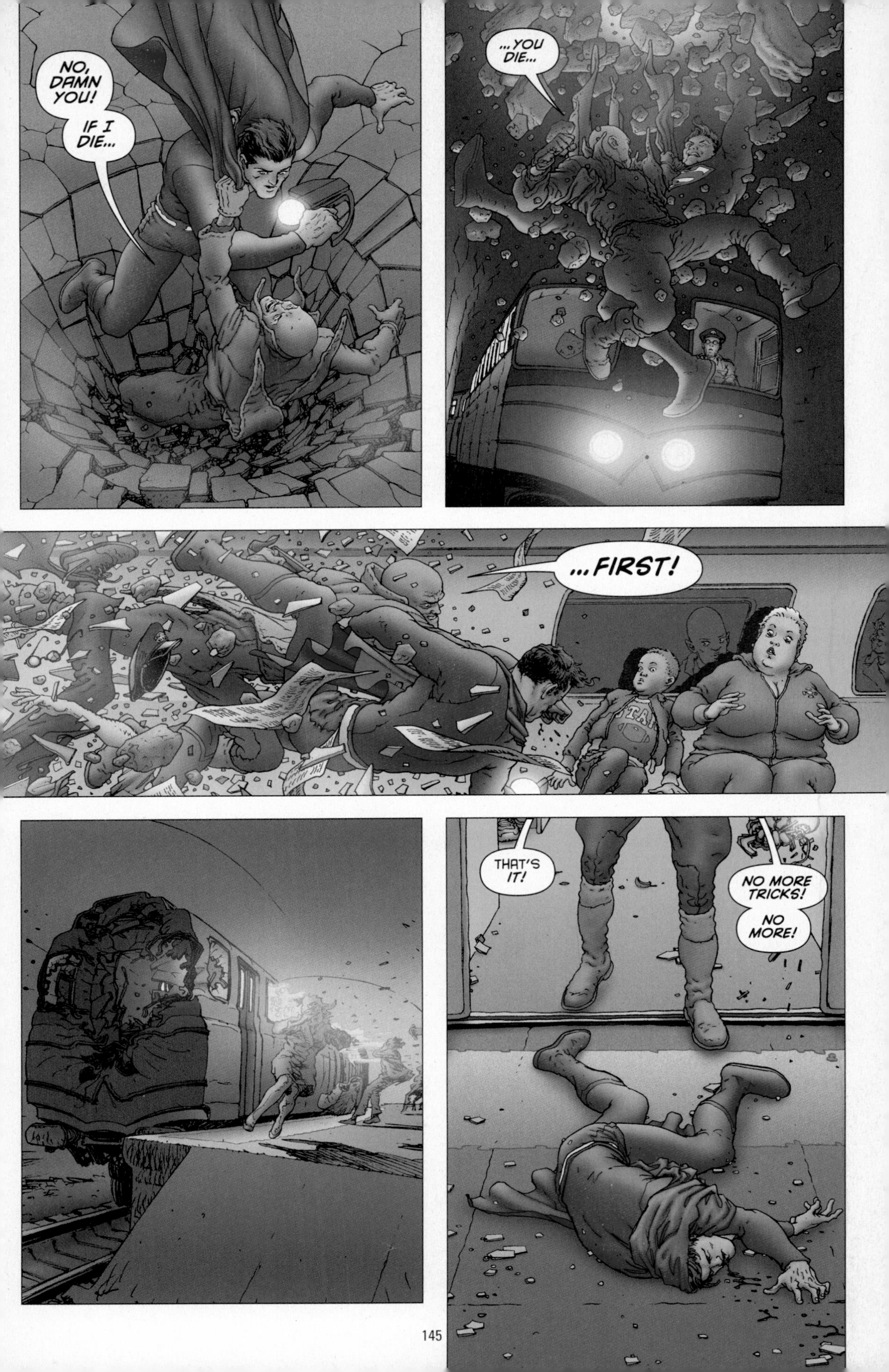
NO, DAMN YOU!
IF I DIE...
...YOU DIE...
...FIRST!
THAT'S IT!
NO MORE TRICKS!
NO MORE!

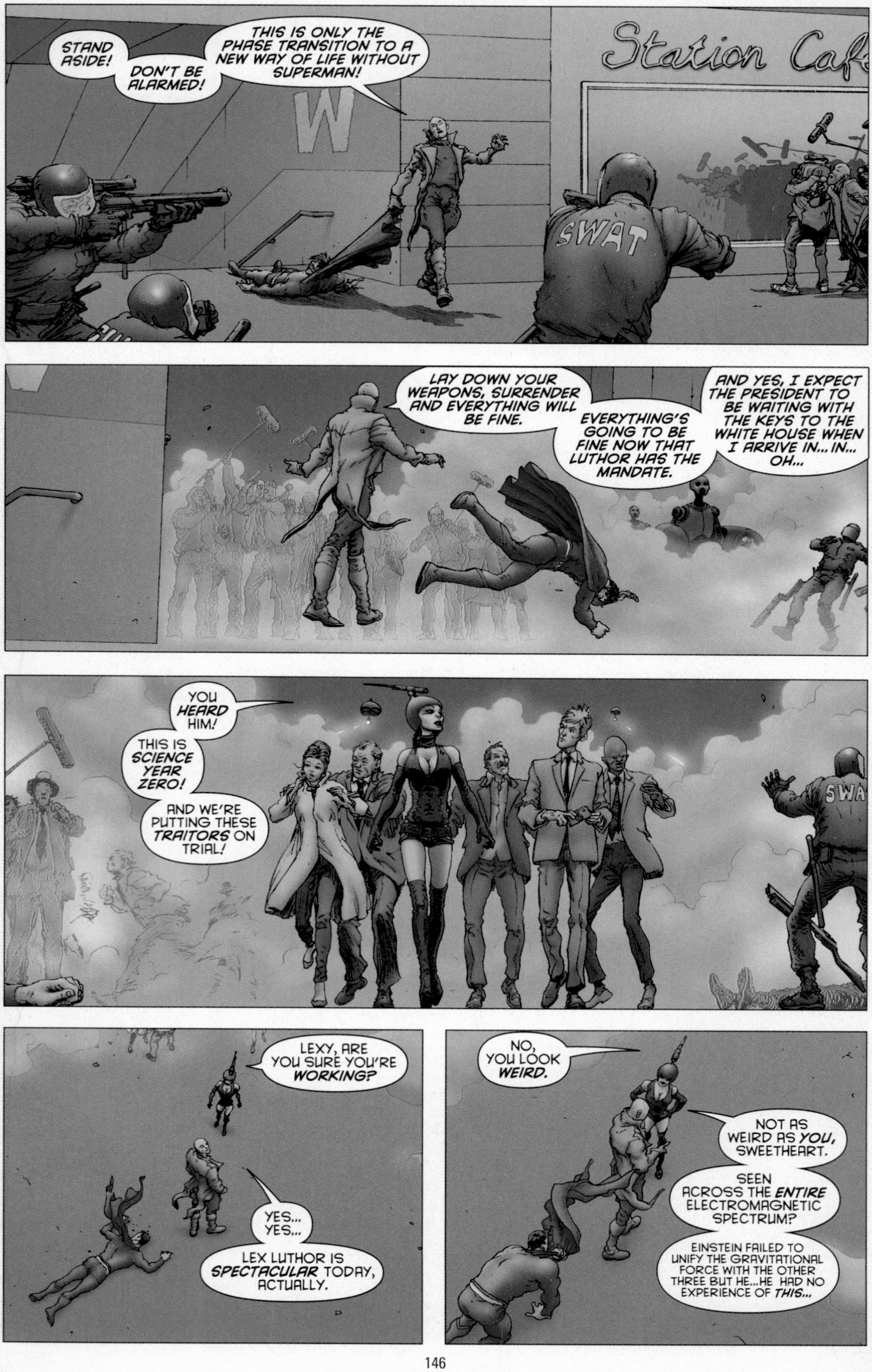
STAND ASIDE!
DON'T BE ALARMED!
THIS IS ONLY THE PHASE TRANSITION TO A NEW WAY OF LIFE WITHOUT SUPERMAN!
Station Caf
W
SWAT
LAY DOWN YOUR WEAPONS, SURRENDER AND EVERYTHING WILL BE FINE.
EVERYTHING'S GOING TO BE FINE NOW THAT LUTHOR HAS THE MANDATE.
AND YES, I EXPECT THE PRESIDENT TO BE WAITING WITH THE KEYS TO THE WHITE HOUSE WHEN I ARRIVE IN... IN... OH...
YOU HEARD HIM!
THIS IS SCIENCE YEAR ZERO!
AND WE'RE PUTTING THESE TRAITORS ON TRIAL!
SWA
LEXY, ARE YOU SURE YOU'RE WORKING?
YES... YES...
LEX LUTHOR IS SPECTACULAR TODAY, ACTUALLY.
NO, YOU LOOK WEIRD.
NOT AS WEIRD AS YOU, SWEETHEART.
SEEN ACROSS THE ENTIRE ELECTROMAGNETIC SPECTRUM?
EINSTEIN FAILED TO UNIFY THE GRAVITATIONAL FORCE WITH THE OTHER THREE BUT HE...HE HAD NO EXPERIENCE OF THIS...

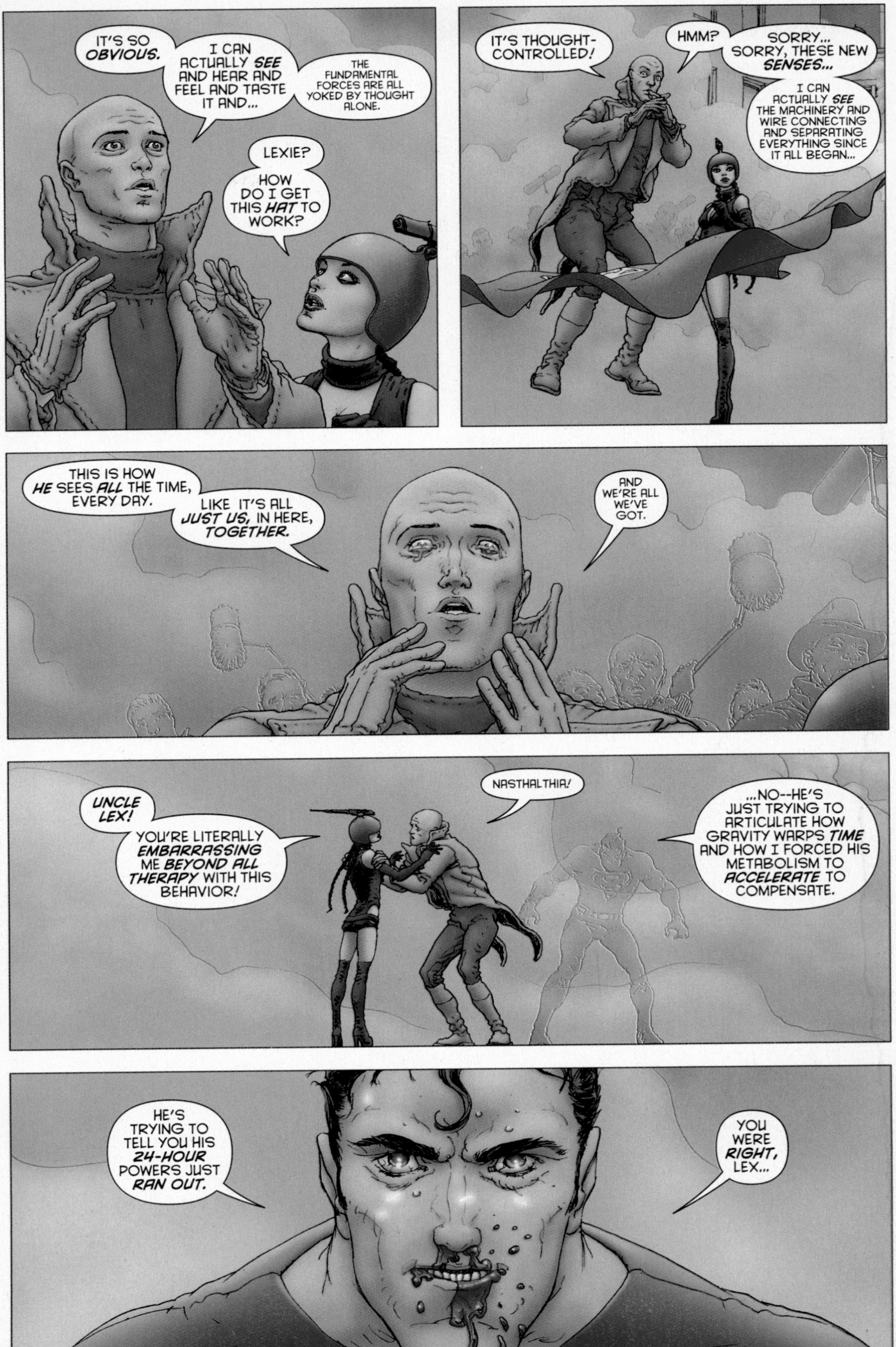
IT'S SO OBVIOUS.
I CAN ACTUALLY SEE AND HEAR AND FEEL AND TASTE IT AND...
THE FUNDAMENTAL FORCES ARE ALL YOKED BY THOUGHT ALONE.
LEXIE?
HOW DO I GET THIS HAT TO WORK?
IT'S THOUGHT-CONTROLLED!
HMM?
SORRY... SORRY, THESE NEW SENSES...
I CAN ACTUALLY SEE THE MACHINERY AND WIRE CONNECTING AND SEPARATING EVERYTHING SINCE IT ALL BEGAN...
THIS IS HOW HE SEES ALL THE TIME, EVERY DAY.
LIKE IT'S ALL JUST US, IN HERE, TOGETHER.
AND WE'RE ALL WE'VE GOT.
UNCLE LEX!
YOU'RE LITERALLY EMBARRASSING ME BEYOND ALL THERAPY WITH THIS BEHAVIOR!
NASTHALTHIA!
...NO--HE'S JUST TRYING TO ARTICULATE HOW GRAVITY WARPS TIME AND HOW I FORCED HIS METABOLISM TO ACCELERATE TO COMPENSATE.
HE'S TRYING TO TELL YOU HIS 24-HOUR POWERS JUST RAN OUT.
YOU WERE RIGHT, LEX...

...BRAIN BEATS *BRAWN* EVERY TIME!

NO! NO! YOU'RE SUPPOSED TO BE *DEAD!*

I HAD IT *TIMED!*

AND...AND YOU THINK I'D BE STUPID ENOUGH NOT TO MAKE *MORE* OF *THIS* FOR MYSELF?

THIS?

I SAW HOW TO *SAVE THE WORLD!*

I COULD HAVE *MADE* EVERYONE *SEE.*

I COULD HAVE SAVED THE WORLD IF IT WASN'T FOR YOU!

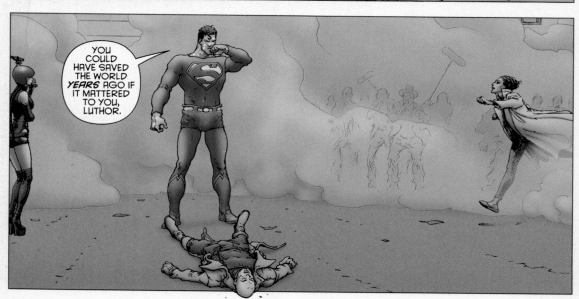

YOU COULD HAVE SAVED THE WORLD *YEARS* AGO IF IT MATTERED TO YOU, LUTHOR.

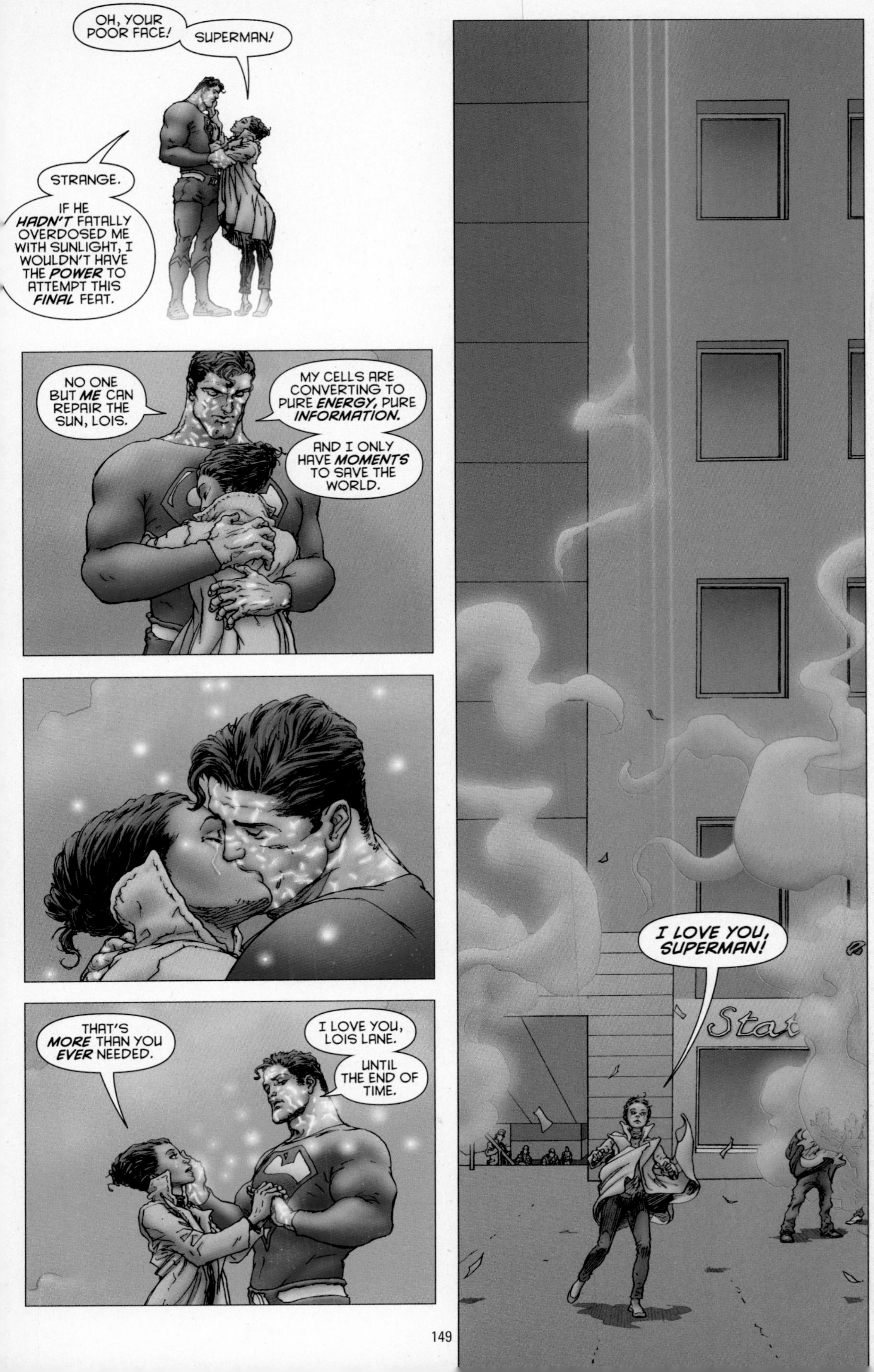
OH, YOUR POOR FACE!
SUPERMAN!
STRANGE.
IF HE HADN'T FATALLY OVERDOSED ME WITH SUNLIGHT, I WOULDN'T HAVE THE POWER TO ATTEMPT THIS FINAL FEAT.
NO ONE BUT ME CAN REPAIR THE SUN, LOIS.
MY CELLS ARE CONVERTING TO PURE ENERGY, PURE INFORMATION.
AND I ONLY HAVE MOMENTS TO SAVE THE WORLD.
THAT'S MORE THAN YOU EVER NEEDED.
I LOVE YOU, LOIS LANE.
UNTIL THE END OF TIME.
I LOVE YOU, SUPERMAN!

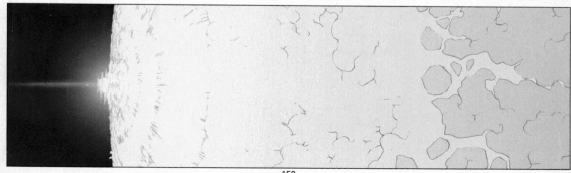

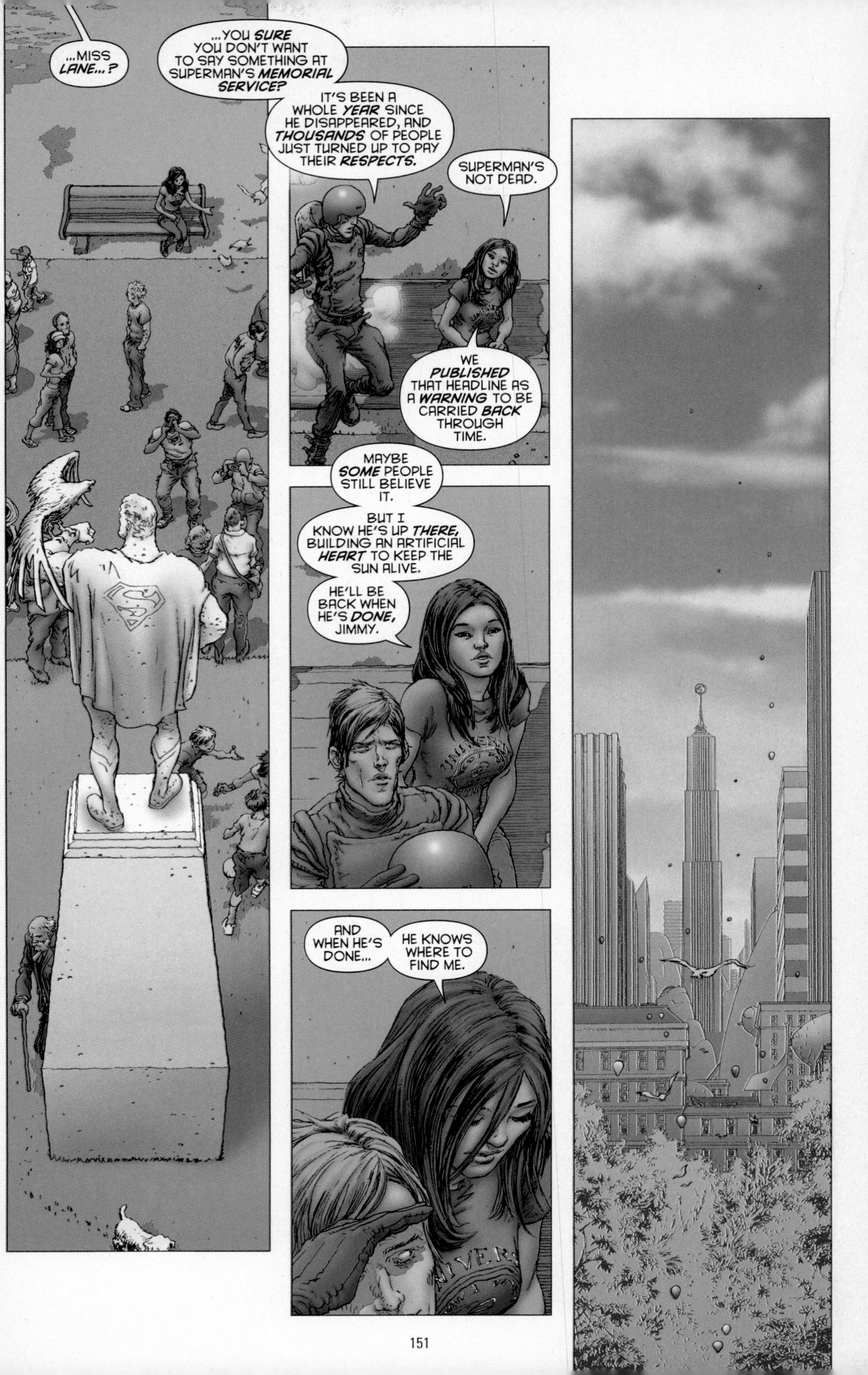
...MISS LANE...?
...YOU SURE YOU DON'T WANT TO SAY SOMETHING AT SUPERMAN'S MEMORIAL SERVICE?
IT'S BEEN A WHOLE YEAR SINCE HE DISAPPEARED, AND THOUSANDS OF PEOPLE JUST TURNED UP TO PAY THEIR RESPECTS.
SUPERMAN'S NOT DEAD.
WE PUBLISHED THAT HEADLINE AS A WARNING TO BE CARRIED BACK THROUGH TIME.
MAYBE SOME PEOPLE STILL BELIEVE IT.
BUT I KNOW HE'S UP THERE, BUILDING AN ARTIFICIAL HEART TO KEEP THE SUN ALIVE.
HE'LL BE BACK WHEN HE'S DONE, JIMMY.
AND WHEN HE'S DONE...
HE KNOWS WHERE TO FIND ME.

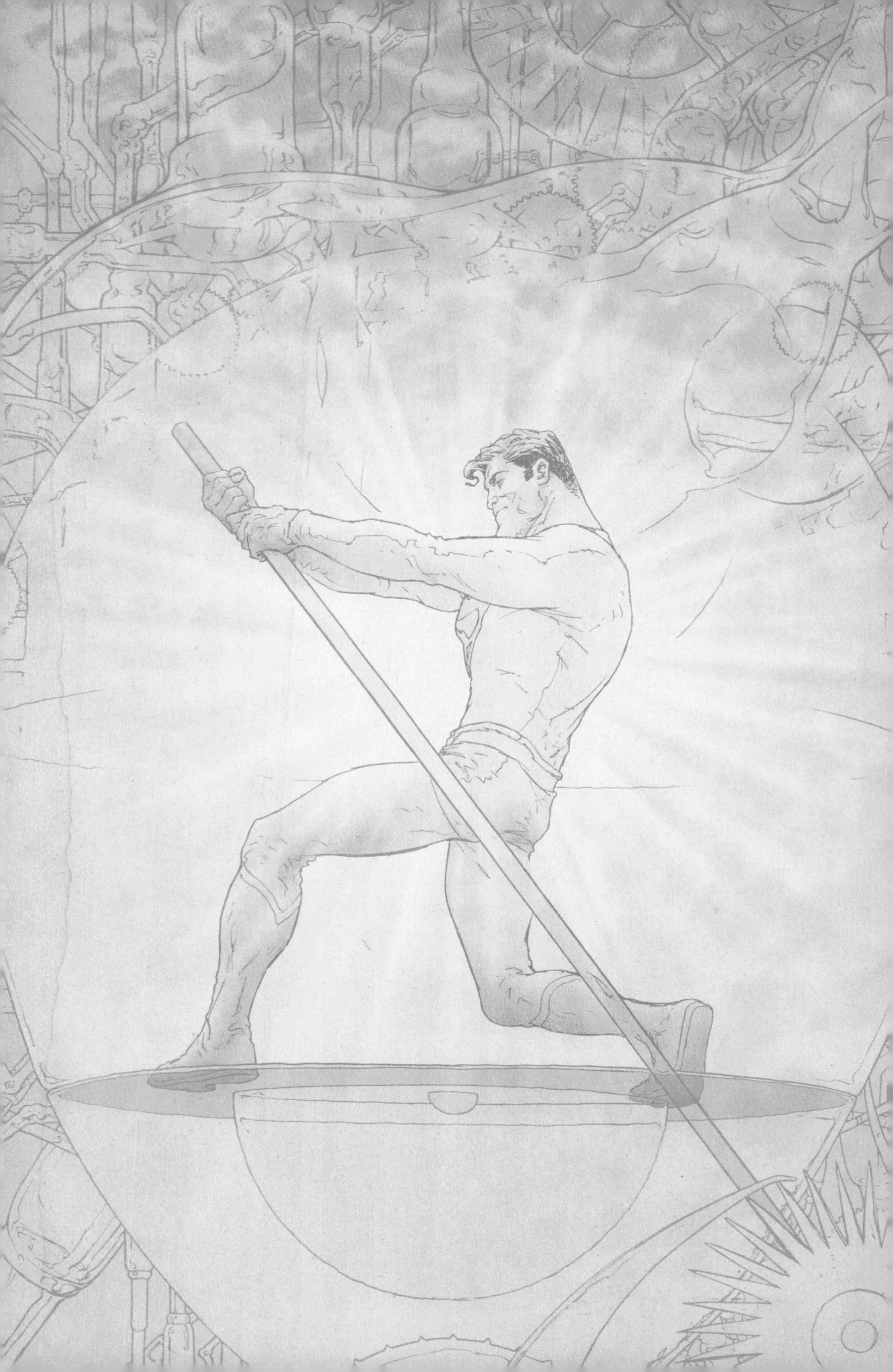

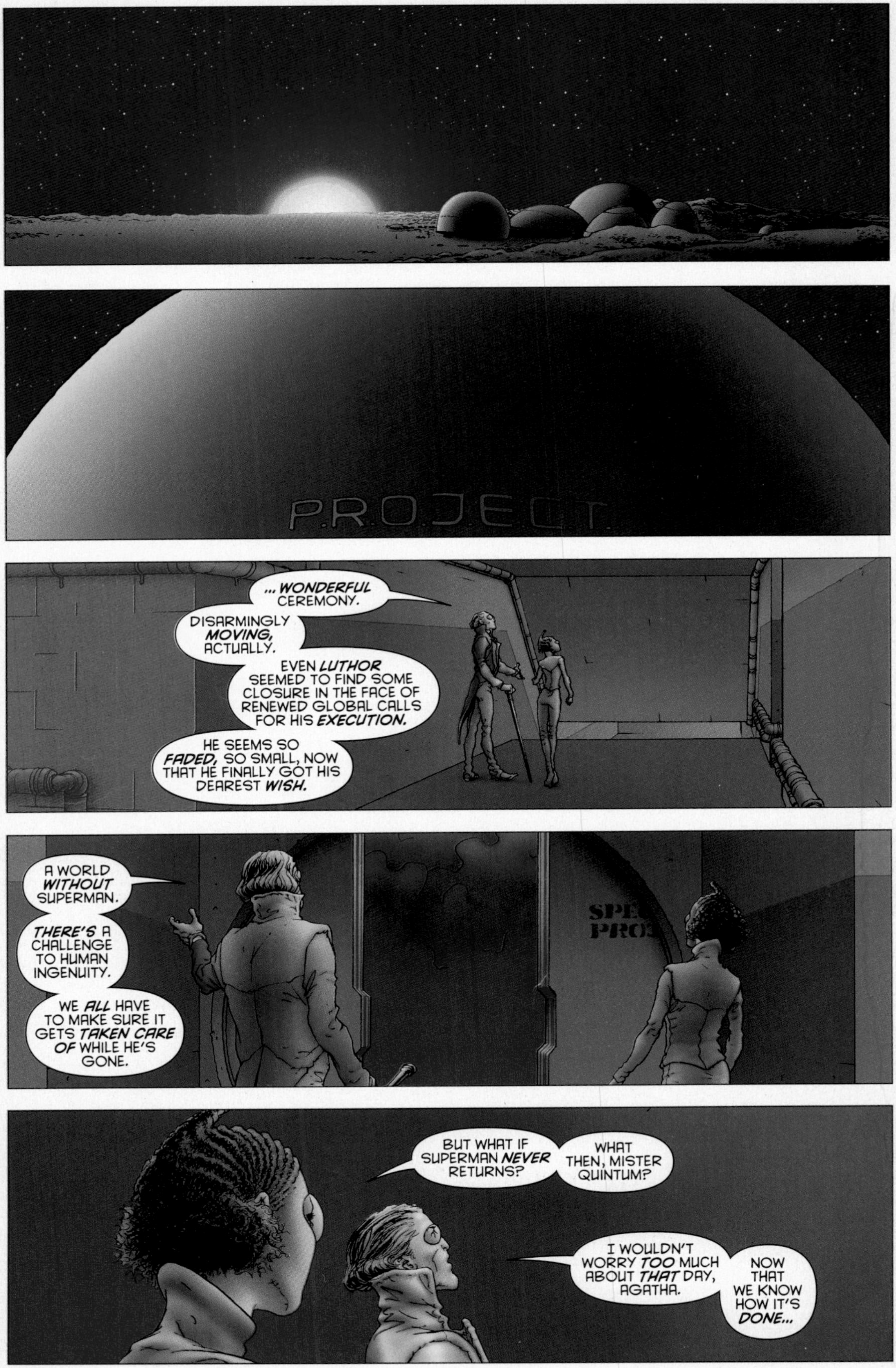
P.R.O.J.E.C.T.
...WONDERFUL CEREMONY.
DISARMINGLY MOVING, ACTUALLY.
EVEN LUTHOR SEEMED TO FIND SOME CLOSURE IN THE FACE OF RENEWED GLOBAL CALLS FOR HIS EXECUTION.
HE SEEMS SO FADED, SO SMALL, NOW THAT HE FINALLY GOT HIS DEAREST WISH.
A WORLD WITHOUT SUPERMAN.
THERE'S A CHALLENGE TO HUMAN INGENUITY.
WE ALL HAVE TO MAKE SURE IT GETS TAKEN CARE OF WHILE HE'S GONE.
BUT WHAT IF SUPERMAN NEVER RETURNS?
WHAT THEN, MISTER QUINTUM?
I WOULDN'T WORRY TOO MUCH ABOUT THAT DAY, AGATHA.
NOW THAT WE KNOW HOW IT'S DONE...

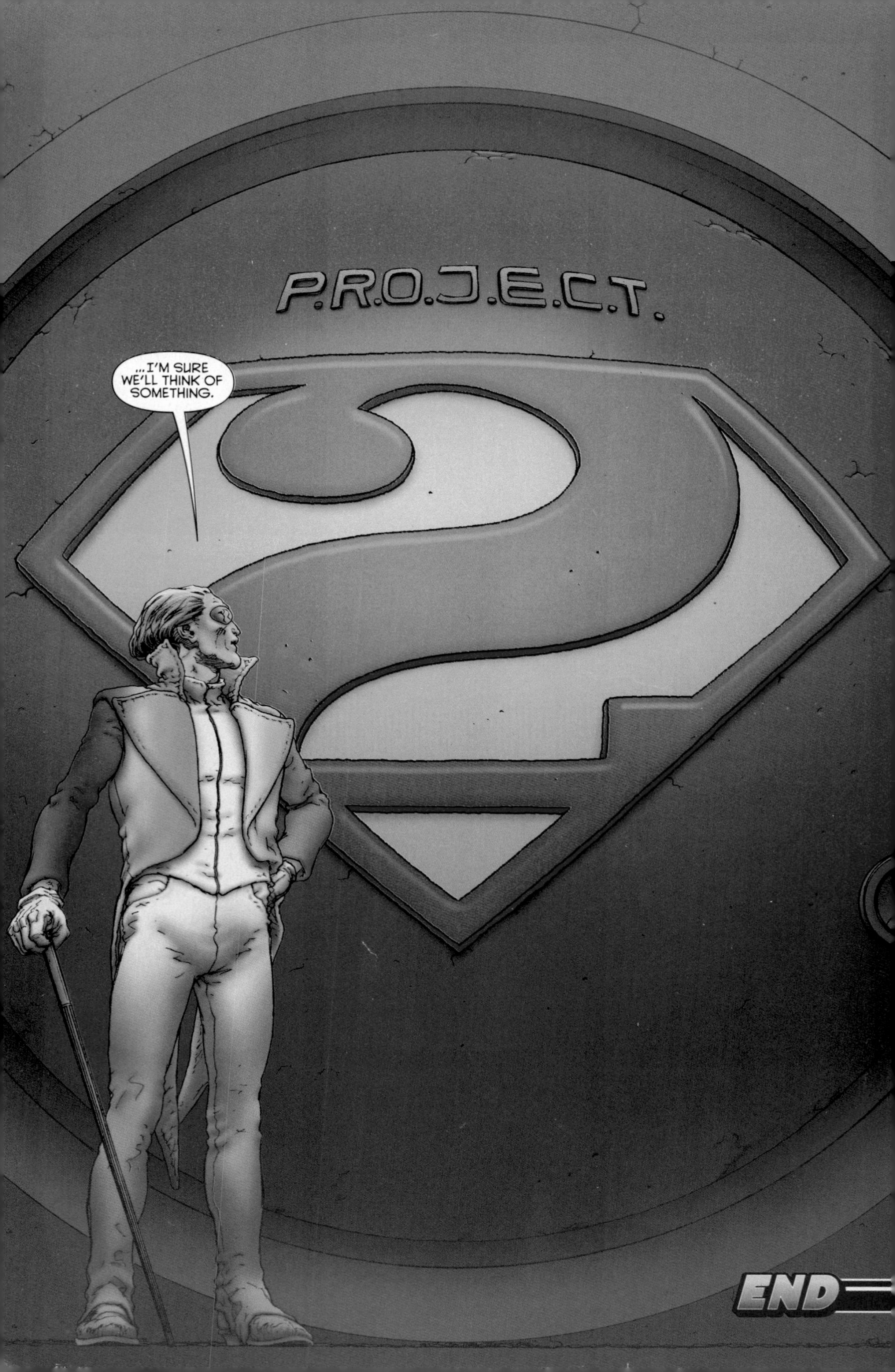
P.R.O.J.E.C.T.
...I'M SURE WE'LL THINK OF SOMETHING.
END

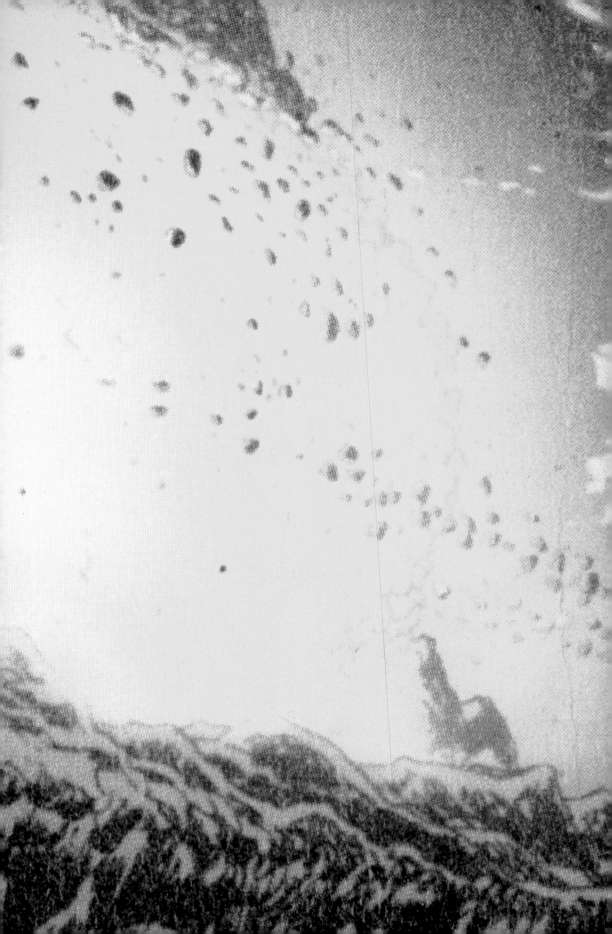

BIOGRAPHIES

GRANT MORRISON

Grant Morrison has been working with DC Comics for 20 years, starting his U.S. career with acclaimed runs on ANIMAL MAN and DOOM PATROL. Since then he has written best-selling titles JLA, BATMAN and for Marvel Comics, *New X-Men*, as well as his subversive creator-owned titles such as THE INVISIBLES, SEAGUY, THE FILTH and WE3. He has been hard at work helping to reinvent the DC Universe in titles from Eisner Award-winning SEVEN SOLDIERS and ALL-STAR SUPERMAN to the hit of 2008, FINAL CRISIS.

In his secret identity, he is a "counterculture" spokesperson, a musician, an award-winning playwright and a chaos magician. He lives and works between L.A. and his homes in Scotland.

FRANK QUITELY

Frank Quitely was born in Glasgow in 1968. Since 1988 he's drawn *The Greens* (self-published), *Blackheart, Missionary Man, Shimura, Inaba,* ten PARADOX PRESS shorts, six VERTIGO shorts, FLEX MENTALLO, 20/20 VISIONS, BATMAN: THE SCOTTISH CONNECTION, THE KINGDOM: OFFSPRING, JLA: EARTH 2 hardcover, THE INVISIBLES, TRANSMETROPOLITAN, THE AUTHORITY, *Captain America, New X-Men,* SANDMAN: ENDLESS NIGHTS, WE3 and now ALL-STAR SUPERMAN. He has also created covers for *Negative Burn, Judge Dredd Megazine, Classic 2000 AD,* JONAH HEX, BOOKS OF MAGICK: LIFE DURING WARTIME, BITE CLUB, AMERICAN VIRGIN and ALL-STAR BATMAN. He lives in Glasgow with his wife and three children. He used to design his own hats and clothing. Currently his favorite hobby is cooking.

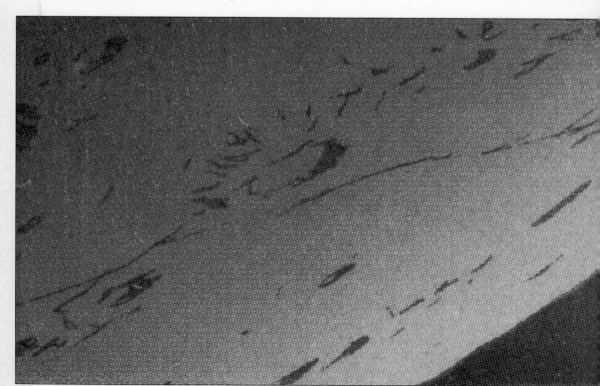

JAMIE GRANT

Jamie Grant first appeared in 1968, Dunfermline, Scotland. As he grew to reading size he began to read A LOT of comics. Later (when bigger) he penned *Blank Expression* (self-published) and painted *Missionary Man* for *Judge Dredd Megazine*, while performing many other demeaning commercial art services in exchange for money (which he spent on comics).

Since 1999 he's lived and got thoroughly wasted in Glasgow, publishing many issues of *Northern Lightz*, an underground anthology comic. He also founded Hope Street Studios (a true comic den) where he crafted the digital inking and coloring techniques applied to Vertigo's WE3 before tackling ALL-STAR SUPERMAN. His favorite music to color comic book super-spandex to is *Devo, the Mothers of Invention* and *Frank Black*.

Jamie's personal coat of arms: "It doesn't take me long to work half an hour. No job too dangerous!"

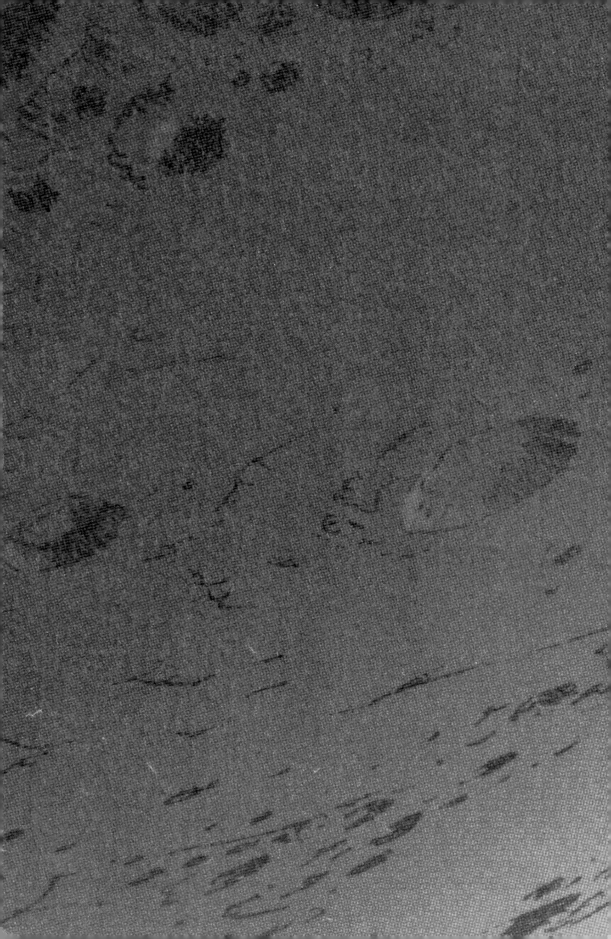